THIS ROUND'S ON ME

LORNE RUBENSTEIN
ON GOLF

Foreword by Curtis Gillespie

McClelland & Stewart

Library and Archives Canada Cataloguing in Publication

Rubenstein, Lorne
    This round's on me : Lorne Rubenstein on golf / foreword by Curtis Gillespie.

ISBN 978-0-7710-7857-6

    1. Golf–Miscellanea. I. Title.

GV965.R828 2009   796.352   C2008-906594-8

We acknowledge the financial support of the Government of Canada through the Book Publishing Industry Development Program and that of the Government of Ontario through the Ontario Media Development Corporation's Ontario Book Initiative. We further acknowledge the support of the Canada Council for the Arts and the Ontario Arts Council for our publishing program.

Typeset in Electra LH by M&S, Toronto
Printed and bound in Canada

This book is printed on acid-free paper that is 100% recycled, ancient-forest friendly (100% post-consumer recycled).

McClelland & Stewart Ltd.
75 Sherbourne Street
Toronto, Ontario
M5A 2P9
www.mcclelland.com

1 2 3 4 5   13 12 11 10 09

For the Roobie-Doobie gang:
Thanks, guys.

CONTENTS

FOREWORD

Curtis Gillespie

In this day and age of relentless multimedia bombardment married to celebrity obsession, a reader – that lonely and old-fashioned figure – has to navigate across a universe of offerings in print and on the Web simply to locate that one thing he or she most craves. That one thing is a voice, a voice that combines subtly skilful writing with solid research, a voice that doesn't need to exclaim its own virtues, a voice that is guided by an optimistic and sympathetic spirit. These are rare finds indeed, in any medium or genre, and such voices are even rarer in the world of sports writing, which has become so dominated by the themes of conflict and sensationalism. It's getting shallow and nasty out there, on both sides of the ropes, and so it has become even more important to find a voice that provides not just pleasure but also a standard to aspire to for how to think and act and relate as we move along in this helter-skelter world.

This is why we value the writing of Lorne Rubenstein so highly. His is that voice. And the fact that he has chosen to add his voice to the chorus on golf is just one more thing that makes this crazy game all the more addictive. Not only is it the world's most challenging and rewarding sport to play (say we, the converted), it also brings one of Canada's most thoughtful writers into our frame. How lucky can a golfer be?

Like many people who know Lorne, I initially met him through his work as a columnist at *The Globe and Mail*. Long before we came face to face, I got to know him through his writing on practically every aspect of the game. It's no exaggeration to say that the main reason I got my original subscription to the *Globe* was so that I wouldn't miss any of his columns. It wasn't until some years later, when Lorne and I had become close friends, that I realized just how much his writing is a reflection of his personality: direct, honest, approachable, well-considered, classy, insatiably curious. When you are in the presence of Lorne's prose you are in a place you can trust, a place you can feel good about, where you're going to get some laughs, where you are going to learn something about golf and about human nature, and where differing views are respected and encouraged. You'll find the evidence of Lorne's breadth of interests throughout this volume, from his touching essay on playing golf with his brother-in-law, Dan, to his theories on the golf swing, to his moving essay on George Knudson, right down to his penetrating observations on what it is that makes Tiger *Tiger*. There is insight, pleasure, and surprise on display in every page of this book.

Of course, anytime a writer publishes an anthology or collection, broader thoughts of legacy and sensibility arise. In other words, once we are able to consider a writer's body of work in one volume (or a significant portion of it, anyway) we want to look for common themes, overarching principles, and, ultimately, the author's prevailing sensibility. We know that Lorne Rubenstein is Canada's pre-eminent golf writer. We know that he has stayed fresh and current over the course of decades. We know that he has written many of Canada's essential books on golf (*Links, Mike Weir: The Road to the Masters*, and *A Season in Dornoch* stand out). All this we know, but the larger question might be: *What does it all add up to? What can we readers take away from his work?*

Well, in Lorne's case, the answer seems rather simple – he's in love with golf, and he wants his readers to be, too – but on closer examination we discover that it's more complex than that. Golf is unique among sports in that it lends itself to writing of a thoughtful and even philosophical bent. First and foremost, one would have to say that Lorne is a golf traditionalist, and he has become even more so as his writing has evolved and as his immersion into the game has deepened. But what does that mean, to say that someone is a "traditionalist"? It's a word that gets tossed around a lot nowadays in golf. It can mean many things. With Lorne, it doesn't mean that he cannot embrace the new. On the contrary, Lorne is as modern a guy as they come in ways that matter. Any of his friends who have had the pleasure of travelling with him will have humorous stories of Lorne organizing his routes based on where he can find bookstores and cafés to check his e-mail. And it's not just in the technological arena that Lorne stays current. Last time I visited Lorne and his wife, Nell, we sat up late watching television and debating the merits of Jon Stewart versus Stephen Colbert, talking about *The Wire*, discussing why there was then no Canadian version of HBO, the pitfalls of blogging, and so much more.

And so to call Lorne a traditionalist is really to say that he values a kind of authenticity that he promotes with every story he writes. It's not just that he likes old-world courses and a style of play that is more about art than power, though you could say both those things of him. I think it has more to do with using the foundation of the past as a platform from which to look into the future, the unknown. This embrace of history, combined with a receptivity to the new, can lead to some sparkling moments, whether you're reading Lorne's work or spending time with him in person. Certainly, some of the most enjoyable rounds of golf I've ever played have been with Lorne, though I can honestly say I hardly remember what I shot in any of them.

I recall one round some years ago in which Lorne and I found ourselves the only players on a challenging golf course on a sunny summer's day. Lorne has never endorsed our current reliance on technology and the golfer's obsession with information and minutiae. *What's my yardage? How many feet is the pin from the left edge? What is the exact direction and speed of the wind?* (The advent of the GPS on the golf course is a dagger in his heart.) On this day, we decided to stop our progress at a par-three of some 180 yards and hit fourteen tee shots each – one with each club in our bag. The results were, in no relation to the order of clubs used, excellent, average, and shockingly bad. It was also about as much fun as you could have on the course. Lorne and I still occasionally play with half a set and the pledge to "eyeball" our yardages.

So, one thing his work stands for is traditionalism, but in a positive, not a reactionary, sense. His work also stands for a kind of sensory authority, a first-hand professionalism, if you will. I reviewed Lorne's book *Mike Weir: The Road to the Masters,* and I suggested that Lorne is the only golf writer in Canada who could have written the book, and that he had "done Canadian golf fans, and all golf fans, a favour, by providing us with a genuine insight into the work, the perseverance, the routine, and the sheer utter self-belief one must have in order to succeed at Weir's level." By this I meant not just that Lorne was uniquely qualified as a writer to write the book – that's obvious – but that it was Lorne's preparation and on-the-ground knowledge that allowed him to write it. He knew Weir, had followed Weir when Weir was, relatively speaking, a nobody; he had talked to people about

Weir; he had encouraged Weir along the way and had grown to like him as a man. In short, Lorne had spent years investing (without calling it that) in his work and his subject matter. He knew thirty years ago, as he knows today, that the proper way to cover a sport is to do it with your own eyes and ears and every other sense you have available, including the sixth you can develop only through years of practising journalism with integrity and thoroughness.

Lorne built his book on Weir the same way he has built virtually every other piece of writing he's given us: by doing the work himself, and doing it right. His idol, among golf writers, has always been Herbert Warren Wind, whose mantra always seemed to be that he would report only on what he had seen directly with his own two eyes. We live in a different and much more complex world than Wind did, and so a journalist and writer in today's environment has no choice but to rely on technology to a certain degree, even if it's just in terms of filing stories electronically and establishing a Web presence. But for Lorne there has never been anything to replace the immediacy of first-hand experience, an experience he then shares so warmly and eloquently with his reader. To this day, I am always surprised, when I have the chance to attend a PGA event, how few golf writers actually get out and tramp around the course. But Lorne is out there, walking, stalking, talking, taking notes, taking it all in. It's part of what makes him great, and it's a lesson any writer in any genre would be well advised to emulate.

If, however, I had to come up with one word that best described Lorne's overall approach to life and writing, it would have to be *curious* – he is relentlessly, yet always agreeably, curious. I truly believe this is what has kept him at the peak of his profession for so many years. He is curious about his own golfing abilities and tendencies. He is curious about golf courses. He is curious about the way golfers of every stripe think and feel and react. But more than anything else, he is simply, and wonderfully, curious about people. All people. I have travelled around the world with Lorne on various occasions to one place or another, and I've never failed to be delighted by his ability to strike up enjoyable and meaningful conversations with people he's just met, on topics that usually have nothing to do with golf.

This, in my opinion, is Lorne's single greatest attribute as a writer – that he never loses sight of the fact that no matter what a person does, or has achieved, or is in the process of trying to attain, that person is at root a human being, someone worthy of respect and interest and, of course, his curiosity. This keeps him fresh and unjaded. So many writers who focus on a single sport – indeed, any writer who immerses him or herself in one sole arena – can end up harbouring a certain bored resentment toward their focus. Not Lorne. If anything, he has become fonder of his sport, more in tune with its subtleties, its unique rhythms. He knows as much as anyone about golf, but he also recognizes that it's too deep a game to pretend to ever fully "know." This is the mark of his essential humility as a writer, an all-too-rare commodity in today's journalistic lineup of obnoxious shouters and annoying non-expert experts.

At his induction into the Canadian Golf Hall of Fame, Lorne's friend Harvey Freedenberg reminded the audience of something Lorne wrote on the occasion of his selection as the first writer-in-residence of the Peter Gzowski Invitational in 1996 (the full essay is included in this volume), words that aptly symbolize his approach to writing about his beloved game: "To write about golf is to allow oneself the luxury of time, because the game takes time. It also gives us time to spend with friends in attractive surroundings, and, often, even alone with ourselves. We need these extended periods. They can nourish us, console us. . . . I feel like a correspondent, writing letters to golfing friends. . . . I write about golf to share some experiences, to find out why the game affects me so. Through writing, through corresponding, it has been my good luck to make friends around the world."

Our good luck, too. Lorne is, simply, wonderful company, and the beauty of it, for those who don't know him, is that reading his work is very much akin to sitting around shooting the breeze with him – stimulating, relaxing, thought-provoking, and good-humoured. The reader of this volume may or may not have met Lorne in person, but, trust me, if you take the time to read this book, you will know him in a very important way – as someone expressing who he is through his writing about others. Lorne is not simply our best golf writer, he is a superb writer who makes golf his subject. He is a dear friend to those who know him and a dear friend to the game of golf. Pour yourself a glass of single malt, find a comfy chair, open this book, and allow yourself the pleasure of reading about golf *and* life, from a person who knows a great deal about both, and who has the gifts to share what he knows.

Acknowledgements

I'd like to thank the editors of *The Globe and Mail* and the many magazines for which I've written. It's been a pleasure and a privilege to roam the world of golf and write about the game.

I also thank my agent, Faith Hamlin, for her encouragement, and, as always, my wife Nell. She's my first reader, and my best critic. A writer once in a while needs tough love, or at least his words do. Nell has offered me this gift for twenty years. It truly is the gift that keeps giving.

Introduction

Maybe it was the time I shot 67 at Uplands in Toronto, where I played as a teenager and into my twenties, that started my obsession with golf. *How did I do that?* Or equally, maybe it was when I shot 71–70–77 to lead the Uplands club championship after fifty-four holes, but then shot 78 in the last round. *How did that happen?* Or maybe watching Moe Norman drill golf balls one after the other without taking any time in between, his feet spread-eagled, his body stiff as a pole stuck in the ground, and hitting them dead straight, showed me that it's possible to play the game in other than conventional ways. Moe played fast, spoke quickly, and broke course records and won tournaments with a swing so far from the norm as to make me want to question the norms; there was room for individuality and creativity in the game. Perhaps it was watching Jack Nicklaus hit a fat pitch shot from close to the seventeenth green at the Mississauga Golf and Country Club near

Toronto, when he was contending in the last round for the 1965 Canadian Open, that helped me realize golf is one confounding game. Nicklaus? Come on. *That didn't happen, did it?* Gene Littler won the tournament, and Nicklaus never did win the Canadian Open, although he finished second seven times.

Then again, maybe golf grabbed me because I enjoyed the hours my dad and I shared in our dawn games at the Don Valley Golf Course around the corner from my home. I still live nearby and I still feel the pull of that course and play there from time to time. What was it about golf and courses and the people who play the game that captured me and wouldn't let go? I started to write about golf professionally in the mid-1970s, and I still ask those questions and try to come up with responses in print. The song "You've Really Got a Hold on Me" wasn't about golf, but in my case, it might as well have been. Golf has had a hold on me and hasn't released its grip. Hmmm. Speaking of the grip, which works better, interlocking or overlapping?

There's so much to write about, because there's always something happening in the game. This means that certain subjects and events demand consideration. This was the case when Mike Weir defeated Tiger Woods in their singles match at the 2007 Presidents Cup, and when Woods's father, Earl, died. Then there's the endless quest for improvement, a staple of golf magazines, golf books, and my own writing. I admit to a sometimes unhealthy fascination with the swing and the mental side of the game – unhealthy because I've probably thought so much about related subjects that my game has suffered. But so what? It's what I do. It's who I am. Golf also happens to be a worldwide sport. It's a culture, and so the game provides opportunities for us to think about other matters. The game is played on a huge landscape, and sometimes it seems almost too manicured; is that a good thing, or does rough, rugged golf engage us more? An eighteen-hole round takes about four hours, when things are moving along reasonably well, and so we have time to slow down. That's useful in a fast-paced Blackberry world, isn't it? I walk a course and I consider whether I'm running myself ragged in other parts of my life. Friends and I discuss politics, film, music – whatever comes up. Sure, we could do this over dinner, but it's somehow more satisfying to talk things over and think things through in the fresh air on the course as we follow our shots around the landscape.

It's no wonder, I suppose, that many of my rounds have led me right back to my desk. Hence the opening chapter, which I've called "Reflections." The chapter focuses on the pleasures of being with friends on the course, and the ways in which golf captures the imagination of so many, transporting us to places where cultures, ideas, languages, and people intersect.

Clearly, I believe in the notion that golf translates oddly well into words, as is apparent in Chapter Two, "Writers and Writing." The subject lends itself to absorbing written analysis that, at its best, captures what a player goes through as he or she tries to capture a championship. The game has also inspired fiction and poetry, and disquisitions on psychology and biomechanics and neurology, yes, neurology. From the time I started reading about golf, I sought out writers I admired. I used to spend hours that turned into days reading Herbert Warren Wind in *The New Yorker*, Peter Dobereiner in *Golf Digest* and the British Sunday newspaper *The Observer*, and Pat Ward-Thomas in the English magazine *Country Life* and what was then the *Manchester Guardian*. Later I met these writers, and enjoyed dinners and walks with them at tournaments around the world. I also came to write about them, and I include in Chapter Two a piece about Herb Wind from the now defunct and much-missed USGA magazine *Golf Journal*.

Reading the writers who influenced me, and later meeting them, helped me appreciate the vast terrain of possible subjects. The swing and its close relation, the mental game, constitute Chapter Three. I've been intrigued by the search for improvement since I picked up a club as a youngster. What made the ball fly just so? Do the hands start the swing, or do the big muscles initiate the action? I still don't know. The golf swing and the mental game are intricately connected, and there's not a golfer who isn't trying to figure out how to improve. I document some of my own quest in my article called "Search for the Perfect Swing." Maybe there's no such thing as the perfect swing, but it's been fun, and sometimes weird – you should see the training contraptions in the room at home my wife Nell calls "the pro shop" – trying to learn more about the mechanics of the swing, and the ways we interfere with our own improvement while trying to increase our chances of getting better.

Golf is a matter of getting from point A to point B – it's whacking a ball across a field to a defined target – which brings us to Chapter Four, about architects, architecture, and courses. I like rugged golf, as is apparent in the pieces I include in this chapter. I don't focus as much on score as, perhaps, I should, simply because I'm so taken with the game's landscapes. I do care about the quality of the shots I hit. I enjoy working on my short game because it's satisfying to save shots. I'm hitting five-irons now where I hit eight-irons a few years ago, and I can't get to par-fours I used to be able to reach easily. A while back I played with 1991 British Open champion Ian Baker-Finch, who told me I shouldn't play courses longer than 6,500 yards. He's right. The older I get, the more it makes sense to play age- and ability-appropriate tees. That's even true for Jack Nicklaus. He played nine holes at last year's Masters with Arnold Palmer and Gary Player – he doesn't play the actual tournament any more – and said that he'd shot his age a couple of weeks before at The Bear's Club in Jupiter, Florida. He played from the members' tees, around 6,800 yards. If Nicklaus, then sixty-eight, chooses to play from the correct tees, shouldn't the rest of us do the same?

Golf at its best is a down-to-earth, walking game. It's playing a few holes in the early morning or evening. It's a shame that so many courses force players to ride. Carts are a boon for people who need them, but it's absurd to force healthy people to ride on so many courses. Too many modern courses make it all but impossible to walk from green to tee. I question whether they should have been built. Golf is a sport, not a lifestyle or an excuse for real-estate development.

As for other forms of golf, I've tried but I can't get excited about indoor or simulated golf, although I appreciate the sensation of making good contact indoors. I grew up hitting balls into a canvas a few feet away during the winters at the Toronto School of Golf in a strip mall, or at another school over a grocery store in the middle of the city. I went out to local fields at the hint of a thaw, and batted balls around. I liked the texture of the game then, as now. I'd stop playing golf if it were stripped of its textures. Maybe that's why I don't use an electronic device to calculate distance. I'd rather use my eyes. I'd rather see and feel the shot.

The less mediated the game, the more a player *feels* it. I refer to "golf on the edge," which I find at the courses I most enjoy. My favourite course in Canada is the Devil's Paintbrush in Caledon, Ontario, where every hole is an adventure, where the ground heaves and rumbles. Many holes are quirky by modern standards. They have deep pot bunkers from which one can sometimes escape only backwards or sideways. Some greens, such as the sixth, have so much pitch and slope it's possible to hit a putt and see it come back to your feet if it didn't have enough speed. Why, sometimes the golfer even has to face away to hit a putt near the hole. Fair? Who cares? This is as it should be. The same could be said of holes at the Old Course, Royal Dornoch, Ballybunion, Bandon Dunes, for example. Golf at these courses is a ground as well as an air game.

Golf on the edge is about self-reliance. The more self-reliant we are, the more freedom we enjoy. We're called upon to perform, but not to depend on something outside ourselves. Golfers who travel to the links of Ireland, Wales, Scotland, and England often return with tales of playing in a gale, or of the ball bouncing all over the place on hard ground, of the breaks of the game. They accept and even welcome conditions they avoid at home. Doesn't this suggest that golfers feel more in tune with the game when it's a raw, almost primal experience? Golf today can so often be four or more hours of sensory deprivation. We drive into a club past a security gate. Somebody takes our name and demands photo ID. The guard informs somebody at "golf operations" that we're arriving. We have to valet-park our car and are then assigned a cart. A GPS monitor on the cart tells us how far we are from the target, and an accompanying advertisement tells us the location of a nearby steakhouse. I'm feeling numb just writing about this virtual experience that is no experience at all.

Golf in its essence is an individual sport, a golfer against himself or herself and the course. I've enjoyed writing about players who have pushed themselves to their limits, and include a look at some of them in Chapter Five, "Profiles." In my opinion, these players are all successes. The challenge of writing about golfers is to capture personality, motivation, and performance. I'm pleased when readers feel I've taken them inside the ropes and perhaps introduced them to new ideas, techniques, and people. The reader will find profiles of the well-known and the lesser-known. In Florida one winter I met the former tour golfer Paul Bondeson, who grew up and played with Nicklaus. Nicklaus believed he could have been one of the great players, but Bondeson had his demons and later suffered a terrible accident. I feel fortunate to have met him and to have had the opportunity to write about such a positive person.

Death, meanwhile, brings into sharp relief what certain people meant to us, and, like many of my colleagues, I have found myself wanting to look back on their lives. In Chapter Six, "Gone Now," I write about famous champions such as Gene Sarazen, Sam Snead, Payne Stewart, and Nick Weslock, and also friends I met along the way, including the great Canadian golfer George Knudson and the writer/broadcaster Peter Gzowski.

In the end, golf is all about people and their stories as they play out on and off the courses of the world. In Canada, no golfer has captured attention to the degree that Mike Weir, the subject of Chapter Seven, has. I've followed him since his early days as a professional, and I wrote the book *Mike Weir: The Road to the Masters*. These pieces introduce the reader to Weir and move to the 2003 Masters and beyond.

As big as Weir has been, and is, in Canada, Tiger Woods, the subject of the concluding chapter, is massive in terms of his impact around the world. I've followed Woods closely, from when he was a junior through his win in the 2008 U.S. Open, where he played with a broken left leg and deteriorated knee. He winced in pain as he won the championship. He had reconstructive knee surgery eight days later and took the rest of the 2008 season off to recover and later train for his return. I feel fortunate to have been writing about golf in the Woods era. It seems fitting to conclude with a chapter about him.

These, then, are the stories to which I've been drawn. I've been writing about golf for more than thirty years, and have tried to convey the feel of the game and the people who play it. I came to writing as a golfer. Having played some competitive amateur golf, I realized that I had too active an imagination to make anything of myself in the professional arena. I could no more control my mind or imagination on the course than I could sprout wings and fly. This was painfully clear to me on many occasions as a junior, but never more so than when I played the 1977 British Amateur at the Ganton Golf Club in

Scarborough, England. I was two up on Welsh international team player Huw Evans with three holes to go, and hit a long drive down the sixteenth fairway. The thought occurred to me that, should I lose the last three holes, I'd lose the match only one down. That's what happened. My mind went places, and not good places. My golf ball followed.

But the same cast of mind that impeded my development as a golfer, and would continue to do so, turned out to be well suited to the writing trade. I've willingly – well, sometimes not so willingly – sacrificed my game in the interests of my work. That's been a small price to pay for getting close to the game. Tom Watson once told me that a writer can get only so close, and no more, and he's right. Still, I've walked inside the ropes at tournaments around the world. My view from the rough has provided me with a ringside seat.

My parents subscribed to *The Globe and Mail*, and I'm lucky they did. The world, and the world of golf, opened to me in its pages. Soon enough I was learning that golf was an international sport, and that its journalism and literature were rich and enriching. I've travelled the world while following the game, and continue to enjoy watching the way the act of trying to make the golf ball behave compels so many of us. As I've tried to convey a sense of the game, I've also tried to make words and sentences and paragraphs behave so that I can set down what I've seen. Thirty years along, I'm still trying. I like to think I've kept my attention focused on what's enduring in this great and confounding game, and I hope that attitude comes through in this collection.

ONE | Reflections

Passion Play

Maclean's | May 24, 1993

The squishiness of the green, still sodden ground beneath my spiked feet; the earthy scent of the now fertile soil and the spray of water as my clubhead contacts the ball; the flight of the ball toward the green; or, often, its helter-skelter path, windborne, clasped to the welcome breezes blowing spring warmth onto the course. These are some of my impressions of early games of golf each spring. Every year for thirty years I have taken to the game anew, wondering what the season will bring. Still, the passion remains for a game that Winston Churchill once derided as being like "chasing a quinine pill around a cow pasture."

Ah, but Churchill was misguided. What did he know of the energizing feeling that courses through a golfer's body when he contacts the ball on the sweet spot of the club face? How could he even dare to speak so maliciously of a game in which even the most horrible hacker can sink a long putt across the hollows and humps of a tricky green, knowing for a moment that he or she is feeling just like Jack Nicklaus or Nancy Lopez? More golfers than ever are celebrating an illogical love of a game in which even the great Ben Hogan, master of the swing, said that he hits only a few shots each round that come off as he imagines.

Can so little success anywhere, on any field of play or in any walk of life, offer such rewards as a golf ball perfectly struck? Golfers know. And never mind the golfer's standard rueful lament. Asked after a round how he played, a golfer can quite rightly answer: "I didn't play my usual game today. Come to think of it, I never play my usual game."

But who needs "usual" games, anyway? Golf, and especially late-spring golf, when hope still is writ large in the golfer's mind, is about reaching for the unusual, the outer limits of what the golfer can do. We golfers are exhorted to "extend" the clubhead, to "swing to the target." Spring golf stretches our vision, pulls us out of our winter selves, huddled for warmth, at last. But winter also propels us forward for golf. The very hibernation it imposes makes the anticipation of a spring round keen indeed. Awakening, sensate again, we believe in ourselves. Against common sense, encouraged by thoughts sharpened over many a winter's night, the golfer believes that he can still play to his potential. That is the promise of the game, the lure that brings the golfer out spring after spring. An odd round down south during the winter does not count. That's a holiday round. Now comes the real thing, in spring.

But what is the real thing? With no apologies to Churchill, or to George Bernard Shaw, who sneered that golf is "a typical capitalist lunacy of upper-class Edwardian England," the fact is that golf is not some backwater foolishness where only the lightweight, the fat cat, and the dopey participate. Many golfers are fit, and more than a few read books, attend plays, keep up with the news, and even make worthwhile contributions to society beyond advising fellow golfers where to place their elbows on the backswing. There is high art and bizarre science enough in striking the ball to satisfy most anybody, and even to capture the imagination of people who, mistakenly thinking they are politically correct, call golf "an old man's game."

No, no, a thousand scorecards no. Think of something Brendan Gill wrote about his father in his memoir *Here At The New Yorker*. Gill's father was "a brilliant surgeon and physician. . . . He hunted, fished, hiked, chopped wood, planted trees, and painted houses, barns, sheds and every other surface a brush could reach. But his favorite outdoor activity was golf. The game amounted to a passion with him."

Passion. Now there's a word often heard in connection with golf. Go figure: "passion," used to describe a game in which nobody even hits anybody, or runs after a ball. The word means "strong emotion; outburst of anger; strong enthusiasm." Roget comes up with such synonyms as "desire, distress, eloquence, fervor, mania, torment, zeal." Golf does inspire these feelings. It might seem crazy, but there's a fellow who shall go unnamed here who has said that his self-esteem rises and falls with his golf. He's an orthopedic surgeon whose family life and career are going beautifully. But he can't figure his golf game out. He can't play his "usual" game.

This fellow, and millions like him around the world, know what a gentleman named Douglas Bertram Wesson meant when he titled his book *I'll Never Be Cured And I Don't Much Care: The History Of An Acute Attack Of Golf And Pertinent Remarks Relating To Various Places Of Treatment.* Exactly. Who cares? Life is fraught with problems, so why should a golfer not be allowed the simple pleasure of an early evening on the course, alone or in company? How good it feels when a warm, drizzling rain tickles one's head. The white flag on the green ahead may be barely discernible as it slaps the air in the dusk, but a shot hit just so will reach the green, and perhaps cuddle up to the flagstick. Is this a dream, only a dream? These spring rounds can make the dream real.

But perhaps it does not matter if the shot is good. Maybe the walk is what matters, the opportunity for silence, for reflection. A round of golf can be a communion with oneself and with nature. Truly, though, the game is rarely played this way nowadays. Most public courses are jammed, and buzz with carts. People accuse one another of playing too slowly. Golfers diligently add up their scores as if they are checking stock quotations; they are too concerned with their scores. The game becomes a sombre affair.

To care too much about score is to lose the rhythm of the game. Judging our shots, we can miss the essential pliability of golf, the way it bends us every which way. Golf is really not about judgment, but about acceptance. The essence of the game is demonstrated when a player drives the ball in the middle of the fairway and lands in a deep, ugly scar of a divot left by a golfer ahead. Accept it. This is the game: golf is played outdoors on grass. It is not possible to control the environment. Let the pliability of the game encourage a suppleness within yourself.

This is what the late George Knudson, Canada's deeply introspective and mightily gifted golfer, alluded to when he suggested that the golfer "give up control to gain control." The player ought to stop thinking about what to do with the golf club at every segment of its route away from and back to the ball. Said Knudson: "Let yourself swing."

Perhaps that sounds too much like Zen golf. But we will risk any accusation of limp thinking because we know that we find almost an altered state when we bounce on the rolling turf, and when we are aware of the high grass swaying in the rough and when we wrap our fingers around a velvety grip and when we swing the club to and fro and when we fall into the grace of the game, an outing that sends us inward.

If we play sensibly, we can discover the sensuality that lurks everywhere on the course. Thinking about slow play, Knudson once said: "I don't know what all the concern is about. Slow play just means that you're going to spend a longer time in a nice place." Take a book along on the course, then. Read a poem. Chat with your companions. Swing, swing, swing. Walk in the woods.

Knudson's comment can be a coda for the game. Spring has been here for weeks, but the season still feels fresh, and we are renewed. As for me, I have scratched the itch long enough. I want grass clippings stuck to the soles of my shoes, mud on my golf ball, dirt on my clubface, the club in my hand while I turn it round and round until it feels right. Care to join me?

Return to Caddying

The Globe and Mail | September 11, 2004

OAKVILLE, ONTARIO

His ball was nearly buried in high, wet rough thirty-five feet from the hole, and a ridge intervened that would take the ball sideways. To the casual observer, it must have looked like a routine shot. But to Richard Zokol, my boss for the two rounds he played in the Bell Canadian Open this week, and to me too – no longer a casual observer but a caddy – the shot was treacherous.

But Zokol was equal to the task. He somehow contrived a shot where he had to be firm through the ball yet have it land softly. The ball rolled across the green's spine, and settled a few feet from the hole. He made the putt for his par and went on to the back nine of the last Canadian Open he'll play at the Glen Abbey Golf Club; he finished with a second successive 75, and will miss the cut to be made today after all golfers complete their second rounds.

"It's a totally different ballgame looking at the ball from on top of it as opposed to being outside the ropes or watching on television," Zokol said after his shot from behind the ninth green. We were walking toward the tenth tee by then. Zokol hadn't made a birdie in twenty-seven holes, and when he finally made one on the par-five thirteenth hole he laughed and said, "I've broken the ice. But I didn't think my first birdie here would come so deep into September."

Zokol was playing his only tournament of the year, and I was caddying in my first tournament since 1982, when I worked a few events for Jim Nelford. We were having a good time out on the Abbey, where birdies were available for the golfer who found the fairways. But the rough was up, and it was tough to score from there. Zokol hit only thirteen of twenty-eight fairways, and that was pretty much the story of his thirty-six holes.

There was much more to the thirty-six holes than Zokol's score. There was the chitchat that we got into with Grant Waite and Scott Simpson, who played in the threesome, and for me there was what amounts to a camaraderie of the caddies. Simpson's caddy, Doug, and Waite's caddy, Andy – caddies don't seem to learn one another's surnames – couldn't have been friendlier or more helpful.

There's also a choreography that goes with caddying. We started on the seventeenth tee at 7:30 yesterday morning after completing only seven holes Thursday before darkness halted play. Zokol hit his three-iron second shot into a greenside bunker, and then came out to a foot. I raked the bunker while Andy cleaned his ball. We also handed the flagstick back and forth, one caddy to another.

It's really a bit of a dance, and there's pleasure in doing it correctly. Similarly, there's pleasure in catching the ball in the wet section of one's towel when the player tosses it to you, and also in throwing it back properly. It's also satisfying to turn the clubs toward the player in the fairway so that he can choose the one he wants, and in always having the pin sheet close at hand.

Of such small moments is caddying made. Yesterday we had to go twenty-nine holes, and the weather couldn't have been more favourable. Simpson noticed how many people were concerned as to whether I'd hold up. I wondered if I looked worse than I felt.

I'd arrived at the course at 5:55, under a quarter-moon and a starry night-morning, and meandered over to the range at 6:25. Portable lights allowed players to hit balls and prepare for their 7:30 start.

It wasn't long before I spotted Vijay Singh on the practice green, using his putting track. Soon Mike Weir came along, ready to go after a course he once despised, but now accepts. There was a nice moment when Weir and Zokol were the only ones left on the practice green, one guy in the prime of his career, another at the end of his PGA Tour career but hoping to play the Champions Tour in a few years.

Later, out on the course, Zokol noticed that Weir had reached six under par for the tournament, and was tied for the lead at that point. "That would be pretty cool if Weirsy wins the tournament on the fiftieth anniversary of the last time a Canadian won it, and also its hundredth anniversary."

A few holes later, Zokol's eye caught the scoreboard behind the sixteenth green. Weir's total through fourteen holes had just been posted.

"Hey, Rube, that's an eight," Zokol said, meaning that Weir had eagled the fifth hole, his fourteenth of the second round, to get to eight under par. He'd taken the lead. "I think Weir's going to win this."

We spoke near the green of how Weir, who would finish at nine-under to hold the lead as play ended for the day, had met most every challenge he'd faced during his remarkable and still relatively short career on the PGA Tour.

Zokol said, "He's a good person and a good player."

The same goes for Zokol. I'd prefer to be caddying this weekend rather than following the tournament from outside the ropes. But I enjoyed life inside the ropes for each of the thirty-six holes. Sure, we missed the cut, but this wasn't about golfing or caddying for our livelihoods, anyway. This was about a couple of friends taking the fair ways with the rough ways, and spending time on a fine course during a national championship.

"Thanks for being part of this," Zokol said to me as we came down the last few holes. "We'll remember this when we're real, real old."

I'll thank Zokol right here, too. The golf's over for us, but we'll still hook up this weekend. We're going to the World Cup of Hockey's semifinal game between Canada and the Czech Republic in Toronto tonight. My feet should be rested by then.

Playing with Dan

The Globe and Mail | August 18, 2005

In the press of major championships, hoopla about the Presidents Cup coming to Canada in 2007, and continued concern across the land about Mike Weir's play, it's easy to forget that golf is – above all – a game, a recreation, for millions of people. Those people don't care much about tour golf. It's background, not foreground.

I was reminded of this the other day during a game with my forty-three-year-old brother-in-law, Dan Kozak, on a charming executive course in north Toronto called Bathurst Glen. He was visiting from his home in Grand Rapids, Michigan, and was keen to get out for his first round of the year. I rustled up some clubs for him and off we went.

The first hole at Bathurst Glen curves gently to the right. Dan set up over the ball, took a couple of practice swings, glanced at his target, and swung smoothly. His ball went out 150 yards in a slight left-to-right arc, the ideal shape for the hole. Dan smiled. So did I. So did my twelve-year-old nephew, Sam Waldman, and his father, Steven.

You're probably wondering, what's the big deal about a 150-yard drive? The big deal is that Dan has Down syndrome, a genetic disorder.

Limitations in intellectual, physical, and language development result. But not, I've learned, in appreciation of a walk on a golf course, of a shot sweetly hit, of a ball soaring toward a target, or of a putt holed.

Dan was wearing his red Tiger Woods shirt, although he said he likes Weir more than Woods. (Clearly, the time he spends in Canada has influenced him.) But what he really likes is just playing the game. Golf for Dan is pure play. He learned well, from his late father, Frank, a fine athlete who graduated from Washington University in St. Louis, Missouri, in 1942, where he'd studied on a football scholarship.

Dan's three sisters, the eldest of whom is my wife, Nell, weren't quite the athletes or sports fans their father might have dreamed of.

But Dan, the youngest and the only boy, needed just a little encouragement from his dad to get thoroughly hooked on sports. He took to golf, and Frank was happy to provide his son with lots of (if not always patient) instruction.

It's fascinating to see how some lessons persist from so long ago. Dan doesn't get much chance to golf at home, where he participates in soccer, swimming, and softball as part of a Special Olympics program. But he retains a straight left arm at the top of his abbreviated swing, and Ben Hogan and George Knudson would have admired his orthodox grip. He swings with the same tempo back and through the ball. He's a pleasure to watch.

Dan's three-wood shot off the ninth tee went straight down the middle – the result of that fluid, directed swing. He grabbed a five-iron and whacked the ball along, having fun, not caring about the score. Dan hit the green over water on the 120-yard seventeenth hole, his ball going right at the cup before finishing fifteen feet past. He three-putted, but so what?

Dan does have trouble with certain shots. He has some difficulty when the ball is above or below his feet (it's a problem with balance), and he's not sure of the pace of putts. But he loves to hole out, so that he can hear the plunk of the ball into the cup.

I also noticed that on the course Dan exhibits a much wider vocabulary.

"Your shadow, your shadow," he told Sam on one green, asking that he move as Sam was casting a long shadow in the early-evening light. I wouldn't have guessed Dan knew the word "shadow." That was my limitation, not his.

Later, on the drive home, I began to engage Dan in more conversation than I normally do. I've been fearful of hurting his feelings if I don't understand what he's saying, but he can handle it. There are lots of ways to communicate, I'd learned from our game. Dan did a little dance on one fairway after a good shot and took a bow after another.

"Great playing with you," Sam had told Dan after we putted out on the final green. "Good job."

Good job, indeed. I told Dan we'll play more golf. Our next chance will likely be his winter vacation with us in Florida. Once a year isn't enough.

Thanks for the lesson, Dan. Thanks for reminding me there's more to the game than professional golf, scoring, and results. Much more.

On the Edge
Travel & Leisure Golf | September 2006

I was in a bookstore in Palm Beach Gardens, Florida, a few weeks ago, and came across a book I had just read a review of, Eugene O'Kelly's *Chasing Daylight*. The author had been diagnosed in May 2005 with glioblastoma multiforme, a brain cancer, and told he had but a few months to live. At the time, O'Kelly was the CEO of KPMG, the global financial firm that employs twenty thousand people. He wasn't unhappy with his life, but he resigned from his job to try to get the most out of the time he had left: to chase daylight. One of the ways he and his wife did this was to play golf into the evening, and to savour each moment as night fell, just as night was falling on his life. He died on September 10, 2005.

I hadn't planned to buy the book, not then anyway, but I did because once I'd picked it up I couldn't stop reading, even as I wandered the aisles. O'Kelly's book isn't exclusively about his love of golf, but the many sections where he addressed his feelings for the game resonated with me. One passage in particular leapt out. He had been writing about finding what he called "perfect moments," and of a particular experience at the Royal Dornoch Golf Club in the Scottish Highlands. O'Kelly felt something special there, "something almost tactile, as if the ground had an energy coming from it.

"I felt a shock come up through the ground," he elaborated. "I could actually feel the energy come right up through my arm and through my hands. It was not an earthquake tremor. I felt extremely aware of something. I can't explain it any other way."

As it happens, in the summer of 2000 my wife and I had lived in Dornoch, above the cozy bookshop in town a few hundred yards from the first tee of that great links at the brink of the North Sea. At home on this edge-of-the-world course, I had enjoyed many perfect moments. O'Kelly was up against a different edge – the edge of his life, although he was only in his mid-fifties. But he was thinking about golf. He'd always felt intensely on the course, and now felt that way even more. His experience confirmed something I had come to believe: that golf is all about the edges.

I feel this most vividly when I'm playing remote courses. Royal Dornoch represents the paradigmatic edge-of-the-world course for me. I'm a member there, and I return as often as possible. Prior to the 2005 British Open at the Old Course at St. Andrews, I spent two weeks in Dornoch and was first out and last in on my final day. I played the first round alone, teeing off not long past dawn, in two hours and fifteen minutes, and I finished the second not long before darkness, at 10:30 p.m., beside a calm, soothing sea and under a starry sky.

Because he was open to having them, O'Kelly also wrote about similar edge experiences and perfect moments at other courses. One occurred late one evening at a course near Lake Tahoe. "You realized, slowly, yet with a certain amount of excitement and even joy, that it was just you on the course," he wrote. "No one else was left. It was no longer late afternoon but the gloaming. Your fellow players had been replaced by fellow shadows."

It's not surprising that golf can come to mean so much to its participants. Maybe it's the "solace of open spaces," to appropriate a title Gretel Ehrlich used for her book about Wyoming, and the way one moves through the roomy landscape of a golf course. There's a definite beginning and a definite end, and so much space to explore in between, all the while doing something mildly physical. It's possible that somebody who is facing death wants to see himself as part of a bigger picture. Maybe being on a course puts one in a landscape that can offer perspective. There's the big sky, the singing birds, walking beside water, freedom, air. Space.

The place where I find the most perfect moments, because I live nearby, is the Devil's Paintbrush course in Caledon, Ontario, thirty-five miles northwest of downtown Toronto. It's my favourite course in my native Canada. The ground heaves wildly, and most of the holes are visible from any spot on the property. I swing, follow the flight of the ball, and feel I can see forever because of the distant views. The summer sky as evening approaches is often clear. Driving home from the 'Brush, as we call it, I feel calm.

I associate these moments at the 'Brush most fondly with my great friend Irv Warsh, who, though in his early eighties, still carries his clubs, eight or nine of them. Irv had his own confrontation with mortality not long ago, when he faced some serious medical issues. He's fine now, and often, as we're walking along, he'll say, "I'm so relaxed I need a pill to tighten up." Back at his home high in the Caledon Hills, surrounded by countryside, we'll listen to some John Coltrane or Miles Davis and not say a word. Words couldn't describe the golf we've shared at the edge.

Of course, there are many ways to enjoy golf. My way isn't the only way. The wonderful thing about the game is that it's so big – a world game played out on an endless variety of landscapes. For me, though, edge golf has it all over most contemporary golf experiences. Driving past a gate where a uniformed guard, possibly sporting a gun in a holster, takes my name, I tense up. Forced to ride a cart on a course, I lose contact with the ground and the opportunity to commune with nature and to walk alongside companions, or to walk alone, if I choose. Sometime there's a mandatory forecaddy telling me, "It's 147 to the front, 164 middle," when I would rather sense the shot and play it as I see and feel it. Clogged with too much information, I close up and often feel the impulse to get away.

I must not be alone in my preference for edge golf, because remote, rugged courses that put as few impediments as possible between the player and the game are enjoying a revival. How else to account for places such as Sand Hills in Nebraska, Bandon Dunes in Oregon, and the Links of North Dakota, all built in recent years? Mike Keiser, the visionary behind Bandon, is an aficionado of "dream golf," the title of Stephen Goodwin's spirited book about the man and his creation. It's edge golf out there, hard by the Pacific Ocean. The golfer can chase daylight until the sun sets over the sea.

That's what my friend Jim Fitchette and I did during a particularly memorable trip to Scotland in the summer of 1990. After arriving in Glasgow on an overnight flight, we went directly to the Longniddry Golf Club, a little-known, rub-you-raw links just west of Muirfield. The wind was up and the ground was firm and the course was empty. If the shot called for a low-running 125-yard five-iron, that's what we hit. Ditto for a hooking drive downwind, aiming for a deep pot bunker on the right because we knew the wind would bring the ball back to the fairway. The round gave us energy. Edge courses always give me energy. How strange that we felt stronger after walking those eighteen holes at Longniddry than we did setting out.

Back in Toronto after our return from Scotland, I was the best man at Jim's wedding. While still on their honeymoon, Jim's wife, Gail, called me. Jim hadn't responded when she called him for dinner. Gail went into the room where he'd been watching a golf tournament, and there was something wrong with his speech. Glioblastoma multiforme – the same disease that would strike down O'Kelly.

This, of course, is another reason O'Kelly's book rang so true to me. Jim was told he had a 5 per cent chance of living five years, and five years is how long he lasted. In that time we played a lot of golf, aware he could have a seizure any second. Jim buffed up his clubs before each round, and we created perfect moments out on the knife-edge of his life, against the certainty of his death. Back then I didn't think of those moments as perfect ones. But having read O'Kelly's book, I do now.

The point of O'Kelly's book, obviously, is that it shouldn't take looming death to motivate us to find perfect moments. They're available anytime, anywhere. But for me and, apparently, for O'Kelly, golf is one place where they happen frequently and vividly. So I'm making sure I walk to the edge as often as I can, in the silence of an early morning or late evening, before the course has filled or after it has emptied, with my clubs on my shoulders, with only my eyes and ears to guide me – no yardage book, no scorecard, no GPS system.

For me, golf is at its best when I can feel the ground and the wind and hear the swish of the clubhead, when my mind is pliant, ready, and open, when I'm in tune with my surroundings. That's when I have my perfect moments.

End-of-Season Thoughts

The Globe and Mail | November 8, 2006

This week's news is that Tiger Woods will design courses, that Paul Azinger will be captain of the 2008 U.S. Ryder Cup team, and that Kingsville, Ontario's Richard Scott, a gifted young man who has won three of the past four Canadian Amateurs, has turned pro.

Yet it seems more important, as the Canadian season wanes, to affirm a fact that's not news but that endures: golf's a recreation for millions, and a living for very few.

Maybe a golf writer needs to be reminded about this more than most people, but it's the thought that kept occurring to me on a mild Monday during a late-afternoon nine holes at the municipal Don Valley course in Toronto. It seemed the ideal way to close the season, at the course where I first played and which this past summer celebrated its fiftieth anniversary.

"Do you want a scorecard?" the starter asked as I approached the first tee. Nope, I sure didn't. "Are you going out to join with somebody?" Nope, I sure wasn't. This would be a walk with a half-set on my shoulders, alone on a course that plays along and across the Don River, and underneath Highway 401. This was about more than score. It was about a quiet game, alone with my thoughts.

My tee shot on the 329-yard first hole was a three-iron down the middle, and then a nine-iron came up short. Ambling along and, for once, not having any swing thoughts – well, only a few – I chipped up close to the hole, tapped in, and continued on my joyful jaunt. On to the second tee and under the 401 I went, hardly hearing the traffic above.

Don Valley's head pro, Dave Richardson – here's a gentleman who cares so much about public golf, and does so much for it – had said the course will stay open until the snow flies. I'd played Don

Valley in cold weather and snow flurries, but this was preferable. The ground was firm, and made for an easy walk.

The 464-yard second hole has changed since I was a kid. The hole used to be a long par-five and the tee was elevated. The tee is now on the floor of the course. The hole still plays along a corridor between trees, and the green remains in a glade. I stood in the fairway for a minute or two, taking in the silence, looking at the golden woods that were carpeted in leaves.

Walking along, I noticed a foursome comprising three middle-aged women pushing their carts and a man of similar vintage pulling his. Another foursome included two young men pulling their clubs and two carrying. One wore jeans, and another an orange and black soccer jersey. Private clubs wouldn't allow them to dress this way. Is it any wonder golf isn't attracting more young players? Too many club rules are inane.

Soon a couple of joggers came along. "Good afternoon," one said. That it was. I remembered rounds as a kid with my late friend Brian Waldman, who lived just up from a dark road in the woods everybody called Ratland. We'd play thirty-six holes in the summer heat and walk up the hill on the other side of the third fairway to his home, where his mother would greet us with refreshments – cold milk, of course.

That was a long time ago. Now, still at Don Valley, the light was fading by the time I played the ninth hole, my last, and so was the season. Packing up my car a few minutes later, I heard the pleasing sound of other golfers whacking the bottoms of their golf shoes together to loosen any mud that had gathered. It's a sound unique to golf.

Back home, I examined a ticket from Don Valley dated May 14, 1987, 3:26 p.m. That turned out to be the last game I played with my father. Heart problems weakened him, and he died two years later. Golf was a way for us to spend time together, and Don Valley was a fine place to do it.

It was also a fine place to play the other day. Golf is about so much more than Tiger Woods, the Ryder Cup, and all things professional.

It's about golf as recreation. It's about Don Valley, and courses across Canada and elsewhere like it. It's about a solitary game on a late-autumn afternoon, and about silence in a noisy world.

TWO | Writers and Writing

Arnold Haultain: Cloaked in Mystery

Golf Journal | October 1992

In 1908, the Houghton-Mifflin Company in Boston published a book, *The Mystery of Golf*. It was written by Arnold Haultain, a man as enigmatic as the sport he sometimes chronicled. That book went on to achieve the status of a much-sought-after classic that, according to Richard Donovan, a bookseller in Endicott, New York, and Joseph Murdoch, co-editor with Donovan of *The Game of Golf and the Printed Word*, 1566–1985, commands up to $750 for a first edition. Its author, however, has remained cloaked in mystery. Who was Arnold Haultain?

Only someone with unyielding attentiveness to the minutiae of life could have written *The Mystery of Golf*, a discussion that treats as its starting point the idea that "In golf the mind plays a curious and important part," and then expands upon that idea by philosophical speculation, psychological introspection, and an examination of neurophysiology. This game with a stationary ball means that golf is a game not of reaction but creation. Therein lies its chief fascination and problem, certainly for Haultain.

Haultain was born in Cannanore, India, of English parents. The son of a major general in the British army, he emigrated with his family to Canada, where he and his brothers Herbert and Charles lived with their parents in Peterborough, Ontario, some one hundred miles northeast of Toronto. Haultain later moved to the city, earning a B.A. in 1879 and an M.A. in 1880 from the University of Toronto. Herbert became a professor of mining and engineering at the university. A building on the campus was eventually named after him.

Arnold Haultain found employment as secretary to one Goldwin Smith, the most influential political writer of his day. Smith was born in England and educated at Eton and Oxford, but left in 1866 to look after his ailing father. Smith moved to Ithaca, New York, after his father's death to take up an appointment at the just-opened Cornell University. He taught history there for two years before moving to Toronto in 1871 to be near family. There, he met Haultain a decade later.

Smith married, and he and his wife lived in a grand home called The Grange, which later became the first site of the Art Gallery of Ontario. It's now a historic site adjacent to the gallery's modern building. It was at this pristine setting that Haultain arrived in 1883, hoping to work for Smith. He was hired and worked for Smith until his employer's death in 1910. Toronto historian Donald Jones has written that Smith's book *The United States: An Outline of Political History* was acclaimed as the best book of its kind. Smith also wrote on the arts, economics, and philosophy; rarely a week passed in which he did not contribute an essay or opinion piece to the *New York Star* or a Toronto paper.

It was into this intellectual milieu that Haultain moved. His responsibilities were, in the main, to attend to Smith's every whim. His employer was a disciplined man who rose early, read and marked up the morning papers, and then took his breakfast. He then met Haultain in the library, where the two would deal with correspondence. Smith was so busy that lunch with Haultain rarely lasted more than seven minutes.

Throughout his employment, Haultain belonged to the Toronto Golf Club, the third-oldest club in North America after Royal Montreal and Royal Quebec. James Barclay, author of the recently published *Golf in Canada: A History*, points out that Haultain may well have witnessed golf on the common at Cove Fields, the first course of the Royal Quebec club. Barclay's research turned up a clipping from Quebec City's *Morning Chronicle* newspaper announcing the Haultain family's arrival at the harbour in September of 1875. The common was three hundred feet above the point where Haultain would have disembarked. Like everyone else, he would then have had to walk up a winding road to the city, passing by Cove Fields.

It is not clear that a glimpse of Cove Fields was Haultain's first exposure to golf. He could have been made aware of the game in India, where the British had exported it. But wherever Haultain may have learned about golf, it is certain that he was part of a golf family. In addition to his brother Herbert, there was his brother Charles, who introduced golf to Fort Macleod in Alberta in the summer of 1895. And a cousin, Frederick W.G. Haultain, became premier of the Northwest Territories – and president of the Regina Golf Club, Saskatchewan.

Arnold Haultain, then, had golf in his blood. He also enjoyed writing and somehow found time to accomplish a good deal of it. He wrote *The War in the Soudan* (1895), *Two Country Walks in Canada* (1903), *The Mystery of Golf* (1908), and *Hints for Lovers* (1908). He edited Goldwin Smith's *Reminiscences* from his employer's writings (1910), assembled *Goldwin Smith, His Life and Opinions* (1913), and *A Selection from Goldwin Smith's Correspondence* (1913). One reviewer of *Life and Opinions* wrote that Haultain must have been a "human dictograph"; it seems that he took down most every word Smith uttered during their years together.

If Haultain played Boswell to Smith's Johnson, it is also true that he was a faithful recorder of impressions he gathered away from The Grange. One can surmise that he thoroughly enjoyed his golf at the Toronto Golf Club. "There are some woods fringing portions of the course most tempting to explore," Haultain rhapsodized, "woods in which I get glimpses of lovable things, and a wealth of colour which for its very loveliness I forgive for hiding my sliced ball."

Haultain's book, to be sure, was not the first time he had written of golf. In 1900 he penned a detailed analysis of then three-time British Open champion Harry Vardon's visit to Canada. Following a long and arduous series of matches in the United States, Vardon played at

Rosedale in Toronto, and then at Royal Montreal. Barclay writes that Haultain was the only reporter who "captured the excitement of the moment; of how it felt to watch the finest golfer in the world display his skills." A sample conveys the rich tone of Haultain's analysis. "Vardon's play was a pure aesthetic pleasure," Haultain wrote, "and the ball as it rose into the clouds, hung for a moment in the firmament, then dropped with the parabolic swerve plumb on the green gave you an emotional thrill only to be compared to that evoked by a work of art."

It seems clear that Haultain thought deeply about the mystery of the game long before *The Mystery of Golf* was published; in fact, a lengthy article, "The Study of Golf," in the September 21, 1901, issue of *Living Age* magazine, is a forerunner of the book. He also wrote a piece called "The Mystery of Golf" in the July 1904 issue of *The Atlantic*. His book is an expanded version of these articles. He writes early in his book that he is "a recent convert to golf." But it is evident that he came to golf long before *The Mystery of Golf* was published in book form.

Alas, it was to be Arnold Haultain's last major contribution to the literature of golf, notwithstanding the additions he made to the book for a 1910 edition. The book is still in print, but Haultain has long since vanished from public discourse. Indeed, he became a mystery himself, leaving Canada and returning to England after Smith's death. He was still a member of the Toronto Golf Club in 1927, but the Torontonian Society Blue Book of that year lists him as residing at Whitechapel Court, in London, England. Little else is known. He died in England in 1941, his movements in his last years as mystifying as the game he so evidently loved and of which he wrote so endearingly.

• • •

The cost of a first edition of The Mystery of Golf *is approaching* $3,000.

Stephen Leacock: Always Keep 'Em Laughing

Golf Journal | November/December 1994

When the time comes to establish a Hall of Fame for golf writers, Stephen Leacock should surely be admitted on the strength of two sketches alone. Leacock, a Canadian who was born in 1869 and died in 1944, wrote "The Golfomaniac" and "A Lesson on the Links: The Application of Mathematics to Golf."

Both essays create characters with whom golfers can identify, indeed, in which they can see themselves and laugh out loud. By the way, we call Leacock Canadian, although he was born in Swanmoor, Hants, England, in 1870; he moved to Georgina, a town some fifty miles northeast of Toronto, in 1876. "My parents migrated," Leacock was likely to say, "and I decided to go with them." There, somehow, he discovered golf.

Leacock is well known as Canada's, and one of the world's, most popular humorists. He wrote sixty books, many of which are classics. Leacock had a day job, too, as a professor of Economics and Political Science at McGill University in Montreal. He became head of the department and remained in that position until he retired in 1936.

Leacock is a major figure in the pantheon of humorists. In Canada there is a Leacock Award for Poetry, a Stephen Leacock Humour Award for prose, and a postage stamp issued in his honour. Leacock also spawned a subculture of people who collect anything and everything to do with him. His papers are in the National Archives of Canada, and he sat for famous portrait photographer Yousuf Karsh, of Ottawa. Karsh also photographed Prime Minister Winston Churchill, for one; the photograph was on the cover of *Life* magazine in 1941. Leacock was a fine subject, what with his thick moustache, the touch of whimsy that always played at the corners of his mouth, the twinkle in his eyes.

Leacock's golfomaniac is quite the fellow. Leacock places him in a suburban train, perhaps travelling into Manhattan for a harrowing day at the office. When his seatmate on the train mentions something, anything, the golfomaniac turns the subject around to golf. Nothing cannot be related to golf, as all golf lovers know.

When the conversation turns to a trip the golfer made to Scotland, he is asked if he saw much of the auld sod. "I saw it all," the golfomaniac responds. "I was on the links at St. Andrews and I visited the Loch Lomond course and the course at Inverness. In fact, I saw everything." Leacock appreciates to what extent our passion for golf can shape our thinking, and demonstrates this exactly. The golfomaniac is asked how long he has played the game and responds that he has done so for but twenty years.

"I don't know what I was doing," he muses out loud. "I wasted about half my life. In fact it wasn't till I was well over thirty that I caught on to the game. I suppose a lot of us look back over our lives and realize what we have lost."

But then again, there is always hope. We may yet play our usual game. Leacock rather adroitly demonstrates how this may come to pass in "A Lesson on the Links," where he applies some elementary lessons of mathematics to the problem of "going round in bogey." "Bogey" used to be a standard of excellence, today's "par."

Leacock sets his calculations out for the reader in exact detail, at the same time invoking the golfomaniac again. As he says: "Let me explain for the few people who never play golf (such as night watchmen, night clerks in hotels, night operators, and astronomers) that 'bogey' is an imaginary player who does each hole at golf in the fewest strokes that a first-class player with ordinary luck ought to need for that hole." How wonderful it would be, Leacock speculates, and one can almost see him rubbing his fingers across his chin in contemplation of the fact, if the ordinary golfer, or "goofer," could do all nine holes of a course in bogey. Leacock assures us that he will.

His reasoning takes off on a wondrous tangent. Having asked how often a golfer really plays his game, his "usual" game, Leacock offers some excuses at first. He is a kind soul, to be sure, and uses his friend Amphibius Jones as an example; dear Mr. Jones is a veritable catalogue, a thesaurus, of golfing excuses that keep him from playing his game. On some days "the light puts him off his game; at other times the dark; so, too, the heat, or again the cold. He is often put off his game because he has been up too late the night before; or similarly because he has been to bed too early the night before." ·

Leacock touches familiar chords here. We golfers use similar reasons to explain opposite results and believe we are being accurate. Who among us has not said we played terribly because we were up too late the night before; and then, a few days later, having played unusually and surprisingly well, explained that we were up so late the night before that we were too exhausted to think and simply let ourselves swing. And we played well.

Leacock also suggests that there are fifty disturbances that could ruin Jones's game, each occurring once each ten days. He then inquires: "What chance is there that a day will come when not a single one of them occurs?"

The formula is brief, a model of clarity as expressed by Leacock. It goes like this: "x over 1 plus x squared over 1 . . . plus x to the nth power over 1 . . . worked out in time and reckoning four games to the week, and allowing for leap years and solar eclipses, comes to about once in 2,930,000 years." And that is when Amphibius Jones can expect to play his usual game. Leacock adds, digging deeper, "And from watching Jones play I think that this is about right."

Oddly enough, no one is certain that Leacock himself was a golfer, let alone a golfomaniac. But it is difficult to see how he could have grasped the essence of the genus "golfer" without having some experience of the game himself.

As it happens, the Karsh portrait of Leacock offers a hint as to whether or not Leacock golfed. Leacock sat for the portrait in the study at his summer home on Lake Couchiching, Ontario, which he called Old Brewery Bay. Two tennis rackets can be seen hanging to one side of a clock. What appears to be a golf club hangs on the other side.

There is also evidence that Leacock's wife, Beatrix, golfed. It is interesting to note that he grew up in a home near Lake Simcoe, Ontario, in the town of Orillia, that looked down on land that would become a club called The Briars. There is some evidence that Leacock had a three-hole course set among the thirty-three acres of Old Brewery Bay. Leacock did much of his writing at this estate set on the estuary between Lakes Simcoe and Couchiching. He is known as the son of Orillia; the town is as proud of Leacock's place there as Brantford, Ontario, is of being Wayne Gretzky's birthplace.

It is pleasant to contemplate Leacock spending some of his summer evenings with a club in his hand, banging a ball around his three holes. His stories might have taken shape during those evenings, when the sun was falling over Lake Couchiching and his golf balls were flying every which way but straight down Old Brewery Bay's fairway. Leacock died March 28, 1944, and fifty years later we are still laughing with him and trying to play our usual games.

Jim Fitchette
The Globe and Mail | January 25, 1995

A number of people write occasionally about golf without making it their primary vocation. For most it is an avocation that derives from their appreciation of the game. One of the finest and most complete writers in this genre, Jim Fitchette, died Sunday at age forty-six.

Jim was one of my closest friends. I was best man at his wedding in 1990 and he was best man at mine three years ago. He read every word in the manuscript of every book I wrote. That's why I dedicated my last book as follows: "For Jim Fitchette, a friend on the fairway and in the rough."

Jim's own work is full of insight and humour. He wrote for *The Globe and Mail*'s golf supplements, for *Score* magazine, for *Golf Digest*. I believe he would have done well had he chosen to write golf full-time rather than teach at York University. But this way we have his golf pieces, while those he taught are better writers for his teaching.

Jim could really get you laughing. He started the Tour de Farce, and produced a hilarious media guide on the various tournaments and players every year. There was, for instance, the Garbage Bag Open. The winner received a green garbage bag, Jim's takeoff on the green jacket that the Masters champion receives. His writings on the Tour de Farce are as fresh and comic as when he wrote them.

Jim introduced golf scenes into his fiction from time to time. He writes in his story "Headache Glasses" about Ben, who is visiting his home in upstate New York and who goes to golf at Chenango Valley State Park. There Ben finds comfort as he recalls a difficult time in his life. He's the first player out, at 6:45 a.m.

"It's a misty morning with lots of fresh dew on the fairways," Jim writes. "I go off alone. Playing golf in the early morning is one of my ideas of heaven. The air is still and moist, everything so green and peaceful, especially here where you feel so isolated, so separate. The holes are surrounded by pines and spruce, and the course is the right length for someone like me, 12-handicap, not too long, 6,200 yards. It's my own world. I like the way my putts make the first lines through the dew."

Jim loved to play golf then, in the early morning, or at dusk. We visited Scotland in July of 1990 for the British Open in St. Andrews.

This was Jim's first visit to the Old Course. We arrived near dark and walked the holes. A misty, soft rain fell while Jim soaked up the centuries-old golf atmosphere. There were almost enough memories during that walk, that visit, for a lifetime. That's because Jim was a detail man; very little escaped him.

It was only a month later when Jim suddenly suffered symptoms that he learned were because of a brain tumour. Jim was told that only 5 per cent of people with that tumour lived five years. He never flinched from the diagnosis.

In fact, Jim kept writing until shortly before his death, and golfed as long as he could. I don't need to write about the courage of his wife Gail and daughter Jessica here. Suffice it to say that they lived through every minute with Jim. As Gail often said, they tried to keep laughing.

Jim eventually wrote a touching story called "An Eloquent Region," an account that while rendered fictionally describes his experiences after learning of his brain tumour. The story was published in the January 1994 issue of *Second Opinion*, a journal of health, faith, and ethics. During the story, Jim's character, Stan, talks about golf with his brother. They speak about their late father. Stan talks about "the way they played golf together and got to know one another."

That's the way it was with Jim. People got to know him when they joined him for a round. He would often go to Westview or The Maples of Ballantrae near Toronto. Or he would play small country courses. He was always trying to improve, and was pleased to write a popular instruction series for *Score* with Canadian professional Ben Kern.

Meanwhile, he derived such satisfaction from a good shot. He ignored the others after a momentary flush of frustration. Jim knew one can't control things in life, not even the flight of the golf ball.

That attitude carried over to the way he wrote golf; Jim had a balanced perspective. He admired the high standards Tom Watson set for himself. He was pleased when gentle Ben Crenshaw won the 1984

Masters, or when Nick Price, another gentleman, won three majors in 1992 and 1994.

Jim also felt like screaming when he read something ridiculous about golf, or when ABC's Brent Musburger betrayed his lack of golf knowledge by saying something silly. He would let out a little shaft on the matter in his articles.

Golf, writing, and reading gave Jim lasting, simple pleasure. His articles and stories gave his growing cast of readers equal pleasure. Many stories remained, unwritten, in his mind. But we're fortunate that Jim wrote what he did, and that he left us the gift of a small but luminous body of work.

In Peaceful Communion

From a booklet for Peter Gzowski's Tournaments for Literacy | June 1996

In one of those happy coincidences that life sometimes offers us, I received word that Peter Gzowski's Invitationals had named me writer-in-residence at The Briars on the eve of my departure for Ireland. As I reflected on my good fortune to have been writing and reading golf, as well as playing this royal and ancient and frustrating and satisfying game for so many years, it occurred to me that Ireland would be the ideal place to think about why golf and words have always existed in peaceful communion with one another, like Guinness – the devil's buttermilk – and the country to which I was about to travel, like Yeats and poetry, like birdies and bogeys, friendship and walks on country courses.

Thinking further about golf, writing, and travelling contentedly in the world in pursuit of both, I remembered that the Irish writer Samuel Beckett, that apparently unhappy gentleman who wrote

Waiting for Godot, also enjoyed golf. Surely he could not have been misanthropic, then. Surely he knew that golf was not at all a good walk spoiled, as Mark Twain once famously said, but a good walk enhanced. Beckett played to a seven handicap, so he either spent a lot of time at the game or else was a natural. And, as all golfers know, there is no such thing in golf as a natural. There is only the unnatural being made more comfortable through practice and application, as is true with writing. Asked the secret of the game, Ben Hogan, a most diligent practitioner of the black art of hitting a white ball into a dark hole sunk into the ground, answered, "The secret is in the dirt." That is, get thyself to the practice field and figure it out. Does this not sound similar to what those of us who would write are advised to do – to put our own seats on the seat of a chair and work it out, find the right words? We're always looking for the feel, and sometimes we have it and sometimes we don't. But we continue our quest for that slight and elusive alteration in tone or rhythm or motion that will improve our games. Such is the promise of golf, of writing, and we can engage ourselves in this search all our lives long.

I like to think that I have been engaged in the search for a better swing, and a better phrase, sentence, paragraph, for most of my adult life. In truth, I have been searching for the better swing since I was a child whacking balls in my backyard in Toronto, and for that passion I have my late father to thank. He loved sports and always would say, "Lorne, you have the shots. I know you do." Neither he nor my mother pushed me to contort myself into a professional golfer, where surely today I would be driving myself even crazier about the game than sometimes I do. There were always books around the house, and some of them were golf books. I remember Arnold Palmer's *Go for Broke* especially. That is what would have happened to me had I given up school and pursued a career as a professional golfer: I would have gone broke.

Happily, there was a world of golf writing, and a full world it was, and is. Packing for Ireland, I needed only to wander into my office at home and glance at the bookshelves to focus again on all those writers whose work I have enjoyed for years, and who have taught me: Bernard Darwin, grandson of Charles, and a man who left the law to write about golf, and who liked to quote Dickens in his pieces; Henry Longhurst, who worked in advertising before writing golf, and who showed a deep appreciation for the finer points of the game when he wrote of the yips, "The yips – once you've had 'em, you've got 'em" (now that's golf writing); and Pat Ward-Thomas, who used to holler his pieces into telephones back to the copy-taker at his newspaper, before computers entered our world. These were some of the writers whose work I read instead of visiting the practice range, or, to be sure, studying my course work in the university library. I still reread them, because they convey the game out of their feelings for the game; they came to golf writing because they loved golf, not because they decided to pursue a particular career in journalism.

Of Darwin, Peter Ryde once wrote: "Darwin had no truck with punchy introductory paragraphs. He thought the way to convey a picture of the day's play, and it no doubt suited him to think so, was to start by taking account of the weather, make a few general comments on the scene before him and on the state of the turf, and then take things as they happened."

That is, Darwin let the leisurely pace of the game dictate his style. Sometimes I think that the fact that golf takes place in an open-air arena of some 150 acres, and that it occurs over a period of four hours or so, encourages the sort of thoughtfulness and contemplation that the most effective writing demonstrates. Playing a round of golf is akin to reading a novel: it takes time and patience. Writing about the game should, I think, reflect these same qualities. To write about golf is to allow oneself the luxury of time, because the game takes time. It also gives us time to spend with friends in attractive surroundings, and, often, even alone with ourselves. We need these extended periods. They can nourish and console us.

Interestingly, people such as Darwin, Longhurst, and Ward-Thomas were not referred to as golf writers, or golf journalists, or golf reporters, or golf columnists. They were called golf correspondents, and in some cases their articles did not include their names. At the end of a piece by Darwin the reader might read only, "From our golf correspondent." Maybe this is what I have always felt about the privilege of setting down words about golf. I feel like a correspondent, writing letters to golfing friends. Now I do so by computer, and via the Internet, but I hope I am still writing letters. That is what I was about to do from Ireland, when I would send back a couple of golfing letters to *The Globe and Mail*. These would, perhaps, lead to letters from readers; all of us, then, golf correspondents.

So with my wife Nell, I set out for Ireland. My clubs were at hand, as well as a few notebooks and pens. I left my computer at home, knowing I would write in pubs, cafés, and golf clubs. Now, as I write, I am in Dublin, at 11:30 at night on the fourth day of our visit. We are in a café on South William Street, and I'm writing on a napkin, having filled the bill and a postcard with the previous paragraphs. Word-soaked in literary Dublin, I felt it was time to begin the pleasant assignment that Peter had set for me. This method of writing is in the noble tradition that Peter himself set some years ago when he, as he likes to say, "wrote on a scotch-stained napkin that I would raise a million dollars for literacy" via golf tournaments. He has done that and more. Words and golf go together, again, as ever.

Words, always words. Tonight Nell and I attended a reading that 1995 Nobel Prize for Literature winner Seamus Heaney gave at the Abbey Theatre. It was the Irish poet's first public reading since he received his award, and we were lucky to find ourselves in Dublin for the occasion. Sitting in the Abbey Theatre, Yeats's gift to world theatre, I was transported by Heaney's reading, by the way he corresponded with the audience. Correspondence: the word keeps coming up in my mind's eye as I imagine golf writers and readers the world over. Golf really is an Esperanto of sport, a universal language. It's spoken everywhere, and can become a means of communication, even when, as we play, we are silent. The flight of our golf balls, tracing paths errant and exact in the sky, often speaks for itself. In that, as through words, we find a shared experience.

I write about golf to share some experiences, to find out why the game affects me so. Through writing, through corresponding, it has been my good luck to make friends around the world. A love of golf turned me into a writer, and somehow both have connected to bring me here, as writer-in-residence for the 1996 PGI. It is a high honour that I cherish. If it brings me into contact with somebody who, over a drink on a warm evening at a sweet course, can offer a tip that will help my putting, well, all the better. A golf tip is nothing more than a few words strung felicitously together, a haiku of sorts, a sonnet, music to my ears, the music of the game, and words that reach from Ballybunion in Ireland to Capilano in Vancouver to Royal Melbourne. An Esperanto, always.

A Golf Odyssey Through Hardy Country

Travel & Leisure Golf | July/August 1999

The third hole at the Isle of Purbeck Golf Club in the county of Dorset, England, is a modest par-four of only 302 yards. There's not a level lie on the fairway, and the humpy, bumpy, firm ground cants sharply right to left, tumbling to a scrubland of thorny bushes. Here, on this rugged course on the Purbeck downland, I've struck gold.

My companion is Howard Singleton, the club president and a man very much disposed to this course. I first saw him when I pulled into the parking lot high on a hill overlooking the course; he was loading his clubs on a pullcart – or trolley, as the English say. As I soon learned, Howard preferred to carry his clubs but had started using the trolley three years ago as a concession to advancing age. Howard Singleton is ninety-six.

Howard loves his golf and takes it in doses of three or four rounds a week, walking, always walking. Howard is ninety-six, it's true, but he still gives the ball a solid thwack. Typically it carries about seventy yards in the air and then, thanks to the hard ground, bounds along another seventy yards or so. He plays briskly and, like me, swings right-handed and putts left-handed. "I see the line better," he tells me.

At the third tee we survey the prospect. Golf holes spread out all around and about us. Flags for the holes sway in the breezes carrying here from the English Channel. I can see forever, it seems, and golf green after golf green is visible, as are the fairways that snake and twirl and, sometimes, run straight as a ruler between the hills and mounds. Clearly this is superb golf country. I have always loved golf on firm ground with a fresh breeze as accompaniment. You can hit a far wider variety of shots because the possibility is always there of running the ball along the ground to your target rather than carrying it there through the air, the only choice available on most American courses.

Howard cracks his tee shot 130 yards down the sloped fairway. The ball bounds madly, then stops in an awkward spot in a bushy copse. No matter. Howard simply fits himself into a stance, then slaps his ball another 130 yards. Watching him, it occurs to me that he could not play many American courses, where water and massive sand traps often mark the passage from tee to green. Because the fairways and greens are accessible along the ground, not only through the air, the course allows players of all ages and abilities to get around. "I reckon I've walked twenty thousand miles here," Howard tells me.

His second shot finishes within twenty-five yards of the green. He then plays a pitch and run between two bunkers that flank the green and clips it perfectly off the turf. It's bouncing along, curving with the right to left slope of the ground. I think Howard's pitch and run has just the right look. It's wending its way toward its ultimate destination, hopping and skipping along, and it looks in all the way. Our senses can get so acute on a golf course, where we're out in the fresh air and scampering along. Johnny Miller once told me it's amazing that a golfer can hit a forty-foot putt and know immediately that it is going to come up one roll shy of the hole.

Howard's ball topples into the hole for a birdie. Later, of course, golf will have its way with him, as it does with all golfers. The bouncy ground can send the ball off-line. When we play through the air, we can believe the flight will be smooth. But bumpy ground teaches humility, self-acceptance, the long view. After all, we are playing a game for a lifetime. It helps to be playing in an environment that really gets me going. I feel so alive here, as if every sense is multiply engaged; the hills, the wind, the views, the walk, the company – being here is a heady experience.

Purbeck is part of what I have come to call "Hardy country." Perhaps no writer is more identified with a particular part of the world than is Thomas Hardy with Dorset and its environs. One can almost feel the writer roaming Purbeck's heavenly golfing ground, for he was a man who loved the land he called Wessex. It is a surpassingly beautiful part of England, green and rural, with dramatic coastal headlands. Happily, I am here with my wife, Nell; she spent a few years in Hardy's company, as it were, writing a doctoral dissertation on his novels and poetry. In Nell's company I am learning to appreciate the landscape here for more than its golfing values alone.

Playing Purbeck, I found it easy to imagine Hardy walking in the area. He lived for a season in 1875 in Swanage, a nearby village where Howard Singleton has lived for thirty years, just down the hill from his beloved course. Surely Hardy would have walked the ridge where Purbeck's holes lie. He described the scene in the novel he was working on at the time, *The Hand of Ethelberta*.

Standing on the top of a giant's grave in this antique land, Ethelberta lifted her eyes to behold two sorts of weather pervading Nature at the same time. Far below on the right hand it was a fine day, and the silver sunbeams lighted up a many-armed inland sea which stretched round an island with fir-trees and gorse, amid brilliant crimson. . . . On the left, quite up to her position, was dark and cloudy weather, shading a valley of heavy greens and browns, which at its further side rose to meet the sea in tall cliffs, suggesting even here at their back how terrible were their aspects seaward in a growling south-west gale.

Carrying Hardy's novels and poetry along, we find many places where we are seeing with almost a double vision: his and ours. We see the way Hardy's "silver sunbeams," along with the "growling south-west gale," affect my golf, for weather is so much part of the game here.

Twice I try to play the Came Down Golf Club near Dorchester, the town that Hardy called Casterbridge, the setting for his famous novel *The Mayor of Casterbridge*. But the course is swathed in fog, and a chilly rain falls when I visit on successive days. Still, I play along in the company of the club captain, Ian Clark, until we reach the eighth hole, called Hardy. It's unplayable in the wet, dreary conditions, and so we call it a day and repair to the clubhouse for tea.

The weather will break, but meanwhile, Nell and I explore Dorchester, a bustling town that probably looks much as it did when Hardy walked its streets. We visit the important places of his life: the thatched cottage in the woods of Higher Bockhampton, where he was born (in 1840) and raised; Max Gate, the brick Victorian home he built in the 1880s, when his novels began to make him a man of means; Stinsford Church, where his heart – literally – rests in the churchyard among his family's graves (his ashes are in Westminster Abbey's Poet's Corner).

And we wander through Dorset, the geographical heart of Hardy's work. A tiny corner of England – about fifty miles east to west and thirty miles north to south – this area is the primary setting for his fourteen novels, and for the more than a thousand poems that are equally his legacy to English literature.

In Evershot, arguably the prettiest of villages in this prettiest of shires, we learn more about Hardy. We've ambled agreeably in the sunshine for an hour or so on a sleepy Saturday morning. We savour a "filled" roll that we purchase in a back-lane bakery. We gaze at the Acorn Inn, the place Tess in *Tess of the d'Urbervilles* avoids on her ill-fated journey to Angel's parents, and then we stumble upon a small thatched house, now dubbed Tess Cottage. It's the spot where Hardy – who called the village Evershead – has her take breakfast on this trek.

Our next stop is Summer Lodge, a country inn that was formerly the dower house of the earls of Ilchester. We're not hungry, but the drawing room is so inviting that we can't pass up a pot of tea. To our considerable surprise, we learn that Hardy was the architect who designed the sunny, light-filled room that seems to bring the gardens right inside. We'd known that the young Hardy was an architect by trade, but legend has it that he wasn't a very good one. Certainly the distinctive shape, brightness, and warmth of this drawing room contradicts that notion. Refreshed, we leave Summer Lodge to search for

Cross-in-Hand, on Batcombe Down, the spot where Tess has a fateful encounter with the sinister Alec d'Urberville.

Hardy filled his work with powerful, memorable – sometimes lurid – events like this one, and it is those events, along with the landscape, that remain in our imaginations long after the intricacies of the plots have faded. Dorset folk have made a cottage industry, so to speak, out of searching for the places where events in the novels and poems "happened" and acquainting flocks of Hardy pilgrims with these sites. Strangely, we are searching the countryside for the fictional places where characters in novels live their fictional lives. So potent is the spell that Hardy wove about his people and their world that, as two more Hardy pilgrims, we use our maps and guidebooks to traverse an imaginary land.

The landscape keeps us mindful of this double vision – the intensely wrought world where Hardy rooted his characters, alongside the ravishing landscape of Dorset that we actually encounter. The verdant hills of lush Frome and Stour river valleys fold around tiny, quiet villages; narrow roads twist between ancient hedgerows; downlands are spread wide with gorse or woods. Hardy's writing reflects this beauty and serenity; yet the landscape itself can also reveal the dark fates that befall many of his characters. Tess's beauty resonates, for instance, in the luxuriant, green world of the dairy lands at Talbothays. Yet her tragic destiny is evident in the grim, barren chalk hills at Flintcomb-Ash, where she works, desperate and alone, as a field hand.

Hardy's Wessex was a place where he could depict the entire human enterprise. Dark mysteries and calamitous turns of fate frequently engulf his characters. He was far from sentimental about the natural world or human nature. But the gentle landscape also mirrors the loveliness in the people, and in their stories – and in his poetry – we sense the fullness of what Thomas Hardy most assuredly knew life offers.

From Dorset we head into the counties of Devon and Cornwall, the haunting "Lower Wessex," along the precipitous Atlantic coast, that had great significance in Hardy's life and work. In 1870, the thirty-year-old architect travelled to Bocastle to plan the restoration of St. Juliot Church. Here he met the vicar's sister-in-law, Emma Lavinia Gifford, who became his first wife. As Emma was to write many years later, "Scarcely any author and his wife could have had a much more romantic meeting . . . with a beautiful seacoast, and the wild Atlantic ocean rolling in with its magnificent waves and sprays." They married in 1874.

We walk down to the garden-encircled rectory – now a private home – where Thomas and Emma would have first laid eyes on each other. Our walk takes us into the little church – again beautifully restored and cared for – where Hardy placed a memorial plaque to Emma after her death in 1912. From there we motor into Bocastle and Tintagel – the legendary birthplace of King Arthur – and hike Beeny Cliff, high above Pentargan Bay. It is easy to see how Hardy was captivated by Emma and by the enchanted lore of Cornwall. Despite the romance of their meeting, though, Hardy and Emma would never return together to this place. Their marriage deteriorated into a tense, difficult relationship. Emma lived out the last years of her life in self-imposed isolation at Max Gate. Hardy returned to Cornwall only after her death. There, the solitary old man transformed their story into what is one of the most moving elegies in the language: "Poems of 1912–13." These twenty-one poems acknowledge the estrangement in unflinching tones, but they also affirm the truth of love, of memory, and of the place "by those haunted heights / The Atlantic smites."

> I see what you are doing: you are leading me on
> To the spots we knew when we haunted here together
> The waterfall, above which the mist-bow shone
> At the then fair hour in the then fair weather,

And the cave just under, with a voice still so hollow
That it seems to call out to me from forty years ago,
When you were all aglow,
And not the ghost that I now frailly follow!
                              – "After a Journey"

As Hardy grieved for a vanished time in his own life, much of his
work both celebrates and mourns a vanishing pastoral world. The
rural workfolk, their dialect, their traditions, their songs, and their
stories suffuse all of Hardy's writing. Yet even in his time, people were
leaving for cities and industrial jobs, and the hitherto timeless rhythms
of a rural world were ceasing.

The drive through Dorset takes us through the seaside town of
Lyme Regis, home of the celebrated novelist John Fowles. In an essay,
Fowles notes that between 1870 and 1914 a labour-intensive system of
agriculture that linked people intimately to the land was converted
"to the final and grim destination of the mechanized and monocul-
ture farming, or agribusiness, of our own time." He adds that "a complete tradition of surviving in rural conditions" disappeared in this
transformation.

Of course the old ways change, even in golf, and it does seem a
loss that the American version of the game is making such startling
inroads in Britain. A mechanized, technical approach to the game is
beginning to prevail. More courses are abuzz with carts. New courses
designed by Americans – Loch Lomond, in Scotland; Mount Juliet, in
Ireland; Oxfordshire, in England – are immaculately maintained but
are largely the product of earth-moving equipment, not nature. Lakes
and the slow play typical of American golf predominate. Pesticides
keep the courses green and lush, and one rarely sees dirt – the dirt of
the earth. A complete tradition of surviving, golf-wise, on rugged,
unruly ground is disappearing.

But not everywhere. Industrialization in golf terms has been slower to reach Hardy country than it has the populated cities and newfangled resorts. One does see the odd golf cart – but it's very odd here, indeed. Pockets of the old ways in golf remain.

Saunton Golf Club, in Devon, with its East and West courses, is one of those places where the old ways persist and enhance the golfing experience. Saunton provides what English course architect Donald Steel once described as "majestic golf on some of the finest natural land you could find anywhere." The view from the white Saunton Sands Hotel that stands sentinel over the sea is enchanting. The courses spread out below, and the dune grasses shimmer in the early evening sunlight. As Steel has written, "Saunton's joys are unconfined." I certainly felt that way after playing the East course on a sunny afternoon when the wind was up and the ball was bouncing merrily along Saunton's firm links turf. By now I had seen a variety of weather in Hardy country. As Hardy wrote, "So do flux and reflux – the rhythm of change – alternate and persist in everything under the sun."

Those rhythms are noticeable on the courses here, where we feel vulnerable to the capriciousness of the bouncing ball. Fine: golf is a better game when it leaves us feeling vulnerable, not protected. A course should call us to spend time in the outdoors, open to the elements, and not enclosed in carts with roofs, isolated on paved cart paths. I felt called to these courses and found the calling more strongly the deeper into old-style golf I ventured. At Trevose Golf and Country Club in Cornwall, I stood on the high first tee and looked up the north Cornish coast. At one point I could see nine or ten greens, and golfers all over the course, telling their own tales through their play.

Perhaps no course has so determinedly resisted modernization as the Royal North Devon Golf Club, in the county of Devon and across Barnstaple Bay from Saunton. The course is also known as Westward Ho!, after the improbably named town that is its home (said to be the only town in the world with an exclamation mark in its name). Mind you, members of Royal North Devon prefer to call it RND. By any name, it's an original; the club was founded in 1864 and is the oldest in England still playing on its original course. It is like nothing else in all the world of golf in that it transports the golfer to another time, back to Hardy's time.

The approach to Royal North Devon is not impressive and belies the treasures that soon become apparent. We drive into a scruffy parking lot where a few ramshackle buildings around it make us think we have dropped in on an abandoned farm. We can't see any golf holes from the parking lot, but as we walk around the buildings – one of which happens to be a low-slung wooden clubhouse, whose delights we shall soon discover – we begin to see what look like golfers out on a vast plain. People are pulling trolleys and taking swings, but the most visible forms of life are not golfers; they are horses and sheep that graze on the ancient linksland.

Farmers, we learn, maintain ancient grazing rights over the land, and the livestock roam freely, as much a part of the scene as the players. A narrow rope around the green protects them from the heavier-footed horses and ponies. But sheep can be out there munching away at the greens. Small piles of "biodegradable hazard" are scattered about on the fairways. Soon this doesn't matter. The animals wander nearby, but all around one finds compelling golf.

Royal North Devon plays across tidal flats, and sometimes the opening holes are damp. I stand on the first tee and have to focus my vision narrowly to pick out a landing spot in the fairway. Make no mistake: although the fairways here are wide, it's still important to find the right segment so that the shot into the green will be along a better angle. And the wind blows – does it ever. I hear it whistling as I work my way into my stance and swing. This is exposed land that exposes the player to elemental golf. At the fourth hole, I come across one of

RND's famous "sleeper" bunkers, shored up with railway ties. The bunker looks fearsome but asks for only a 170-yard carry. The fifth is a wicked par-three where the green sits up above one of those massive bunkers and all but hangs out over the sea. Today, downwind, I hit a half-wedge to the 136-yard hole. But against the wind, the shot can require a three-iron. Downwind or against the wind, I think of something a golf teacher once told me: never do anything at the expense of balance. It's an admonition especially relevant to golf at RND.

Ah, the ways that golf takes us to our limits. Can I quiet my rushing mind and negotiate my way around RND's well-known rushes? These are challenging hazards, but there's always a way around or over these spiky grasses that shoot ten feet in the air and cut like needles into those who dare to look for golf balls in the area. Menacing rushes notwithstanding, there is a delicious feeling of freedom at Royal North Devon: the land, flat except for some of the green sites, appears to go on forever. The last fairways must be some of the widest in golf, but now I must find a way to hit the ball low into the howling wind that bends the flagstick at the last green. A burn only three feet wide runs across the fairway short of the green, and I must get across. But at the same time, I don't want to hit the ball high in the air where the wind will take it. High enough but low enough – of such puzzles is golf on natural, untamed ground made.

Later there is comfort in the clubhouse, a treasure trove of museum-quality holdings. An oil painting of J.H. Taylor, the English professional who learned his golf here, dominates the main room that looks out on the course. Taylor won British Opens in 1894, 1895, 1900, 1909, and 1913. There are racks of antique wooden clubs, medals, and more paintings. I can't think of a better way to spend a golf day in England than to have a round here, or two, and then examine the golfing relics before lunch and a game of snooker in the clubhouse.

I am so taken with the club that I ask Mark Reid, a club member with whom I have played, to secure for me an application for overseas membership. I fill it out on the spot, and in a month learn that my application has been approved. So before long I'll be back at RND often. While I'm there, I'll be sure to ring Howard Singleton over at Purbeck. My guess is he'll be up for another round.

Herbert Warren Wind
Golf Journal | September 2002

On a crisp, sky-blue afternoon, a man dressed in his customary jacket, tie, and tweed cap enters his favourite village restaurant, near his residence in Bedford, Massachusetts. This elegant man in his mid-eighties has seen it all in golf, and written about it for some fifty years, for *Sports Illustrated, The New Yorker,* in important books. He lives now in a nearby assisted-living facility. The gentleman is Herbert Warren Wind, to whom the PGA of America in 1992 gave its lifetime achievement award in journalism and the USGA in 1995 awarded its highest honour, the Bob Jones Award (the only writer to have been so honoured). Wind is too modest to speak of these awards, or even of his writing. His words speak for themselves.

Wind is accompanied by Robert Macdonald, the publisher of Flagstick Books, which issues reprints of old titles. Macdonald started the imprint under the name "The Classics of Golf," and Wind wrote a foreword for each book. The imprint's name was changed when Wind could no longer write the forewords, due to declining health.

"I'm in pretty good shape," says Wind, having removed his cap (a gentleman never wears a hat in a restaurant). He has written books with Gene Sarazen, Ben Hogan, and Jack Nicklaus, and his scholarly *The Story of American Golf* is an important reference source. "But my eyes aren't so good. I don't read much any more, so I lose the sense of what's going on."

Wind provided generations of readers with a clear sense of what was going on. He joined *The New Yorker* in 1948, working on unsigned pieces for "The Talk of the Town" and later writing profiles. His first golf piece for the magazine was a profile of designer Robert Trent Jones, published on the occasion of the 1951 U.S. Open at Oakland Hills Country Club. In 1954, Wind went to work for *Sports Illustrated* as its golf writer, and in 1957 the magazine published a series of instructional pieces that Wind worked on with Hogan; the book *Five Lessons: The Modern Fundamentals of Golf,* comprising these lessons, has never been out of print and remains the best-selling work of golf instruction.

Wind left *Sports Illustrated* in 1960; he returned to *The New Yorker* two years later. Over the next twenty-five years, he contributed sixty timeless essays on golf for "The Sporting Scene," a department he helped found. Wind's writing called to many aspiring journalists. I read and collected early *Sports Illustrated* magazines and still have the issues that led to the book with Hogan. My files bulge with *New Yorker* issues that included his essays; I always looked forward to his reports from the Masters.

Whatever Wind wrote, his readers could be sure he had staked out his territory, done his research, and tended meticulously to each word and phrase. Brad Klein, a course architecture writer, once called Wind and asked how he was doing. "Oh, I'm just polishing up a few sentences," he said.

Writer Kaye Kessler refers to Wind as a "golf walker," a writer who prefers the course to the press room. The *New York Times* Pulitzer-winning sports columnist Dave Anderson walked many courses with Wind, and for years enjoyed what came to be known as the Herbert Warren Wind dinner at the Masters.

Some people wonder whether Wind would find an audience with

today's thirty-second-attention-span readers, given that his pieces ran at 15,000 words. He needed space and time to give his subject its due; it had to be put into historical perspective, fleshed out. He rewarded reading, evenings in a favourite chair, letting his writing take you somewhere.

"Oh, Herb would find readers even now because he's a great writer," Anderson says. Macdonald adds: "You could argue that Herb is the greatest American sportswriter. He puts golf into a context. It's not the be-all and end-all."

• • •

"What's rather nice about it is that it's like no other place in the area," Wind says of the restaurant, Dalya's. "The menu is limited but the choices are very good. But before we eat, shouldn't we have a drink?" Wind orders a vodka. "A nice, pleasant drink," he says.

He asks Macdonald what books he's issuing. Macdonald says he's publishing some books Wind wrote – the *On the Tour with Harry Sprague* series. He concocted the idea of letters between a writer and a fictional pro who's having problems with his game. The books have long been out of print. "I'm so pleased to hear the books are still alive because of your publishing them," Wind says, beaming.

During lunch, Wind touches on subjects and places he's loved and written about, such as St. Andrews, "The only place I know where people play three or four times, and when they come back the locals remember you and say, 'Hello, Tom, good to see you.'"

One need only look at any Wind essay to appreciate that he sees the game as part of a larger tapestry. To him, golf is a part of sporting "culture," and so he introduced cultural allusions into his work. He might touch on something that the novelist Anthony Trollope wrote, or refer to an Alfred Hitchcock film, or a passage from Herman

Melville's *Moby Dick*. In 1958, covering the Masters for *Sports Illustrated*, Wind casually tossed off the term "Amen Corner" in reference to the stretch of the eleventh, twelfth, and thirteenth holes at Augusta National. He was familiar with a jazz number by Mezz Mezzrow called "Shoutin' at the Amen Corner." When I learned this as a kid, I went right out and found Mezzrow's autobiography.

Wind's words sent me from golf to jazz. He transported a reader, and implied in the least intrusive way without saying so, that one would be enriched by coming along for the journey. One could learn, as he had, that golf was about, well, more than golf. Wind learned about the world from reading, long before he wrote about golf.

Born in Brockton, Massachusetts, Wind came to love sports, playing and following them. His father was in the shoe leather business and belonged to the Thorny Lea club. Herbert started to play at age ten. There were two golf books in the house, *Down the Fairway*, a Bob Jones biography, and *The Duffer's Handbook of Golf*, by Grantland Rice. Wind also seemed to absorb whole *The American Golfer* magazine.

"In my time growing up in Brockton, there was nothing to do between school and dinner," he says. "So you read. You read not only golf, but also seventeenth-, eighteenth-, and nineteenth-century literature. There was no television, so you became a good reader. It gave you so much you couldn't get elsewhere."

Wind's writing career began at the *Brockton Enterprise* newspaper, where he was invited to write a golf column when he was eighteen. Writing the column gave him "what writing does for anyone," he says. "A good feeling. I liked people coming up to me, saying, 'I like what you wrote,' or, 'I disagree with you.'"

Wind's course was set. He attended Yale University, and in his senior year contributed a golf column to the *Yale Daily News*. He then took a degree in English Literature at Cambridge University in

England and, at twenty-two, met famed English golf writer Bernard Darwin, then sixty-three. Darwin's "high standards about golf and life suited Herb perfectly," Macdonald says, "and appealed to his perfectionist ways." Following graduation from Cambridge, Wind did his military service and then landed at *The New Yorker.*

By then a worldly young man, Wind began a writing life that has enriched every reader who has come across his work. There's his love of history, for example. To read his 1984 essay on St. Andrews and the British Open is to learn just enough of the town's medieval origins and appreciate how its history bears upon its relationship to the game.

"There was something about the town that appealed to intellectuals . . ." he wrote. "Writers as different in personality as Thomas Carlyle, Anthony Trollope, and Charles Kingsley were regular visitors, as were Sir Edwin Landseer, Sir John Millais, and other painters of the top order. It would be wrong, however, to play down the salient part that the ever increasing reputation of St. Andrews as the cradle of golf played in the recovery of the 'auld grey toun.'" He had also pointed out that "at the very end of the sixteenth century and during much of the seventeenth St. Andrews was ravaged by plagues that killed off most of its inhabitants and left it little more than a ghost town."

There it is: ancient history and golf, in one paragraph, unforced, easy to read, enriching. Ben Crenshaw, an avid reader of Wind's work, calls it "impossibly good. Every time you read him you get a history lesson, a golf lesson, and a life lesson. To write like that you have to love golf."

I always felt I was sitting at the feet of a master when I read Wind. I feel that today, enjoying this long lunch with him and his friend. I feel privileged to have made his acquaintance over the years, to have walked Augusta National and the Old Course with him. My first Wind walk was during the 1982 Masters: we followed Byron Nelson and Gene Sarazen as they played a ceremonial nine holes to open the event; I remember Wind saying Nelson, then seventy, was looking "chirpy," and remarking of the people following, "There's a different mood in this crowd. It's an esprit. The people seem lost in the game. I don't think we'll have a more pleasant walk all week." A month later, I read his assessment in *The New Yorker*.

Wind is a writer through and through, even if he's not actually writing anything any more. His conversation is that of a writer, someone who cares about words. Wind enjoys a lively debate.

"All right, Robbie," he says to Macdonald, "let me have your five favourite courses in the world."

Macdonald offers up the Old Course, Royal Dornoch, Muirfield, Royal County Down, and Cypress Point, then asks for Wind's choices.

"I don't think I can do it," Wind says, playfully.

"Oh yes you can," Macdonald shoots back.

"Well, all right then. The Old Course, Ballybunion, Dornoch, Cypress Point, and Merion. St. Andrews just gives you so many good greens," Wind concludes, leaning back in his chair. "Now, let's have some dessert."

There is no denying the wistful feeling that washes over me while I visit with Wind. There's the matter of his declining health, even apart from his vision problems. His memory is slipping, and he repeats himself occasionally during conversation. Here is a great man of letters, a man from an era now passing. Magazines rarely publish long pieces such as those he favoured. His body of work is evidence that the game is worth examining, that it's a good game, and will endure.

Wind's writing offers lessons. Perhaps because he was a competitive amateur, Wind never used the word "choke." He knew what it was like to lose one's form while competing. After Greg Norman shot 75 to Fuzzy Zoeller's 67 in their playoff for the 1984 U.S. Open at Winged Foot, he wrote: "All in all, [Norman] had one of those days that anyone who plays golf understands only too well. Whatever your degree of proficiency, some days you can hit the ball so sweetly that you wish a large audience of friends were on hand just to see how gifted a shotmaker you are. Then, the next day, for no reason you can understand and then correct, you look as if you'd never played the game before."

What's the lesson? It is, simply: Show empathy in your writing. Golf is difficult.

Our lunch over, we make our way to the car. "I'm so pleased we had this chat," Wind says as we drive back through the meandering, rural roads. "I don't get the chance to be with people who love golf and writing as you fellows do."

Back at his residence, Wind sits in the lounge with us for a few minutes. He's tiring, but insists on walking us to our cars. A woman is giving a tour of the facility, and we come upon her and her guests in the foyer. "We do a lot here," she says. "There are many activities. People come in and lecture, people from Harvard and other schools. We have concerts as well, from many noted musicians."

Wind can't help but overhear her spiel. He adds, "Yes, and a few high-handicappers also find their way here."

We say goodbye in the parking lot. "I hope to see you again," Wind tells me. I hope so too.

"He said some sweet things, didn't he?" Macdonald says after Wind has left. "He always walks out to the car with you, too. You know, I was very lucky to know him. To read Herb and then to get to know him has provided me with a wonderful education. I learned everything about golf from him."

Back home, I find a letter that Wind wrote in 1999 in response to a note I'd sent him. His words are written, not typed. They sit softly on the page. "It's hard to believe but the Masters is just around the corner," it reads. "That's where you and I met many years ago. I thought that the Augusta National played superbly last year. I was also impressed by how the huge crowds were marshalled. Thank you again for your thoughtful letter. I hope that you have a fine spring on and off the golf course."

Wind helped me, and all his readers, have that fine spring, and the other seasons, too. He still does. We have his writing, and what writing it is.

• • •

Herb Wind died on May 30, 2005, at the age of eighty-eight. Charles McGrath of The New York Times wrote in Golf Digest that he "was to golf writing what his friend and idol was to golf itself." His nephew Bill Scheft, a writer himself, organized a memorial for him at the Yale Club in New York City the following September. He wrote that he anticipated "the kind of evening Herb would have loved, especially if everyone was talking about someone other than him." That was Herb; the story was about golfers and the game at large, not about him.

Herb never did write an autobiography, although readers could discern through his work what kind of man he was. He was a fine man, a refined man, a decent man. He also knew his meteorology. It was pleasant to recall the time he went out to watch a round at the 1984 Open, when it was being played at the Old Course. Herb wore a shirt and tie, a sweater, and a jacket. He carried an overcoat. The weather was warm and sunny, but Herb wanted to be prepared. He was always prepared, and it showed.

Herb was inducted into the World Golf Hall of Fame on November 10, 2008.

THREE | The Swing and the Psychology

Letter from Ben Hogan

The Globe and Mail | May 22, 1993

Some thirty-five years ago, Ben Hogan taught ten fellows for a week. He later wrote one of his students a letter. A chain of circumstances has led to the arrival here of a copy of that letter. It offers insights into the mind of a golfer who mastered the flight of the golf ball.

Hogan wrote his thirteen-page letter in longhand. His own stick figures illustrate the positions in the swing he believes enable a golfer to hit the tee shot – "the key that opens the door to good golf."

Hogan immediately sets forth his point of view. "Clubs alone do not make a golf game. Acquiring the proper technique is the only way that a solid game of golf can be developed. It is difficult and almost impossible to analyze the swing of a top pro. None of them can describe what they do entirely so that the average golfer can copy them."

This comment puts the lie to the instructional books pros have written. But Hogan himself wrote *Five Lessons: The Modern Fundamentals of Golf*, a bible for many players. To give Hogan his due, that was his one main contribution to the genre, outside of an early work he called *Power Golf*. He refused to write more books.

Hogan's letter is written differently than his book, which Herbert Warren Wind shaped. The letter is almost a folk-art distillation of his book, written in a naive manner, which is not to say that it is not intelligent, but that it is simple and appealing.

The stick figures that Hogan draws, for example, are effective. He brooks no criticism anyway, by saying their use "was explained to me in detail by one of the greatest pros to play the game, so their [*sic*] is no need to verify or justify its practicality and basic soundness."

"One of the greatest pros" was Walter Hagen. Hagen to Hogan – there's something poetic about the lineage.

But Hogan was a more mechanical player than Hagen, whose

idea of golf was to hit the ball and find it. Hogan's idea was to move the ball around from point A to point B, with no variation tolerated. He practised when he wasn't playing. Golf was Hogan's life, and he learned it in detail.

He writes in his letter of the importance of the grip, and anticipates, or even introduces, the modern emphasis on swinging with the bigger muscles of the body and keeping the hands out of the swing as much as possible. This will reduce the chance that the clubhead will waver, a major source of error.

"The basis of a sound swing is correct leg work and body position," Hogan decrees. He wants the golfer to keep his centre of gravity in one place during the swing; that means keeping one's head still, a tenet of golf much challenged today.

"Difficult you say, impossible, ridiculous you say," Hogan writes. "Why, look how Babe Ruth leaned into the ball when he hit it. Pictures of the Babe verify the fact that he did use his legs with tremendous effect and his head remained in one place throughout his murderous assault of the baseball and golf ball."

Hogan sets up such an assault by bending his knees slightly at address. Then comes the key move.

"The most important part of a good golf swing," he advises, "is to take the club back correctly so as to keep the head in one place. This can be accomplished in only one correct way – by moving the left knee in toward the right knee while moving the left shoulder in a slight downward arc. This will take the club away from the ball without using the hands at all."

That knee motion begins the powerful and accurate swing. The starting move helps the golfer turn his hips and shoulders. The left heel comes off the ground, and from the top of the swing the golfer is told to set it back on the ground and bring the right shoulder slightly down "as the hands, arms, and feet work spontaneously."

Hogan's summarizing tip is that one should have a feeling at the top of the swing that the groin muscles on the inside of the right leg are tightening. "This subtle feeling of tightness there tells you that you have made the correct move back from the ball."

The letter that Hogan wrote was, presumably, free advice to his pupils. It is worth noting that former Toronto Maple Leafs star Frank Mahovlich and his brother Pete, who starred for the Montreal Canadiens, recently played Shady Oaks in Fort Worth, Texas, where Hogan plays. (Pete is a coach in the Central Hockey League in Fort Worth.) They met Hogan for five minutes in the clubhouse, and were favoured with a brief lesson – more free advice from "Bantam Ben."

The ten disciples who visited Hogan in the 1950s weren't as fortunate. Each paid $500 to spend a week with him, plenty of money then. But if it included follow-up by letter, maybe that was a small price to pay. Hogan, after all, was the best, deadly accurate, and not a man given to many words. His detailed letter is a revelation.

The Yips

SCOREGolf Magazine | July 1993

That esteemed golf writer Henry Longhurst said of the yips, "Once you've had 'em, you've got 'em," and indeed, once he had them, it was only a matter of time until the yips forced him to give up playing the game. Other people have called the condition "whisky fingers," or "the twitches." We are speaking of the unspeakable, a debilitating nervous condition that usually affects golfers on short putts and for which Tommy Armour coined the term "the yips."

Armour won three Canadian Opens as well as the 1927 U.S. Open, the 1930 PGA Championship, and the 1931 British Open, so obviously he was able to make a few putts. But he, like many golfers, became anxious when he was near the hole, and on the seventy-first hole of the British Open he yipped a two-footer. He left himself with a three-foot putt to win the championship, and he somehow holed it; not, however, without terror. "I took a new grip," Armour said, "holding the hands as tightly as I could and with stiff wrists, and took a different stance. . . . From the instant the club left the ball on the backswing I was blind and unconscious." But the ball dropped and Armour won the Open. Still, he knew he had suffered an attack of the yips.

Make no mistake: we are speaking of a malady that does attack and is career-threatening. It is a disease of the mind that finds expression in the fingers and, hence, in the putting stroke. "Whoops," exclaims the golfer afflicted with the horror. "What happened there? The putter seemed to go off in my hands. I was standing over the ball and froze." Or, in another version, "I felt okay over the ball, took the blade back nice and slow, and then my right hand took over and the blade jumped."

The mind reels at the memories of golfers who suffered from the yips. Tom Watson hit the ball beautifully, tee to green, during the 1991 Masters. But he appeared shaky over short putts, although not on longer putts, where the yips strike only occasionally and rarely for very long.

Watson knew he would have to make short putts if he hoped to win that Masters. On Saturday evening he worked with David Leadbetter on the practice green at the Augusta National Golf Club. Watson hit short putts with his eyes closed, a common strategy to relax oneself and nullify the worry about striking the ball properly. The idea is that a golfer will make a smooth, almost carefree, accelerating stroke if the visual cues are withdrawn. Watson rolled the ball nicely during his practice session, and then mis-hit a short putt for par on the first hole in the last round. But for the yips around the hole, Watson would surely have won the Masters. He lost by one shot to Ian Woosnam.

Yes, the mind snaps at the memories. Canadian Stan Leonard was as frenzied as a fevered child every time he stood over a putt during the 1983 Peter Jackson Champions tournament at the Earl Grey club in Calgary. The yips had also affected the poor man's chipping and short pitching. He could no better than lunge at the ball, his hands flying on their own, out of control. It wasn't easy to avert one's eyes at this public display of a private demon. It was impossible to turn away.

But what are, or, more properly, is, the yips, exactly? Bernhard Langer, the 1985 and 1993 Masters champion, has suffered more than any contemporary golfer. He's had the yips three times and overcome the condition three times, which must offer hope to yippers everywhere. That does not mean Langer understands where the yips comes from, or that he is confident the sickening problem will not return. He knows better.

Nick Price, the 1992 PGA Championship winner, remembers playing with Langer on the European Tour. Langer didn't want to walk onto a green. Here is a golfer who four-putted from six feet during the 1977 German Close championship. He used to average forty putts per round.

"It's a weird situation," Langer says. "The yips can come back any time, and I haven't found anyone out there who understands them. Believe me, I have tried all sorts of remedies and talked to many people."

Langer wasn't aware that the yips is part of a class of motor difficulties called "focal occupational dystonias." Baylor College of Medicine neuropsychologist Dr. Fran Pirozzolo works with many touring pros, one of whom is Mark O'Meara, and has written on the subject. He believes the yips represents golf's Dracula.

A group of doctors studied the yips and reported their findings in the February 1989 issue of the journal *Neurology*. Their clinical definition of the yips as one of the focal dystonias is illuminating.

"The 'yips' is a motor phenomenon that affects golfers and consists of involuntary movements occurring in the course of the execution of focused, finely controlled, skilled motor behaviour. The movements emerge particularly during putting and are less evident during chipping or driving. The nature of the involuntary movements has been difficult to characterize but golfers have used the following descriptive terms: yips, twitches, staggers, waggles, jitters, jerks, or 'them,' suggesting various components of muscle spasm, cramp, tremor, or myoclonus."

For a horrifying, if all too accurate, rendition of the minutiae of the yips, we turn to the Englishman Harry Vardon, who won six British Opens as well as the 1900 U.S. Open. He was Bobby Jones's idol, just as Jones became Jack Nicklaus's hero. Superb golfer though Vardon was, he had a long-time case of the yips, perhaps brought on by a short stay in a sanatorium when that was the only way to treat tuberculosis. Here is Vardon on the tremble in his right hand that was his primary symptom of the yips. Audrey Howell writes of the matter in her biography of Vardon.

"As I stood addressing the ball, I would watch for my right hand to jump," Vardon recalls. "At the end of two seconds I would not be looking at the ball at all. My gaze would have become riveted to my right hand. I simply could not resist the desire to discover what it was going to do. Directly, I felt that it was about to jump. I would snatch at the ball in a desperate effort to play the shot before the involuntary movement would take effect."

This is material fit for a nightmare, and many golfers are familiar with the images and feelings. Sam Snead had the yips, which I watched during the 1966 PGA Championship at Firestone Country Club's South course in Akron, Ohio. Snead could not make a putt the first nine holes of this particular round and looked especially anxious when he faced one. So it was on the tenth hole, if memory serves, that he went to a croquet style of putting, whereby he straddled the line of the hole. The United States Golf Association, in its infinite wisdom to confound yippers, decided this was illegal. Snead eventually altered his style to putt by still facing the hole but with the ball and putter at his side. Some years later I played a round with Snead. He said with no particular relish that all golfers who are accurate ball-strikers can expect the yips to attack them after age forty.

"You hit the ball close to the hole so often, you start to think you should make all those birdie putts. But nobody does, and it gets to you." So said Slammin' Sammy Snead.

But back to Vardon for more Gothic description.

"Up would go my head and body with a start and off would go the ball – anywhere but on the proper line. Such was the outcome of a loss of confidence . . . I could always tell when I was about to have relief. If no jump came on the first green, I knew I was safe for the round."

But Vardon, like Armour, Snead, and Ben Hogan, always had to contend with the yips. At age fifty he led the 1920 U.S. Open by four shots with seven holes to play. A furious storm blew in over the Inverness Club in Toledo, Ohio. Vardon three-putted from the thirteenth through the fifteenth, and all was soon lost. Howell writes that "Vardon cursed the illness which, over the years, had left him with an uncontrollable twitch in his right arm muscle."

What of modern golfers? Has science helped them in their attempts to avoid or overcome the yips? First, Nick Faldo.

"Oh, thanks," he says when asked about the yips during the 1992 Johnnie Walker World Championship at Tryall Golf Club near Montego Bay, Jamaica, as if to speak the word is to bring on the malaise. He offers a comment, but only a brief one. Remember, though, that this is a golfer who often asks his caddy, Fanny Sunesson, to stand behind him on short putts so that he can be sure of his line. The less confusion, the better. Faldo believes in science.

"It's mental, isn't it?" Faldo says of the yips. "Just got to think the right things." Faldo must have done that. He went on to win the Johnnie Walker.

Here's Corey Pavin: "The only thing the yips can be is a lack of confidence over the putt. You have a bad feeling that you're not lined up, or that you've misread the putt. There's a lot of negative thought. You need a positive outlook to make your decisions count. There's no chance otherwise. You have to overcome the flinch, that's the thing."

Paul Azinger: "Some people say it's neurological, but I don't believe it. The yips are a flinch of some sort, an inability to make a short putt that probably begins in the mind. I've never had them yet [notice that 'yet']. But I feel fear over every putt. You just try not to hit it until you feel ready to make it."

That could mean a golfer stands over the ball forever. It may also be why some yippers freeze and can only get the blade back with that twitchy jerk that resembles somebody snapping his hands away from a hot burner. What to do, what to do?

Start with the idea, as teacher David Leadbetter suggests, that putting is individual, different for every player. That opens the territory for personal solutions. Tom Kite and Fred Couples have gone to putting cross-handed for the most part. Davis Love III follows Dr. Bob Rotella's advice to look once at the hole and almost simultaneously make his stroke. Numerous golfers have gone to the long putter, all in order, Leadbetter believes, "to make a stroke and let the ball get in the way."

"People get tense and tight," Leadbetter continues. "A lot of the solution is in developing a routine every time. I still think that practising with one's eyes closed is helpful, because the eyes can do damage in watching the putter head. It's a serious problem, and I believe it happens because at some point golfers realize a putt has the least margin of error of any shot. Years of realizing that, and the fact that you may have been a good putter, and you soon expect to hole every putt."

But Langer's experience indicates that the yips can strike any time, to a golfer of any age. He first suffered when he was eighteen, at the start of his career.

"The main reason for me, I think, was that I grew up in Germany playing on slow greens for my first ten years in the game," Langer says. "Then I played a tournament in Spain where the greens were lightning fast. I couldn't control the ball, kept hitting it at the wrong speed. That, combined with a pressure to succeed because I had no money and wanted to stay out there, led me to feel tense with the putter and triggered tension and fear."

That noxious mixture caused Langer to flinch for many years. All the positive thinking in the world didn't help, for, as Langer observes, "You can't stand over the ball and say you are going to make it when you haven't been making putts."

Langer sought the proper mechanics. Seve Ballesteros noticed that Langer's putter had no loft and was too light. This was in late 1980, and Langer tried another putter. He putted adequately for two years, and then, another attack.

"I went to cross-handed then, and that lasted six years. In all that time, and even until now, I haven't met anyone who could tell me what the yips are all about. What sort of reaction is it, chemical, mental, something in your body? I don't know."

Langer tried putting conventionally on putts of fifteen feet or longer, and cross-handed on shorter putts. Kite uses a version of this, choosing one way or the other depending on how he feels. Langer putted well quite often. He seemed to have conquered the yips once and for all.

But that wasn't the case. His stroke shortened and his wrists broke down through impact. He five-putted the seventeenth green on his way to an 80 during the 1988 British Open at Royal Lytham and St Annes.

Langer kept trying to devise a way to putt, and came up with an astonishing method after seeing Johnny Miller and Larry Rinker use variations. He clasps his left forearm with his right thumb while putting cross-handed. The fingers of his right hand curl under the forearm and putter. The method locks his right wrist in place. The ball rolls smoothly. Azinger says that most golfers would rank Langer as one of the five best putters in the world.

So it goes in the world of the yips. Langer speaks of his trials in a quiet voice. He is trying to take as many moving parts as possible out of his putting stroke, trying to keep his hands and wrists out of his stroke. The problem, he knows, comes from the small muscles. For now, anyway, Langer has a handle on it.

It was therefore ironic that it fell upon Langer to have to make a six-foot putt on the last hole in the final match of the 1991 Ryder Cup at the Ocean Course in Kiawah Island, South Carolina, for Europe to retain the trophy. He missed, but only because he and his caddy decided on the wrong line. Langer did hit a good putt. It came off the blade smoothly, and rolled rather than staggered to the hole.

A week later, Langer faced a fifteen-foot putt on the last hole to get into a playoff at the German Masters. He rolled the ball into the heart of the cup, and then won the playoff. No shakes, no worries because of the missed putt at the Ryder Cup. No yips.

Maybe Longhurst was not quite right, then. Once you've had 'em, all right, you've got 'em, but you can also deal with 'em. Well, you can try. Good luck.

On Denial

Golf Journal | March/April 1994

Have you ever blamed the wind for a shot that flew off course? Ever examined a discoloration on a green after you missed a putt? Ever stared at a member of your group who moved at the top of your swing? There's a story about a golfer who hit a shot into the woods and then glared at his companion before accusing him of causing his bad shot. "I saw the whites of your shoes when I was coming down into the ball," he said preposterously but, to be sure, understandably. Indeed, he was rather cunning. He was using "denial," an important mechanism that sports psychologists agree is crucial to good golf. Champion golfers in particular deny that they cause their own mistakes, especially during the course of a round.

Many examples make the point. Nick Price missed an eighteen-inch par putt on the last hole during his first-day match against Irishman David Feherty in the Dunhill Cup at the Old Course last October. That gave Feherty the match. Price's putt was virtually a tap-in, and so he was shocked to watch as his putt spun out of the hole and finished behind it; it seemed ridiculous that he could miss such a short putt. Naturally, Price had to deny his responsibility in the matter. Price turned to Feherty as they walked off the green and said he had been putting through his own shadow. It wasn't his fault, not at all.

A similar incident has become legend at the Canadian Open. Jack Nicklaus designed the Glen Abbey Golf Club near Toronto, where the Canadian Open has been played every year but one since 1977. Nicklaus has finished second or tied for second three times at Glen Abbey. In 1985, when he lost to Curtis Strange, the great man came up with a truly inventive reason for his defeat.

Nicklaus and Strange were tied and playing together. Nicklaus hit the green in two on the par-five sixteenth hole, but missed a crucial three-foot birdie putt. Strange went on to win, while Nicklaus related a very interesting excuse for his error. "Just as I was over the ball," he said without any hesitation, "the sun cast a glint over the blade of my putter." Nicklaus was distracted, the ball missed the hole, and he was on his way to another second-place finish. But he had preserved the feeling that many top players share and that, according to psychologists, allows them to go on during a round: the mistake was not their fault.

Davis Love III, for one, believes Nicklaus in particular is a master at using denial, the "it couldn't have been me" idea. He points out that professionals employ the strategy on the greens more than anywhere else. "If you've hit a good putt that didn't go in," Love points out, "then something must have happened."

Something happened, all right, to appropriate the title of a Joseph Heller novel. That something is outside the golfer's sphere of responsibility, or so he believes. Greg Norman hit what looked a perfect putt last August on the seventy-second green at Inverness Club in Toledo at the PGA Championship. Had the twenty-foot birdie putt gone in, Norman would have won the tournament. But the ball spun out of the hole, and then Norman lost the tournament to Paul Azinger on the second hole of their sudden-death playoff.

"We call that 'getting painted,' in our profession," Norman explained after the tournament. "The hole was painted [with white paint] right to the rim. It gets hard and crusty, and the ball can spin out instead of in." Who's to argue? But certainly Norman's was a novel explanation. It helped him handle his extreme disappointment. It was also perfectly understandable.

"I have found that golfers use denial widely," says Dr. Richard Coop, a professor of Educational Psychology at the University of North Carolina in Chapel Hill. Coop works with Payne Stewart, Larry Mize, Scott Simpson, and Corey Pavin, among others. "Golf is so hard to play well over a long haul. You need to put the blame for mistakes elsewhere, at least in the short term. It's important to be your own best friend on the course."

Coop's point seems to be that the most successful golfers are able to deflect blame for their errors elsewhere while they are involved in a round. A golfer could presumably be engulfed by feeling at fault for every little mistake, every bad bounce of the ball. Hence the spectacle of a golfer looking up to the treetops when his ball is carried away from his target. The implication is that the wind changed direction and conveyed his ball hither and yon. Or a golfer tosses blades of grass into the air after his shot; again, the wind changed. Sometimes a golfer will wring his club after he doesn't make solid contact with the ball, as if to say that the grips were damp and he could not hold on properly. These are all examples of short-term denial, an important and often overlooked mechanism that can serve players well.

"In psychology we refer to what we call 'attribution theory,'" explains Dr. Fran Pirozzolo, chief of neuropsychology service at Baylor College of Medicine in Houston. "This has to do with the ways in which people describe themselves, as successes or failures. Clinical and experimental studies show that peak performers [that is, golfers such as Price and Nicklaus] have an internal explanation for success and external ones for failure."

Pirozzolo has worked with Norman, Mark O'Meara, Steve Elkington, Joey Sindelar, and Bill Britton, as well as 1992 U.S. Amateur champion Justin Leonard. Like Coop, he believes that denial, employed properly, can be an effective tool in dealing with the mental strains of golf. Players use the strategy all the time. O'Meara showed this endearingly on the eleventh hole during the Doral Ryder Open last year, when he hit a routine bunker shot fifteen feet past the hole. His reaction was to stare at the sand. Of course – his shot went too far because there was something wrong with the sand. A few minutes later, meanwhile, Azinger missed a ten-foot birdie putt on the fourteenth hole. Walking to the tee, Azinger said, "The grain held that one up. I had it read right." The grain. Of course.

Such explanations are humorous when considered later, but this should not diminish their significance. At the same time, both Coop and Pirozzolo agree that denial, taken too far, can harm a player's chances for long-term success. The simple reason is that there is indeed a cause for every error on the course. But smart golfers accept their mistakes on the course without feeling they need to change everything immediately. They work on their games later, no longer denying the part they themselves may have played. In fact, they may have even acknowledged their responsibility to themselves on the course, but only privately and briefly. They rarely would blame themselves publicly for their errors. Top athletes have an essential and fundamental detachment from their own unsuccessful performance.

The phenomenon may apply in all sports. The extraordinary New York Giants pitcher Christy Mathewson, who played during the early part of this century, once said something pertinent to this discussion. His comments are worth capturing in whole.

"An alibi is sound and needed in all competition," Mathewson explained. "I mean in the highest brackets. One of the foundations of success in sport is confidence in yourself. You can't afford to admit that any opponent is better than you are. So, if you lose to him there must be a reason – a bad break. You must have an alibi to show why you lost. If you haven't one, you must fake one. Your self-confidence must be maintained.

"Always have that alibi. But keep it to yourself. That's where it belongs. Don't spread it around. Lose gracefully in the open. To yourself, lose bitterly – but learn! You can learn little from victory. You can learn everything from defeat."

Mathewson's words may be taken as an anthem for top golfers, except that many do make their alibis public after their rounds. But then they are off to practice. They know they cannot maintain the alibi forever.

"I agree that it is important to keep the alibi to yourself," Coop says, knowing that golfers don't always do this. "But it's more important to use it, really use it, only on the course. If you let golf get to you too much while playing, the game can overwhelm you."

Coop tries to help his players achieve a helpful detachment on the course, and then gets them to correct their errors away from the course. "It's crucial that the player get back to thinking about his mistakes rationally," Coop adds, "to understand that he really did hit that driver badly."

Alibis, then, are central to effective play. Even casual golfers know this. What else are they preparing themselves for but errors when they chat on the first tee with their companions, saying, "I haven't played in months." They are making sure they won't expect too much from themselves; presto, poor play is not their responsibility. After all, how could it have been different?

There are golfers, however, and plenty of them, who are hard on themselves on and off the course. These players, Pirozzolo observes, rarely reach their potential. They persist in blaming themselves and can't even take credit for their successes. Their successes are the accidents; they expect their failures. These people haven't learned to use denial.

"I think it's part of our American way of life," Pirozzolo says. "We believe we are responsible for everything that happens to us, and so we believe we can push to great lengths and then succeed. But that doesn't always happen. We can't achieve perfection. We need to be more flexible." A major part of this flexibility is the ability to incorporate a healthy denial into one's approach to golf. Pirozzolo refers to this as understanding that the source of error, on the course, is remote from oneself. Failure, then, does not become a stable part of one's character. The golfer can learn to internalize success and externalize failure. It's all part of playing well. After all, how bad can the wind really be on the twelfth hole at the Augusta National Golf Club? One would think by watching the competitors in the Masters on the tee who swirl grass clippings in the air and glare at the treetops around the green that there is something mystical going on in the area. Hasn't anybody ever just hit a bad shot to this green? Or, to take another angle on the subject, hasn't a golfer ever hit a good shot when a camera clicks? Does he credit the click of the camera for his good shot? Of course not, but golfers are quick to blame a cameraman for their poor shots.

A final, telling example: two-time U.S. Amateur champion Jay Sigel was competing in the first round of qualifying for the 1989 championship at Merion. Sigel double-bogeyed the opening hole, then made a nine on the par-five second hole, shanking his second shot out of bounds from deep grass. He went on to recover from his potentially devastating start and qualified for match play.

Washington psychiatrist Ted Beal, an avid amateur golfer, was watching Sigel that day. "I couldn't believe he was disintegrating like that," Beal says now. "The way my head would work, I'd figure I'm out. Instead, he played brilliantly and went on to qualify." Beal wondered about Sigel's mental processes and chatted with him after the round.

"I asked him what he was thinking about after the nine on the second hole," Beal remembers. "Was he worried about qualifying? Sigel answered, 'No, I didn't think it was a problem.'" To this day, Beal recalls the incident and his conversation with Sigel vividly. "My hunch is that the nine he made just didn't enter his mind."

It didn't, at least not consciously. Sigel remembered the experience somewhat differently. "That was unbelievable," he told writer James Finegan. "I wanted to hop on the trolley, the P&W, and just keep going. I thought that my career had ended right there."

There you have it – denial par excellence. Call it an "ego defence mechanism," as Coop does. Or speak about "external reasons for failure," as does Pirozzolo. Or think about what Beal mentions is a tendency of highly successful people, that they can hold "multiple contrasting simultaneous thoughts." Golfers such as Sigel and Nicklaus can be bothered and detached at the same time. The decisive factor is that these golfers maintain their detachment while they play. Denial keeps them going, and it's one important reason Nicklaus has won twenty majors, including his two U.S. Amateurs, and why Sigel was the country's best amateur for years. Now, if the rest of us could only learn to use denial. How well we might play.

• • •

Tiger Woods missed a four-foot birdie putt on the first extra hole that would have won his third-round match against Nick O'Hern in the 2007 Accenture Match Play Championship. O'Hern won the match on the next hole. Woods said a ball mark deflected his putt to the right of the hole on the birdie putt he missed. "I was so enthralled with the line and where I had to start it. It was just left centre, go ahead and hit it, and I didn't see the ball mark. All I had to do is just fix it, and it's in."

No way could Woods have hit a poor putt. Denial lives.

Theodore Jorgensen: The Physics of Golf

The Globe and Mail | April 15, 2006

Along the way to winning the 2003 Masters, Mike Weir studied the golf swing closely; he still does. One of the books he read was *The Physics of Golf*, by Theodore Jorgensen. I sent the book to Weir because I thought he'd find it interesting, and I mention this because Jorgensen died on April 4. He was 100.

Weir said he liked a lot of what Jorgensen wrote. Apparently, many people did. The American Institute of Physics published the book in 1994, and it remains the institute's best-selling title. Jorgensen spent twenty-five years researching and writing the book.

Earlier this year, I was supposed to visit Jorgensen in his hometown of Lincoln, Nebraska, for a story about him. But when I called his wife, Dorothy, to make the arrangements, she told me he'd fallen and moved from their home into an assisted-living residence. She said he wasn't up to seeing a visitor then, so I never did make the trip.

Jorgensen was an emeritus professor of Physics at the University of Nebraska at Lincoln. He took up golf at sixty and immediately was taken with the game. He couldn't hit the ball properly, even though he read instruction books. Then came May 9, 1968, when he made an entry in his workbook.

"Would an investigation into the physics of the swing of a golf club help improve my game?" he asked. His quest began that day and never stopped.

His associate, Roger Kirby, now the chairman of Nebraska's Department of Physics and Astronomy, told me when I called him a few months ago: "He always likes to talk about golf, and he won't mince words."

That wasn't surprising, given what Jorgensen had done before in a world far removed from golf. Having received his doctorate in Theoretical Physics in 1935 from Harvard University, he taught for a few years at Nebraska while doing some research. He was called on to work on the Manhattan Project in Los Alamos, New Mexico. This led, of course, to the development of the atom bomb.

Jorgensen's responsibility was to measure the size of the explosion that the atom bomb would set off. Talking to the *Lincoln Journal Star* last year, he said: "Some people thought the universe would blow up. We knew we were on the edge of a new world."

Jorgensen and his family eventually returned from Los Alamos to Lincoln, where he began and directed an atomic accelerator program at the university. His first wife died in 1959 and he remarried in 1960. His second wife, Dorothy, was a golfer.

Jorgensen set his practised mind to work studying the golf swing. His wife said: "One of the things physicists do is try to analyze situations that involve physics. How to swing a club is an interesting problem that leads you to ask questions. Computers were just becoming available, and Ted had to learn how to program them on his own."

His studies proved challenging, even for a man who understood quantum physics. He continually revised *The Physics of Golf*, and wondered whether Tiger Woods read it. Jorgensen wasn't convinced that equipment was of much value when it came to a golfer improving his swing, something every aficionado should take to heart when about to spend hundreds of dollars on the latest, greatest high-tech driver.

"Any golfer who wishes to improve his swing must work on himself," Jorgensen wrote. "He is the one who makes his clubs go through their motions. The secret of golf is in the swing. As one knowledgeable golfer put it: 'The effect of equipment is found to be in small percentages here and there, but these never add up to very much.'"

It's not possible here to outline the crucial elements of Jorgensen's penetrating studies. But here's something he said that is crucial to all efficient and powerful swings: "The feeling of the pull of the left shoulder on the left arm has been emphasized [in the book] because this means of supplying energy to the swing is not brought into the conscious level by many [right-handed] golfers."

Bobby Jones believed in this, and so did Jimmy Ballard, who taught major championship winners such as Hal Sutton and Curtis Strange.

Jorgensen was obviously an amazing man. I regret that I didn't make it to Lincoln to meet him. But there's his book, which is worth reading – and reading again and again, for insight into the swing, and the mind of a brilliant man.

Stack & Tilt

Golf World | April 20, 2007

Swing coaches Andy Plummer and Mike Bennett are known on the PGA Tour as "the scientists," and also "the whisperers" for the quiet way they go about their business. Their database includes more than a million – yes, a million – photographs of golfers at various stages of their swings. The centrepiece of their approach is that the most efficient swing is one in which the golfer stays centred over the ball during the backswing, while keeping his weight on the front foot. There is no effort to transfer weight. They've drawn this conclusion from their studies, and it's nearly revolutionary. Most instruction maintains that a golfer must load into the back foot to create torque and power.

Aaron Baddeley has won twice since he began working with Plummer and Bennett in fall 2005. Dean Wilson, Will MacKenzie, and Eric Axley each won his first PGA Tour event last year; Plummer and Bennett have worked with more first-time winners in the last eight months than anybody. Mike Weir, the 2003 Masters champion, has been with them since late last fall. Cameras and computers in hand, the duo intends to turn golf instruction upside down, or, in their view, right side up. Their files and binders are full of lines and circles and grids, because their work relies heavily on the geometry of the swing.

"You have to look at a lot of pictures of players in the same exact spot," Plummer says. "All of them have different stances, and all of them have different postures. If that's the case, then those aren't really fundamentals." But, he and Bennett claim, staying centred over the ball is a fundamental, perhaps *the* fundamental.

"I started with these guys two years ago when I couldn't hit the ball," Wilson says during a practice round one afternoon at the Honda Classic in Palm Beach Gardens, Florida, as Plummer walks along. "I was working as hard as I could with a teacher, and I couldn't hit the ball anywhere where I wanted to. I felt like a hack. Luckily, I ran into these guys."

Wilson goes on: "The great classic swingers, the best players, Hogan, Snead, Nicklaus, they all look like they're on top of the ball. They don't load up on their right side or restrict their hip turn. Nicklaus says you should load up to your right side, but all his weight's here." Wilson is pointing to his left foot.

Nicklaus agrees with Wilson, and, by extension, with Plummer and Bennett. "I don't believe in a lateral shift," he says. "Of course not. I believe in staying on the ball." Asked what he thinks about teachers who advocate a weight shift, he answers, "They don't know how to play."

As for Baddeley, he credits his recent success to his more centred swing, although the idea perplexed him at first. "I had to get around a couple of things when I started to work with Mike and Andy, like staying centred instead of getting behind the ball, and having my hands and arms in on my backswing. My swing's now a little shorter, and my hands are more down. I really, really enjoy working with these guys."

Plummer and Bennett have gained credibility among their fellow teaching pros, even while their approach comes in for some criticism.

"They've obviously had some success," says David Leadbetter, who worked with Baddeley before Plummer and Bennett. "I like what they've done with Aaron, the shortness of his action. There's a look of the old reverse C in the finish position [of their players], so you hope the guys they work with have seriously mobile backs. The interesting thing to me about them is how much time they spend looking at cameras. You just wonder if by doing that, you actually own what you're doing, or are you just borrowing it, and how long it will last and if it will stand up. It's a method, not *the* method."

• • •

Careers, like golf balls, have trajectories. Plummer, a Kentuckian, and Bennett, from upstate New York, each planned a path to the PGA Tour. But they struggled while playing college golf and found themselves adrift in a sea of instruction.

Plummer, forty, attended Austin Peay University in Clarksville, Tennessee, for a year, and then transferred to Eastern Kentucky University, where he was on the golf team while majoring in Economics with a minor in Statistics. But he became his team's worst ball-striker. No matter how many crates of balls he hit, or how much he studied books and tapes, he got worse.

"I couldn't figure out what was going on," he says. "I was getting not just a little worse, I couldn't hit it at all. None of the guys on my team wanted to be my partner. I went from a guy who averaged 72 or 73 in my twenty-round qualifier for the team to a guy who was shooting 90."

Bennett, thirty-nine, traversed a similar path. He played junior golf at the Skaneateles Country Club in the Finger Lakes region of upstate New York. He attended East Tennessee University in Johnson City for a year, and, like Plummer, saw his game deteriorate despite intensive studies. "It was unbelievable," he says. "I had all this information and no idea which parts were helping and which were hurting."

Plummer's and Bennett's trajectories intersected after they'd become familiar with Homer Kelley's fascinating cult book *The Golfing Machine*. Their games improved after intensive study of the book, based on engineering principles. They came to know Mac O'Grady, the eccentric, knowledgeable former PGA Tour winner who studied Kelley's landmark work. Players such as Grant Waite and Steve Elkington have long thought O'Grady's swing is a model of efficiency and power. O'Grady, Bennett says, "taught us how to classify [swing patterns and variations]. That was the biggest light going on. If you want to do a study, the essence of science is classification. That's page one."

O'Grady introduced Plummer and Bennett to Grant Waite, with whom he was working, and Waite introduced them to Wilson. One player begat another, in nearly biblical fashion. Last year, in short order, Wilson won the International, MacKenzie the Reno-Tahoe Open, and Axley the Valero Texas Open. Wilson introduced Weir to the coaches, and he began to work with them after ten years with instructor Mike Wilson. He couldn't prevent what he told Bennett and Plummer was a problem of "drifting" off the ball – the weight shift.

Bennett travelled to Thailand with Weir last month for the Johnnie Walker Classic in March. Weir took Plummer's copy of *The Golfing Machine*. He shot 66–78–68–67 to finish fifth, four shots behind winner Anton Haig. Weir kept drawing the ball too much in the second round, and couldn't stop, although he knew what to do. But as spring wore on, Weir said he had gained a deeper understanding of Plummer's and Bennett's material, and that staying centred was feeling more natural. He continues to be impressed with the diligence of his teachers.

Plummer and Bennett have started working recently with Brad Faxon, who acknowledges taking more lessons from more teachers than just about anybody during his twenty-four years on tour. Faxon was aware of their growing reputation when he approached them earlier this year. "You have to have a guy win to make it as a coach out here," Faxon says. "You have a guy who hits perfect shots all the time, and he finishes fiftieth, nobody's going to want to see him."

Faxon, according to Plummer and Bennett, is a textbook case of what to do wrong, and he agrees. "I moved my centre too far off the ball, I had too flat of a shoulder turn, and my centre stayed way behind on the downswing, with my spine angle way back. They changed me in minutes," Faxon says of their first meeting. Of his ball-striking during tournaments, he adds, "From where I've been, it's not easy to do, but I'm seeing results. The stuff that they're teaching, they'll be teaching the same stuff in thirty years. It's won't go out of vogue."

Of course, many swing theories have come and gone over the years. The list, including some methods that remain popular, includes Jimmy Ballard's "connection" approach; Eddie Merrins's "Swing the Handle, Not the Clubhead"; Jim McLean's "X-Factor"; and Leadbetter's teaching of the swing as based around big muscles and two pivot points. "There's a miracle out there every week," says McLean.

That the Plummer-Bennett way may not be for everyone is evidenced by Jason Gore's recent return to his long-time teacher, Mike Miller, after a period with the duo. "I was trying to do something that I'm not physically able to do," says Gore, a barrel-chested man with short arms. Says instructor Jim Suttie: "Certain people are not built to do that. If you have a flexibility issue, you can't do that [swing as Plummer and Bennett advocate]."

Plummer and Bennett can demonstrate what they preach. Bennett plans to go to Tour Qualifying School in the fall, "not so much that it's my dream to play out here but to prove that I can still hit the ball and chip and putt well enough to play at that level. It's more that quest than wanting the lifestyle of playing week in and week out." Few if any swing coaches have taken the gamble of putting their games on such public display.

Bennett and Plummer are each married, with no children. They have established a research facility near Villanova University in Philadelphia, in part to house their increasingly sophisticated cameras and computers. They're also working on a relationship with a course or resort as a main location. Meanwhile, they speak in one voice. "They never contradict each other," Weir says. "They're always on the same page, which gives me confidence." Waite refers to their teaching as "an inconvenient truth. It is different, and that's what I call it, an inconvenient truth."

Bennett's and Plummer's long-term goals are both simple and audacious. "I think we're going to force the other instructors to use a little more detail or truer measurements to explain why the ball's flying where it's flying," Bennett says. "You can't just stand there and say, 'Oh, that was a good shot, that was a bad shot.' The players are going to demand better instructions. A lot of guys have been taught right off the tour."

Says Plummer: "Our goal is to change the way people think about how to swing a golf club, change the whole paradigm. To have the credibility to do that, the guys we're working with have to play well. They have to be able to demonstrate that it works. I know it works."

In Search of the Swing

The Globe and Mail | September 1, 2007

Mark Burke and Tom Monaghan are golf teachers who run a company called the Next Golf Adventure. They work in Vancouver, where they try to help befuddled golfers improve, and they do the same on the resort courses where they play host to small groups. They were recently in Toronto, where they fell into a discussion at dinner with Laird White, an instructor at the Eagles Nest Golf Club.

"We were wondering why most golfers don't seem to improve," Burke said soon after their conversation.

Golfers' handicaps remain stagnant, despite improvements in equipment, course conditions, and advances in the science of the swing. According to the National Golf Foundation data from 2005, the average handicap index for men has remained about fifteen and for women about twenty-three for decades. The NGF, based in Jupiter, Florida, is the primary research and consulting organization for the industry.

Burke, Monaghan, and White are excellent teachers who study the game closely. But none of the threesome was able to come up with a specific reason or reasons why most golfers don't improve, no matter how much instruction they take or how much they practise. But White did offer an interesting idea in a later discussion.

"The forty-five-minute lesson or a package of five lessons doesn't work," White said of the industry standards. "I'm part of that, too. I book those lessons."

White's view makes sense, but maybe there's more to it.

Bill Madonna, for one, refuses to take on students for less than at least a day that includes on-course instruction. Ideally, he'd like to work with a student for at least six months.

I recently spent a morning with Madonna, a *Golf Magazine* top-100 teacher and PGA master teaching professional, at the Grand Niagara course in Niagara Falls, Ontario. Madonna's academy is in Orlando, but he's been teaching there this summer and will continue through this month.

Madonna faced a formidable task.

My handicap has gone from three to nine in the past ten years. I've developed a re-grip and a hitch in my backswing, followed by a few loops to reroute the path of my club back to impact and a bewildering tendency to collapse my left side through the ball. I turn a ten-degree driver into an eighteen-degree five-wood as I deloft the clubhead and scoop the ball at impact. I turn a five-iron into an eight-iron.

Under a hot sun, Madonna settled into his work with me.

He noticed I was lined up so far to the right that I had no choice but to reroute the club to get back to the ball properly.

Madonna introduced me to his CHEF system of alignment: club behind the ball first, head over it, then eyes to the target and, finally, shift the feet into position. He also showed me, on video, that I stopped moving my left side through the ball. I could only flip my hands at the ball, thereby adding loft to the club.

I'd seen this before, when a smart young techie named Matt Bryce in Toronto took me through the MATT system: motion analysis by TaylorMade. And the late Ben Kern, then the head professional at the National Golf Club in Woodbridge, Ontario, had pointed out my collapsed side. Norm Moote, a disciple of George Knudson, worked with me to move my body correctly back from the ball and through impact to the finish. Mark Evershed tried to get me into a better position at impact through emphasizing a flat left wrist at the ball.

I've worked hard on Madonna's suggestions during the few weeks since I saw him. However, I've been unable to correct my mistakes. My body won't do what I want it to do. It's not as if I haven't tried, and I intend to continue trying. Madonna believes that more extension through the ball is the key to my attaining proper impact position. Knudson felt that way, and so does Moote. I believe they're right.

Still, I can do that in my practice swing, but my failure to do it in my real swing raises a fundamental question: Why is it so difficult to make changes in one's real swing? Is a golfer's swing like a signature, all but immutable?

The difficulty lies not only with amateurs, but with golfers right up to the very best. Major champions such as Seve Ballesteros and Ian Baker-Finch lost their swings to such an extent that they had to withdraw from competitive golf. Craig Perks, the 2002 Players Championship winner, for some reason tried to improve his swing after the tournament. He's had nothing but trouble since and is thinking of leaving the game. Bruce Lietzke, the 1978 and 1982 Canadian Open winner, meanwhile, has never tried to change his swing. He rarely practises, and he said more golfers than anybody wants to believe have lost their games while trying to retool their swings.

Still, most every golfer believes improvement is possible. Golf magazines know this, which is why instruction dominates their covers and fills their pages. I have at hand the Canadian magazine *SCOREGolf* from June, dubbed the Special Instruction Issue. Next to it, glaring at me as if to scold, is the April/May of 1981 issue, which I edited. The cover tells the reader that inside is advice on curing five nasty habits.

Then there's the current issue of *Golf Magazine,* featuring the "No Backswing Swing." Jim Suttie and his associate T.J. Tomasi describe their research that shows a golfer can eliminate a vast number of errors by starting the swing at the top, thereby resembling a baseball batter at address more than a golfer.

Golf Digest, meanwhile, has been advocating the hot "stack and tilt" method, as taught by Andy Plummer and Mike Bennett. Mike Weir switched to stack and tilt late last fall, in the interests of more consistency and less chance of injury. The idea is to stay centred over the ball and not to shift weight during the backswing.

I've written about and tried the no-backswing swing. I've stacked and tilted. I'm promiscuous when it comes to trying different approaches. Plummer and Bennett believe golfers should improve immediately if advised to make the proper corrections. That's not been the case with me, no matter what I try, or, I daresay, with the majority of golfers

But I like to practise and to field-test. Did I mention that I've written instruction books with Knudson and also with Nick Price and David Leadbetter? Still, my problems remain. Johnny Miller once said that a good player takes loft off a club at impact while a lesser player adds loft. It hurt to read that. It hurts to remember it now.

I've had endless instruction to try to attain a valid impact position. Tom Watson once told me that impact is all that matters, and I believed him. But confusion reigns. Leadbetter examined my swing a few years ago and said, "With the shape of your swing, I wouldn't try to do anything but fade the ball." Not long after that, I joined Chuck Cook for a game. Cook, the late Payne Stewart's swing coach, said nothing about my swing until we reached the fourteenth hole at the National, Canada's ultimate examination of one's game.

"You know, I've been watching the shape of your swing," Cook said, "and if I were you, I wouldn't try to do anything but hook the ball." Each top teacher offered me opposite advice.

And so it goes, a steady stream of advice. I've already informed my family of my epitaph: "Finally, no more swing thoughts."

For now, though, I think of my instructors and their instructions. Patti McGowan, then a Leadbetter instructor, advised me during a two-day clinic to hoist a hefty medicine ball and turn my chest to the right before releasing it toward an imaginary wall, thereby learning the feeling of getting behind the golf ball. Rick Rhoads at the San

Francisco Golf Club told me I had an unusual eye-line problem that caused me to toss my head back at the start of my backswing. Jack Nicklaus's teacher, Jack Grout, suggested I get my upper body behind the ball at the top. Moe Norman wanted me to swing long and low through the ball.

Then there was the legendary Bob Toski, the PGA Tour's leading money-winner in 1954 and the first inductee into the World Golf Teachers Hall of Fame. He's eighty and can still drive the ball 275 yards. Toski yelled at me one day on the range at the Medalist Golf Club in Hobe Sound, Florida. "Stop thinking," he said. "Just hit the damn ball."

If I could, I would.

• • •

This article generated an overwhelming number of e-mails, from people who, like me, have had far too much instruction and who are confused, to teachers offering to help me. I was tempted to try every suggestion, but I restrained myself. It wasn't easy.

FOUR | Architects, Architecture, Courses

Crenshaw and Coore: A Team For The Ages

Links Magazine | January/February 1999

It all began with a mutual love of books. The result: a partnership between Bill Coore and Ben Crenshaw that has produced a short but impressive roster of fascinating golf course designs.

The two first met in the early 1980s when a Texas developer asked them to collaborate on a course. A Virginia native, Coore had been discharged from the military and, by 1969, was working as a general labourer on a course that Pete Dye was designing. A Classical Greek major at Wake Forest University, Coore had planned to continue his literary studies at Duke University and then become a college professor. Then the job with Dye came available. An avid reader, Coore readily took to the classic books on architecture that Dye had in his library.

Meanwhile, Crenshaw had long nurtured a love of golf books, particularly those about architecture. His home library includes Bernard Darwin's *The Golf Courses of the British Isles*, published in 1910 (to which Crenshaw contributed a foreword in a recent edition), Charles Blair Macdonald's *Scotland's Gift: Golf*, and Alister MacKenzie's *Golf Architecture*, to name a few. Crenshaw has read and studied them all.

Although the course in Texas was never built, Coore and Crenshaw found they were kindred spirits and that they had read the same books. They talked about design ideas for a year. In 1985, Coore and Crenshaw founded their firm of the same name. "Our love of the same books became the foundation of our partnership," Coore says.

Both men appreciated classical architecture, with its emphasis on strategic design, where golfers are provided options. To Coore and Crenshaw, golf is more than a target game where one throws the ball in the air toward a predetermined point, knowing it will stop just about where it lands. Golf is also a ground game, and they like to bring the bounce back into it. They like sprawling bunkers with ragged edges, reminiscent, where possible, of Royal Melbourne's bunkers.

And, of course, both are big fans of the Augusta National Golf Club, which MacKenzie designed in collaboration with Bobby Jones. It's appropriate that Crenshaw's two major victories were at the 1984 and 1995 Masters. Augusta National rewards study, and Crenshaw likes nothing better than a course that doesn't overwhelm a player, a course whose subtleties reveal themselves over time.

"Augusta National has somehow stood up even with all the changes in the game," Crenshaw says. "Even the tee shot at the eighteenth, which is essentially blind, stands up. I don't understand why people don't like blind shots. Nearly every blind shot or semi-blind shot on a good course is well defined."

Augusta National also provides generous fairways, which encourage the golfer to take a freewheeling swing at the ball from the tee. But that doesn't mean the player can hit it anywhere. The idea is to find the most favourable angle from which to approach the green. It's a thinking golfer's course, and Crenshaw and Coore advocate courses that make the golfer think.

A good example is the North course at Talking Stick in Pima, Arizona, near Scottsdale, where Coore lives. The land is so flat that it's difficult to imagine designing a golf course worth playing here. Yet the course defines the word "minimalism." To play this course that doesn't have three feet of elevation change on it is to see what Crenshaw and Coore can do with, well, very little. To them, a little means quite a lot.

"Talking Stick was an exercise for us in starting with nothing," Crenshaw says one autumn morning while he and Coore walk a piece of property on the north shore of Long Island, where they are designing a course. "It was dead flat. So we said, 'Let's see if we can concentrate on strategy and try to induce optional routes for golfers.' Our central idea was to move land just enough so that somebody standing just off the perimeter of the property could discern the barest of undulation in the land. If the land was just barely moving to that person's eye, that was good. Two, three, or four feet of movement was fine."

You can't get more minimal than that. Crenshaw and Coore like to perform non-invasive surgery on land when designing their courses, and the marketplace has responded with consistent interest. The company has made a name for itself at Kapalua's Plantation course, Talking Stick, Cuscowilla, located midway between Augusta and Atlanta, and the Warren Golf Course in South Bend, Indiana, which it designed for the University of Notre Dame. Then there's Sand Hills, the course for which they are best known.

Sand Hills is eighty miles north of North Platte in the high plains and cattle country of Nebraska. The architects worked for a year on the routing because so many intriguing possibilities presented themselves; they found 136 potential holes on the property. In the end they created a timeless course where the holes flit in and about massive dunes, and where the greens sit in naturally occurring areas for the most part. The dunes range from two or three feet high to more than a hundred feet. As Crenshaw says of the sandy, rolling terrain, "I think you'd be hard-pressed to find a better site."

Maybe anybody could have done a wonderful course at Sand Hills. Or maybe architects other than Coore and Crenshaw would still have moved vast quantities of dirt. It takes an essentially humble nature to leave well enough alone, or to tease a landscape gently to bring out its finer qualities. Crenshaw and Coore were able to do that at Sand Hills. At Talking Stick, meanwhile, they moved just enough dirt to make a course where a golfer has to think because the ball can roll off greens into hollows and across humps. To miss a shot by a little on a Crenshaw and Coore course is often to miss it by a lot. Golf is a ball game, so they create courses where it matters how the ground affects the ball.

"I still think shot-making and finesse matter in the game," Crenshaw points out. "It shouldn't be all about power. That's why we could not lay out a course that's 7,400 yards long. The way to deal with people hitting the ball farther, or at least one way, is to have rough and tight fairways. That means that straight hitting is a requirement. But I hate to see courses that have so much rough they look like jungles."

What to do, then, in this era of 300-yard drives, in this era where young golfers come up expecting to hit 525-yard par-fives with a driver and an iron? "It's all about creating a requirement for strategy," Crenshaw says. "We try to have running fairways and entrances that are firm enough to make a golfer plan his shot accordingly. But that's not always easy in North America, because turf conditions are such that it's difficult to get the ground firm enough. Another way to handle the issue of length, though, is to create interesting greens that require judgment on the approach shots and with the putting."

Crenshaw and Coore's greens reward close inspection. Clearly, Augusta National and the Old Course at St. Andrews have influenced them. The greens at these classic courses are huge and undulating. They don't have sharp changes of elevation, in that ridges don't run through the greens; happily for the golfer, they lack what Crenshaw calls "independent" contours. Yet they move. They swing. They reflect Crenshaw's appreciation of something that John Low, a past captain of the Royal and Ancient Golf Club of St. Andrews, once said.

"He wrote, 'Undulation is the soul of the game,'" Crenshaw recalls. "That's what makes the game exciting and forces a player to search his soul. He was right. You don't want something flat and innocuous, because then the thinking part of the game will be a little on the dull side."

As flat as the ground at Talking Stick is, its fairways and greens are decidedly not flat and innocuous. Those few feet of undulation that Crenshaw and Coore introduced provide enough motion that a golfer must think about where he lands his ball. On the putting surface, the golfer needs to judge pace and line expertly, because a ball rolled just off line can run way off course. Golf is an art as well as a science, and Crenshaw and Coore want to make sure it stays that way. They do so by their philosophy of minimalism.

The greens at Cuscowilla, meanwhile, demonstrate the ground features to which Crenshaw refers. They're large and undulating and put one in mind of the greens at the Old Course and Royal Dornoch in the Scottish Highlands, where Crenshaw has played. Fairways bleed into greens so that a unity prevails. The running shot is welcomed; Crenshaw and Coore invite players to decide among a variety of options, which can introduce confusion into a golfer's mind. They allow the possibility of a variety of shots and therefore demand that the golfer pick one and settle on it.

That's one of the things Crenshaw and Coore are doing on a fall day at their new course, called Friar's Head, on the north shore of Long Island. The terrain is sandy, which is ideal for a golf course because it drains well and helps generate some bounce in the ground. Friar's Head overlooks Long Island Sound, and one can see the city of New Haven from the course.

"It's a wonderful piece of property," Crenshaw explains. "It goes up into the dunes on the north shore, then into flattish terrain. Our job is to meld the two quietly together. We didn't want to load up one nine in the dunes and the other in the flatter land." This approach reflects the way in which Crenshaw and Coore are consistent from course to course.

"Crenshaw and Coore have championed minimalism because they carefully select their work and only work on maximalist sites where virtually no earthmoving is needed," says Brad Klein, a design critic and author of the illuminating book *Rough Meditations*. That is, the duo picks sites that are strong already. Klein, while an admirer of their work, does feel their approach can limit creativity.

"I sometimes think they actually hurt themselves by refusing to move much," he elaborates, "and I'd like to see them experiment more boldly with the occasional multi-path fairway. But nobody has a better sense of native contours, and no one is willing to build courses that measure only 6,600 to 6,800 yards from the back tees. They rely upon timeless ground features – ground contours and angles of approach, not length – to create the demands and appeals of their work."

Says Coore: "Our comfort zone is in areas where we don't have to move a lot of dirt. I did that once in south Texas, before Ben and I got together. It was a housing project, and there were many days when I stood there and felt things were getting out of control. Since then I determined I wouldn't do such a project again."

Coore says he and Crenshaw moved 500,000 yards of dirt at Talking Stick, but quickly points out that this was for two courses, and that most of the dirt-moving was for flood control and drainage reasons. "We look for sites that look like golf," Coore says. "We've looked at sites where Tom Fazio and his people have done courses and moved a lot of dirt, and I'm always amazed at the beautiful work they do on such properties. But it's not the kind of land where we like to work. We try to stress detail work. I'm afraid if we took a project where we had to move a lot of dirt that so much energy would go into doing this that we'd lose our attention to detail."

Listen closely to Crenshaw and Coore and you will hear that word "together" often. They want a golfer to feel that the holes are together. Their job is to meld different terrain "quietly together."

The phrase could also serve as a coda for how they like to work: quietly together. "Bill has been a blessing to my life," Crenshaw says.

"He's a soulmate. We share the same philosophy and have fun with what we do. I've learned a lot from him and I continue to learn from him. He sees things from a practical standpoint."

Crenshaw the philosopher/historian and Coore the practical thinker go well together. They work on only a couple of projects a year and spend plenty of time on-site, and so far have produced one high-quality course after another. These are still early days, but already they have authored a library of masterworks. They are sure to add more fascinating volumes to their small but elegant collection.

• • •

Crenshaw and Coore have indeed added more fascinating volumes. The list now includes Bandon Trails in Bandon, Oregon, Colorado Golf Club in Parker, Colorado, and the Saguaro course at We-Ko-Pa in Fort McDowell, Arizona. Both men continue to believe that undulation is the soul of golf.

Augusta National Syndrome

The Globe and Mail | April 8, 2002

The Masters starts Thursday, and with it comes the Augusta National syndrome – the vivid, green landscape generates in club golfers an unrealistic expectation that the courses they play should also look "perfect."

Such expectations create difficulties for course superintendents, massive greenkeeping budgets, higher costs for playing the game, and, often, intense water usage and application of chemicals. If only golfers would realize that Augusta National's dazzling appearance, which plays so well on television, bears as much relationship to how their courses should look as the women in *Sports Illustrated*'s annual swim-suit issue do to normal human beings.

Who knows how much cosmetic enhancement, airbrushing, and other special effects are used to help morph somebody into an *SI* swimsuit celebrity?

Similarly, every year millions of dollars are spent turning Augusta National into a golf course that is as much a dreamscape as a landscape. The club heavily overseeds its warm-weather Bermuda grass and fairways with rye grass during the fall so that it will be green come spring. And Augusta National shuts down in May and doesn't reopen until October.

The way to counteract the Augusta National syndrome is to allow a course to go brown. Brad Klein, a course architecture critic for *Golfweek* magazine and a consultant to clubs looking to modify their courses, advises that "Green is beautiful, but brown is better." He tells clubs to shut off their water, to neglect the rough so that it can grow wilder, and to go native. Thirsty turfgrass develops deeper roots as it searches for water, and is therefore a healthier plant. It will also look more golden than green, anathema to the networks that televise golf tournaments. But what's wrong with a honey-hued playing surface?

Nothing, except that most golfers wrongly believe a green course is a wonderful course. To many, Augusta National represents the epitome of how a course should look and play – not a chance of a "bad" lie on the fairways, greens as smooth as glass, chance reduced to as near zero as possible in an outdoor environment.

Golfers in Canada and the United States wish they could play in such elegant surroundings, and much of the Masters appeal rests on their longings. But course superintendents groan, and costs grow as they try to grow green.

"Every course is unique," Blake McMaster, superintendent at the Royal Montreal Golf Club, said recently. "Even within a course there are different microclimates and soil conditions that restrict what you can do."

The Royal Montreal's Blue Course was host to the Canadian Open last year, and McMaster said there were five different soil types on the greens for that event.

"Augusta National's greens have a consistent grass," he said. "And there's a lot you can do when money isn't a factor and you can close the course and work on it."

He points out that a different look to a course can work well, even as he tries to get Royal Montreal as green as possible. He also knows that golfers, superintendents, and course owners will in all likelihood have to get used to less-than-green conditions because this look will be forced on them.

"Pesticide and environmental issues will force us to change," McMaster said. "The pesticide lobby is very strong. We'll need to get back to fewer maintained areas on the course. This isn't all bad. The game can be more fun when you don't have perfect lies all the time."

McMaster pointed out that Royal Montreal's members travel often to Scotland, so they know the virtues of the less-manicured courses there. There is a lot of pleasure to be derived from brown, or brownish, golf.

I've certainly learned this during some twenty visits to Scotland, but never more so than during the summer of 2000, which I spent in Dornoch, far north in the Scottish Highlands. I came away and remain convinced that we've turned golf in North America into something it wasn't meant to be: artificial, tarted up, "perfect."

The Scottish Amateur was played at Royal Dornoch that summer. Bobby Mackay, the club's greenkeeper, followed the play one afternoon. He could feel his shoes crunching on the firm fairways, and enjoyed the sensation. He spoke of putting just enough water on the fairways "to keep the grass alive," not green, but a golden brown. "It's traditional greenkeeping," he said.

The climates of the Scottish Highlands and Augusta, Georgia, are vastly different. But notwithstanding differences in temperatures, soils, and precipitation, the most important distinction is between two philosophies of the conditions under which golf should be played: Augusta's controlled greenery, or the relatively hands-off approach of Dornoch.

Golf in Scotland, where the game was born, was never meant to be a fair game. If the ball bounced on the fairways or deflected over splotchy marks on the greens, so be it. A player needed mental resilience to deal with the rub of the green. Golf in America, where the game has become so hot it's cool to play it, has become all too fair. Conditions are immaculate; bad things aren't allowed to happen to good golfers. Something basic to the game is lost; one's experience is muffled. But, perhaps, not lost or muffled forever if we realize that Augusta National is a one-off, not something to emulate.

Steve Smyers, an architect and fine amateur golfer based in Lakeland, Florida, has played championships in the United States and Britain, and he knows that.

"There's a trend now among avid golfers, and owners and super-intendents who care, to move away from the idea that green is the only way to go," Smyers said. "The idea is that when a course is brown because of dry conditions, let it be brown. If it's green because of rain, that's also okay."

Donald Steel, a British architect who played the 1970 British Open at the Old Course in St. Andrews, is also a fan of drier, browner conditions, and of educating golfers toward this view. One summer day he was playing the Redtail Golf Course in St. Thomas, Ontario, his first design in North America. He liked what he saw.

"It's nice to see the fairways browning up," Steel said then. Redtail's owners want their fairways to shade toward brown. Steel, who prefers minimal maintenance, has since designed Cherokee Plantation in South Carolina, Carnegie Abbey in Rhode Island, and a course on Martha's Vineyard that will open in May.

Think about brown versus green while you follow the Masters. Consider what Klein wrote in an essay about Augusta National, published in his collection *Rough Meditations*. After referring to Augusta's impeccable conditions, Klein wrote of what the viewer doesn't see: "Augusta National's maintenance budget, which is next only to the CIA's allotment as a closely guarded state secret. Half the year the layout is closed; plastic liners are placed over the bunkers to prevent contamination, and permeable cloth tents are erected over some of the greens in summer to shade putting surfaces. The green at the 12th hole has underground pipes for both refrigeration and heating."

I like to recall what Steel said that day at Redtail. "This is what I think summer fairways should look like. Some people equate quality with emerald green. I don't."

Strokes of Genius: Stanley Thompson's Courses

Report on Business Magazine | March 2003

Here's a tip if you want to look really clever during the upcoming golf season: study up on legendary Canadian course architect Stanley Thompson, who designed or remodelled 145 courses across the country from 1920 until his death in 1953, at the age of fifty-nine. Read *The Toronto Terror*, Jim Barclay's book on Thompson. Then join the Stanley Thompson Society, an eminently worthwhile organization whose president is Bill Newton, Thompson's great-nephew.

Why Thompson? Well, along with Robert Trent Jones, Sr., and Donald Ross, he was a founding member of the American Society of Golf Course Architects in 1947, and its president in 1949. His heyday was a period known as the golden age of golf course architecture, when the emphasis was on subtlety rather than power. There's not a finer quintet of courses in any country than his Capilano in West Vancouver, Banff Springs and Jasper National Park in Alberta, St. George's in Toronto, and the Highlands Links in Cape Breton, Nova Scotia, one of the great remote courses in the world.

Sadly, some of his masterworks have already been lost, and others compromised by developers, green committees, and architects who, while undoubtedly well-meaning, have altered Thompson's work in disturbing ways. "It's akin to putting vinyl siding on a Frank Lloyd Wright house," as Bill Newton puts it.

York Downs in north Toronto was simply moved to a new site in the northeast suburbs. The original golf course became a municipal park after a short incarnation as a public course, and while it's tough to argue against a private club becoming a public park, some courses – or at least holes – should be considered heritage sites, like important buildings.

Thompson is, after all, far and away Canada's most significant contributor to the world of course design. Consider what Alister MacKenzie, who designed the Augusta National, among many other primo courses in the United States, said after he visited the Thompson-designed Jasper course in 1928: "During the last twenty years I have inspected all the reputed best golf courses in Britain, Ireland, the continents of Europe, North America, and Australia, but not one has created such a favourable and vivid impression on my mind as Jasper."

How did Thompson make such an impression on MacKenzie? There's a hint in his hard-to-find monograph *About Golf Courses, Their Construction and Upkeep*. "In clearing fairways, it is good to have an eye to the beautiful," Thompson wrote, realizing that golf is a game for all the senses, not just the feeling that comes from meeting the ball squarely. He liked streams and steep bunkers with sand flashed up on their faces. He put a little healthy fear into the player's mind by sinking greens into low spots and perching them atop high spots.

He was a master of the risk/reward philosophy of course design. The par-five fifteenth at Highlands Links, which invites golfers to take a bold line to the left over a shoulder of the fairway, is an exemplary illustration. Hit the spot and the ball will bounce forward, opening up the line to the green, now reachable in two shots. But miss a little too much to the left and there's trouble.

Thompson knew golf comprehensively. He and his four brothers were first-rate players. Nicol, the eldest, was the highly respected pro at the Hamilton Golf and Country Club for more than thirty-five years, finishing second in the 1913 Canadian Open. Frank won the 1921 and 1924 Canadian Amateur Championships. Stanley was a good stick himself, posting the lowest score in the qualifying round of the 1923 Canadian Amateur, when he shot 72 with borrowed clubs (his own were stolen). His usual set included a complement of only five clubs.

But Thompson's finest achievements were his designs. We should ensure the preservation of Capilano, one of the world's most beautiful courses, built on hilly, difficult, often sidehill terrain with views of Vancouver and the sea. Parks Canada should never let the Highlands Links in Cape Breton Highlands National Park disappear, as it nearly did until it was resuscitated during the mid-1990s. As for Banff, the decision to change its routing to accommodate a new clubhouse and pro shop was a disaster. The stunning first hole that played in front of the imposing Banff Springs Hotel, with a tee shot from a high point across the Bow River, became the fifteenth hole. It's still, without a doubt, a tremendous hole, but Thompson knew that its true value was as the opening hole. The setting and the shot got the heart pounding.

Then there's Jasper, proving that Thompson was nothing if not whimsical. He built the course for the Canadian National Railways, which owned the property. One day, he was playing the course with Sir Henry Thornton, then the president of CNR. Gazing down toward the green from the high tee on the 231-yard par-three ninth, Thornton noticed the curvy mounds that framed the putting surface. They reminded him of a full-figured woman.

"Mr. Thompson," Thornton admonished the proud architect, "we have been friends for many years. I never thought you'd have the audacity to do this to the Canadian National." Thompson did smooth out some of the curves, but they still retain a rather distinctive shape. The hole is called Cleopatra to this day.

"He had a great feel for what I call the movement of land masses," Robert Trent Jones, Sr., once said of Thompson. He sure did.

Donald Steel

Golf Journal | March/April 2003

On a late May day in England, the man who would change our ideas of golf course design is having a walk without clubs over the rolling land of the West Sussex Golf Club, an hour southeast of London. Donald Steel, who played in the 1970 British Open at the Old Course and who has written lucidly on the game for forty years, has designed courses in some twenty-five countries, and spoken widely around the world on all facets of golf. He's golf's Renaissance man. Yet, in the United States and Canada, he's still largely unknown.

Soon, surely, this will change and these golfers too will understand what he could yet accomplish: a return to golf's simple virtues, where players walk and use the ground as much as the air for their shots, where the game provides an adventure in landscape.

"It's a shame to allow beautiful views to be closed," Steel points out, looking at a dense stand of trees that have grown and impeded the golfer's ability to see across the course to the modest clubhouse. "So many rubbish trees have been planted here, and the heather that used to provide contrast to the greenery and penalize the errant shot has been lost. Heather needs air to flourish. I'm on the board here and I've been leading the crusade to get this lovely course back to where it used to be."

Steel, sixty-five, is a quiet man for a crusader. His accomplishments and views are, nonetheless, substantial forces around the world – except in North America. In the last three years, however, his first three U.S. courses have opened: Cherokee Plantation in South Carolina (1999); Carnegie Abbey in Rhode Island (2000); and last May, the Vineyard Golf Club on Martha's Vineyard, in Massachusetts. (Steel's first North American design, the highly praised Redtail Golf Course in St. Thomas, Ontario, opened in 1992.) These courses, along with the attention his redesign of Royal Liverpool Golf Club will receive leading up to the 2006 British Open, will no doubt make Steel more of a household – or clubhouse – name in the United States.

"I'm not suggesting that we denude the place of trees," Steel continues as he walks around West Sussex, also known as Pulborough for the village in which it's located. "But it's important that one uses trees more like a perimeter, as a frame on a painting. This would also enable the golfer to see the undulations in the ground. We have such lovely views of the Sussex Downs here. When [Bernard] Darwin came here he spoke of a sea of sand and open splendour."

Darwin was an English golf writer who wrote for *The Times* in London and the magazine *Country Life* into the 1950s – and a semifinalist in the 1921 British Amateur. He wrote and he could play, much the same as Steel.

"Donald is very quiet," says Peter Alliss, the well-known ABC and BBC television commentator, and a contemporary of Steel's. "Yet he has been amazingly successful in his golf course business and his writing." John Hopkins, golf writer for *The Times*, adds, "I think of Donald as an eighteenth-century man. I could imagine him as the son of a vicar in a Scottish village who goes on to become minister. We have a saying in Britain that a person is very sound. Donald is very sound."

Steel chooses his words carefully and presents them as if fully formed on paper. Of writing, he says, "When all is said and done, when writers are confronted by a blank page or blank screen, they are on their own. Writing is an expression."

Of playing the game: "I have never met any player, amateur or professional, who hasn't benefited from going slightly slower than that which seems natural to him."

Of golf course design: "Too many of our modern courses don't look like golf courses that our ancestors would recognize. I played so much of my competitive golf on links and still believe it represents the very best type of golf. Links, with their feeling of freedom, are far more invigorating and suitable for everyone in offering a variety of shot selection."

On public speaking, of which he does a lot: "I love listening to well-delivered sermons, poetry, commentary, addresses, eulogies, interviews. I still turn weak at the knees when I hear Martin Luther King's 'I Have a Dream.' Sadly, the standard of oratory among world statesmen and on TV and radio today is abysmal."

• • •

Back at his home in Chichester, an ancient town, Steel sits down to the lunch that his wife, Rachel, has prepared. The row house backs onto a stream and a meadow that extends as far as the eye can see. Steel is sitting in the garden, which robins and thrushes visited during the morning. He has a notebook in which he has recorded the more than sixty bird species he has seen in the garden in the past twenty years. Over a lunch of smoked salmon, a variety of breads, drinks, and ice cream, he shares his background.

Born outside London, he first hit a golf ball as a seven-year-old in 1944, when World War II bombs still occasionally rained upon the city. He played rugby, cricket, and golf, and was proficient at all. At twenty-three, after graduating from Cambridge University, he started writing golf for *The Sunday Telegraph*, a London newspaper. That was in 1961. Forty years later, by the time Steel completed his modifications to Royal Liverpool, he had become a man of many words and many courses all over the world.

Steel wrote about golf for *The Sunday Telegraph* for thirty years and contributed "A Golf Commentary" to *Country Life*. He has worked as a course architect since 1965, when he apprenticed himself to the English firm of Ken Cotton, Frank Pennink, and Charles Lawrie. In 1975, along with fellow journalist Peter Ryde, Steel co-edited *The Encyclopedia of Golf*, a comprehensive reference work. He started his own design firm in 1987 and, in 1992, wrote *Classic Golf Links of England, Scotland, Wales and Ireland*, another standard reference. He is a student of wine, enjoys attending horse races at nearby Goodwood track, is widely sought after as a public speaker, and likes nothing more than a few holes of evening golf.

Steel came to course design because of a feeling for the land and the openness he craves. He was raised on the edge of London, within range of the big city but also near countryside. His father was a surgeon and medical director of a large hospital; his mother was a nurse. But Steel wanted to be a farmer for as long as he can remember.

"I hadn't seen a farm and there was no history of farming in our family," he says. "However, I have always had a close affinity with the country rather than the town, and hate to see what is happening to agriculture and to country ways and traditions in Britain."

Steel's concern manifested itself in his choice of study at Cambridge: agriculture. He was better at languages, and he enjoyed reading widely and getting a liberal education. But he sensed that studying agriculture would serve him well, and it has in his work as a course designer, given the importance of knowing soils, grasses, and drainage.

Cambridge encouraged its students to expand their interests beyond the classroom. "Great advice," Steel says. He played golf for Cambridge, and has long been a member of the Oxford & Cambridge Golfing Society and a fan of its noted competition, which takes place the first week of every January at Rye Golf Club (outside London), no matter the weather. Steel has also been involved, both as a player and a supporter, in the Halford Hewitt annual competition, the national event for British public school golfers. These are match-play tournaments. Steel is an amateur golf and match-play aficionado.

Steel's interest in sports was not limited to playing them. He read widely, taking advantage of a golf literature that was in its golden age when he was young. British newspapers were full of top-notch writing, usually from people who both played well *and* wrote lucidly: Darwin, Ryde, Leonard Crawley, Pat Ward-Thomas, and Henry Longhurst. Steel absorbed their views and styles.

"Apart from being good writers with an easy style," Steel recalls, "this group impressed because they wrote responsibly and sympathetically without shirking an issue that needed a critical approach."

Crawley in particular took Steel under his wing. He encouraged Steel to buy as many of Darwin's books as he could find; "a sound investment," for a young writer, Steel notes. Crawley watched over the young man's prose, too.

The 1961 British Open at Royal Birkdale was the first Steel covered. Arnold Palmer won, and he won again the next year at Royal Troon, which Steel also covered. Steel could not have chosen a more interesting moment to take up the work; Palmer's victories demonstrated that golf had become a sport of international scope.

Steel, who had been reading Herbert Warren Wind, the dean of writers in the United States, was thrilled to be a part of it all. "I was surrounded by senior colleagues to whom I was like a fond nephew," Steel says. "They were all unbelievably kind in every respect and encouraged me without ever telling me how to write. You can never attempt to copy a style, but they inspired a passion in me. They were all strongly contrasting characters. Herb Wind called them the Crazy Gang after a vaudeville group fashionable on the London stage in post-war years."

Crawley not only helped Steel sharpen his pen, but also his game. Steel has kept a letter that Crawley wrote him, which reads, in part: "You have a very fine putting stroke, but you are a little inclined to let the glue run out of your neck and look up too early. That is why you occasionally miss when you ought not to." Of the three-time Walker Cupper, Steel says, "He was a great player with a beautiful slow tempo."

Steel loved to watch excellent golfers, even if he couldn't easily adopt the slow tempo that he so admired. He was a hands player; Crawley referred to Steel as a golfer who employed a "quick flick," a style that took Steel to the 1970 British Open at the Old Course.

Steel studied the methods of all the great players of the day and earlier and has written often of them. But more than anybody's teachings, he remembers Crawley's. "You can't get balance without footwork, and you can't get footwork unless you learn it without a ball," Crawley told him. And so Steel would practise his swing without a ball.

Humble by nature, Steel has never minded taking advice. From

Longhurst he learned that "there was no occasion so solemn that couldn't be enhanced by a touch of humour." He recalls that Longhurst and the writers of his day trusted their own judgment and wrote what they thought in the days before golfers were trotted out to speak to the press in a formal interview. "Interviews," Steel says, "have been a bad influence on golf writing."

While competing and writing about golf, Steel had many opportunities to examine fine courses and form opinions about the sources of their appeal. He accepted an invitation in 1962 from English architect Ken Cotton to visit the site of a course he was designing with his partners. "This was a journalistic exercise for me," Steel says, "and I enjoyed it immensely."

A few years after this "journalistic exercise," Steel was invited to join the Cotton, Pennink, and Lawrie Company. Michael Bonallack, the five-time British Amateur winner and, until 1999, the long-time secretary of the R&A, has also been associated with the firm. Bonallack had met Steel during their university days and knew that he was a very good player with a keen sense of the game's enduring values. He was also impressed with Steel's writing, and wasn't surprised when he became a successful course architect.

"His love of the game shows in his writing and in his architecture," Bonallack says. "The courses he builds are fair, traditional courses. Donald is a great believer that a golf course should not be penal, that while it should challenge you, it should also give you options. He is not a great believer in water unless it's already there, because he reckons it's a lazy form of architecture. His bunkers are real bunkers. If you hit into them, you have a problem."

"Writing is an expression of one's personality and deeply held beliefs," says Steel. Roger Fowler Wright, his first sports editor at *The Telegraph*, wrote in a 1961 letter to him, "If you doubt the wisdom of saying something, it is probably better left out."

This might also be taken as a coda for Steel's design philosophy. The art is in what is left out as much as, or more than, what is said, or put in. He honed his design philosophy with Cotton, Pennink, and Lawrie, and then went out on his own in 1987. In 1992 he designed Redtail, which features narrow, undulating fairways bordered by fescue, fewer than thirty deep pot bunkers, and smallish greens that invariably are firm and fast. The layout invites the golfer to employ a ground as well as an air game. He likes to introduce these options at all his courses.

"I admire our old established courses [in England] like Sunningdale and Ganton," Steel says. "In America, Pine Valley, the National, Shinnecock, Seminole, and Kittansett."

Steel's work has been described as minimalist, a handy description, he says, "of allowing the land to do the talking and not twisting it out of shape. Can you really say that many modern courses are a natural part of the landscape?" Still, he points out, earthmoving is sometimes the only way to produce a course.

"I have no problem with that and am happy to build courses that way, if it's the only way," he allows. To prove his point, Steel, after lunch, leads a field trip to the Mill Ride course that he designed on what was once three polo fields. He points out the area around the clubhouse that constituted the fields, and that now sways and swirls: he converted it to golf country by moving just enough dirt.

Welshman Dave Thomas, a four-time Ryder Cup player and now a course architect, believes that Steel is most at home in a traditional setting. "He's done work for the R&A, yes, but I feel his setting is really a member's course and not a championship course. Donald goes where he wants to go, which is wonderful. He knows his place, and we all have our place."

Steel's own preferred place is a links. "Nowhere in the world is there anything else that compares; indeed, nothing that comes close," he writes in *Classic Golf Links*. "There is a joyous sense of space and freedom about most seaside links, a feeling of escape that makes you glad to be alive."

Steel brings that joy to his work because he sees golf as a game. Spending time with Steel, one thinks of the dedication Eduardo Galeano, a Uruguayan writer, offered in his book *Soccer in Sun and Shadow*. He refers to children he had noticed playing soccer and singing, "We lost, we won, either way we had fun."

Above all, Steel wants golfers to have fun. Although he makes his living from the game, he is truly an "amateur," in the meaning of "for the love of" rather than "for the business of." If he were writing today he would be more likely to report on the Walker Cup than the Ryder Cup. And then, no doubt, he would be just as likely to discuss the events and the people in them at some dinner or another.

Steel, it should be noted, abhors the notion of being paid for speaking engagements. "Charging fees for speaking is anathema to me," Steel says. Hopkins, of *The Times*, recalls Steel speaking after a high court judge and former captain of the R&A at an Association of Golf Writers dinner. The judge, Hopkins says, "was absolutely brilliant. But Donald suffered not a jot by comparison with this brilliant speaker who used words all day long."

Maybe Steel told the story from the second round of the 1970 British Open. "I teed off on the sixteenth and, as I approached my ball over to the left, was confronted by Arnold Palmer charging down the third. When he saw me, he said, 'Hello Donald, what are you doing here?' 'Well,' I replied, 'I am sullying the championship you came to save.' 'Wonderful,' he said, and off he went."

That's vintage Steel, a golfer with heart, humour, and knowledge who, through his play, writing, architecture, and speaking, has contacted the game at more points than almost anyone. "A lot of architecture," he says, "is about observing. Playing with and watching the best players gave me plenty to observe. You have to notice what you see."

Steel settles into a chair to watch a European Tour event on television. He talks about The Vineyards, and his hope that it will demonstrate that a course doesn't have to be elaborate to enchant and challenge. "The architect's job is to provide options for the player," he says. "So many American courses ask only for one club for each shot. It's best when one can play almost any club for a particular shot. Choice is what confuses a golfer and adds interest. Too many courses focus on water and excessive use of bunkers. But I do think a large section of American golfers would prefer the old style."

As Steel's presence in the United States grows, that large section may indeed become *very* large.

• • •

At seventy-one, Steel has had nearly fifty years of satisfying Winston Churchill's notion that "A man is fortunate if his work and pleasure are one." Steel the architect continues to work in that area, although not on a full-time basis. He was president of the English Golf Union in 2006. With Peter Lewis, he wrote Traditions & Change, *the third volume in the history of the R&A. Meanwhile, he continues to enjoy public speaking and playing the game.*

The Sod Couple: Pete and Alice Dye
Report on Business Magazine | June 2004

The 2004 recipient of the PGA of America's First Lady of Golf award and the winner of the organization's Distinguished Service award greet me in their charming one-storey home in Delray Beach, Florida, not far from the Atlantic. Pete and Alice Dye are golf's most decorated couple this year – celebrated for their course designs that grace many landscapes.

The Dyes can still shoot their age from time to time. Alice, seventy-seven, has won two U.S. Senior Women's Amateur championships and two Canadian Senior Ladies' championships. Pete, seventy-eight, won the 1958 Indiana State Amateur, and played in five U.S. Amateurs and one U.S. Open. They're players in every sense of the word.

They're also deft on a bulldozer, fashioning courses that both beguile and bedevil golfers. The word "diabolical" is often used to describe their work. Most famously, there's the par-three seventeenth hole at the Tournament Players Club (TPC) in Ponte Vedra Beach, Florida. This is the home course of the PGA Tour, and it hosts the annual Players Championship. The seventeenth is only 132 yards from the back tee, but it plays to an island green. It's golf's most copied hole, and probably its most fearsome.

"You know where everybody is coming from on the hole," Pete Dye says as we sit poolside on a dreamy late-winter south Florida day. "It's not like a par-four or par-five where everybody is hitting their approach shots from a different place. Here you start from 130 yards from the back, maybe 120 from a tee just forward, or 90 yards from the furthest-forward tee. Everybody who plays the game of golf can hit the ball that far."

Dye likes to watch the golfer he calls "John Q. Public" play the hole as much as he does the tour pros. He's aware of the fear that every golfer feels on the tee, and the thrill players get when they hit the green. "It's the greatest thing in the world for that player," he says. "Then the next three players are in the water. He's king for a day. Watch a foursome and somebody always seems to get on the green, whether the group is full of 80-, 90-, or 110-shooters."

While Pete Dye is credited with designing the TPC at Sawgrass's Stadium Course, partner Alice – the first female member of the

American Society of Golf Course Architects and its first woman president – was the visionary behind the course's seventeenth hole. Pete had dug a huge amount of sand out from the area and used it as the base for greens around the course. But he couldn't find a place for the seventeenth. Along came Alice.

"Pete told me he had just this little lump of dirt left," Alice says as she takes a chair by the pool. "I suggested he enlarge the area and build up an island green. There was an island green up the road at another course, but there was room around it to land the ball before you got in the water. Nobody had done a hole where it was either-or – green or water. So Pete built the green."

He initially built it so that the back third of the green sloped down to the water. The hole already looked terrifying, but now it was verging on unplayable. Alice again intervened.

"I looked at that and told Pete, 'I can just see this on TV during the tournament. The wind will be blowing from the tee to the green and the TV guy will say, "Ladies and gentlemen, it's two in the afternoon and the first group is still on the green because no balls will stay on the green."' So Pete levelled out the back of the green. They can play the hole now."

Golfers hit some 150,000 balls a year into the water surrounding the seventeenth. Even the best players are not immune: the pros hit thirty balls into the water during the Players Championship in March, which Adam Scott won.

As famous as the seventeenth hole has become since the first Players was held at Sawgrass in 1982, it would be wrong to ignore the Dyes' other courses. The Ocean Course on Kiawah Island, South Carolina, hosted the 1991 Ryder Cup. That same year, John Daly won the PGA Championship at the Dye-designed Crooked Stick course in Indianapolis, Indiana. Their Stadium Course at PGA West in La Quinta, California, is one of the courses used for the annual

Bob Hope Chrysler Classic, which Mike Weir won last year. Harbour Town Golf Links on Hilton Head Island, South Carolina, hosts a PGA Tour event every spring. Whistling Straits, near Sheboygan, Wisconsin, while still only a few years old, will host the PGA Championship in August.

Still, the PGA of America probably wouldn't be giving awards to the Dyes for their course design alone, as impressive as those designs are. The Dyes have done much more for golf. Consider what they did many years ago for a young Scottish caddy named Andy Coogan.

Coogan was caddying for Alice at Carnoustie when she invited him to visit the United States as the Dyes' guest. He spent two years with them while attending school and working summers in a golf shop. Coogan ended up in Melbourne, Australia, where he became a successful salesman for a watch company. The Dyes and Coogan lost touch for years, but reunited when the couple visited Melbourne. Coogan presented Pete with a watch as a gift. As Alice writes, "Pete [called] it his $20,000 watch, referring to Andy's expenses while in our care."

The Dyes have donated time and money to the game. Brad Klein, a fan of the Dyes who writes on course architecture, asked if Pete would design the new Wintonbury Hills Golf Course, located in Bloomfield, Connecticut, near Klein's home, for free. Dye accepted the commission, but charged a fee: one dollar.

When it's time to leave, I glance at the books on the Dyes' shelves: *The World of Golf*, an old tome by Garden G. Smith; the coffee-table book *Classic Barns*; *Golf for Women*, by George Duncan. We speak for a moment about Royal Dornoch, my favourite course, and I learn that the Dyes at first called their firm The Dornoch Company. They'd visited the course in the Scottish Highlands, and recommended it to New Yorker writer Herbert Warren Wind. Wind later wrote in "North to the Links of Dornoch" that Pete had told him of the course's "ageless aura." "People who read that said Pete didn't know what an 'ageless aura' meant," Alice says, smirking at her husband.

The First Lady of Golf will receive her award on May 26 at the Bomhard Theater in Louisville, Kentucky, the night before the Senior PGA Championship starts at the Valhalla Golf Club. Her collaborator will be honoured with his Distinguished Service prize on August 11 at the Milwaukee Theater, the night before the PGA Championship starts at Whistling Straits.

As they walk me out, we pass their black German Shepherd, Sixty, who's slumbering in a corner of the front room. They wish me well and invite me to play some time. I'd like that.

• • •

Pete Dye was inducted into the World Golf Hall of Fame on November 10, 2008.

Course Rankings: What About Them?
SCOREGolf Magazine | July 2004

I'm writing this for all the golfers at all the clubs that won't make it into *SCOREGolf*'s Top 100 list, published in this issue. I'm writing this for all the golfers at all the clubs who love where they play. I play at such a club, Maple Downs, in wooded, rolling countryside north of Toronto – or what was once north of Toronto but is almost part of the sprawling city today. Still, my fellow members feel it's their retreat, and they're proud of the club.

They should be, too. But I'm sure I'll have to remind them not to worry that the course didn't make the Top 100. I'll remind them that there's more to the game than rankings, even as I participate on *SCOREGolf's* panel. Rankings aren't scientific. But golfers feel hit hard when their favourite course doesn't make the greatest-hits list.

It's all relative, too. I belonged to the National in Woodbridge, Ontario, for fifteen years. It's one of the two or three toughest tests in the land – the new Eagles Nest Golf Club, just down the road from Maple Downs, also belongs in this group. The National is a pure golf club and many of its members become all but crazed when it's not ranked number one.

As I write, I don't know where the National will rank this year, but I do know that its members didn't appreciate falling from number one. Maple Downs members, meanwhile, have long felt the course belonged in the Top 100. Whether or not it does, Maple, which is celebrating its fiftieth anniversary this year, and many other courses, are delightful places to play.

Maple's former head professional, Irv Lightstone, was always telling me that the course was Top 100 material. Irv, bless him, was, and is, always on me about how much the PGA Tour pros liked the course when they played it prior to the 1988 Canadian Open. Richard Zokol thought the course was first-rate. Nick Price remembers the peace he felt while out on its billowing, tree-lined fairways.

I feel that way when I show up at Maple Downs early on a weekday morning, sling a half-dozen clubs over my shoulder, and head out for a solitary round. I've written that golf is a game that gives loners freedom of expression. I guess I'm part loner. I like the crisp air and the freshly cut greens at Maple in the morning. I like the truce that solitary golf calls with the overactive mind. Walking in nature among Maple's enormous trees, I walk with myself.

There, swinging in solitary silence, I appreciate the attention that course superintendent Steve Holmes, his assistant Jay Weiss, and their crew give the course. There's no place I'd rather be. Golfers across

Canada feel similarly about their courses. I'd feel the same way, I'm sure, if I played regularly at Bally Hally in Saint John's, Newfoundland, Cataraqui in Kingston, Niakwa in Winnipeg, Mayfair in Edmonton, or Royal Colwood in Victoria.

I find so much to take in and enjoy at Maple, a terrific members' course. I particularly like the bumps and knobs on the fairway at the par-five ninth, and don't mind at all when a shot I've curved a bit too much bounces into the rough. I like the way the tenth fairway plummets from a high ridge down to the green, and the view back across the course from the sixteenth green, another high point. There are many high points during a game at Maple. Golf is all about views, near and distant. It's about how we perceive it, our points of view.

The same goes for a course, and for course rankings, even those that rankle. Sure, Maple, like a lot of courses across Canada, could use a few more hundred yards to test today's long-ball hitters. It could be toughened up in a number of ways, but so what? The course rewards power as it is – accurate power – and also demands crafty shots into and around the greens. Maple is a good enough course. Plenty good enough.

That said, a golf club is more than its course. I've greeted old friends and met new ones at Maple. Irving Feldman, my friend of some forty years – he's family, really – accompanied me on one early-morning round. We were out in the middle of the course, two buddies who had shared happy and sad times together, births and deaths, single malts and double-bogeys, when Irv stopped in his spikeless tracks and burst out, "I love this place. I love this game."

Irv didn't really play golf until about fifteen years ago. To him, Maple Downs is the number-one club in Canada. Maple's members all feel this way. One fellow told me, "This is a great place. Don't let anybody tell you different."

Maple Downs, and hundreds of clubs across Canada, are tops

with the golfers who hang out there. *SCOREGolf*'s rankings allow room at the top for only a few clubs. But there's room in golfers' hearts for so many more. That's why I salute Maple Downs. If you were writing this column, you would salute your own club. That's exactly as it should be.

Uplands Is Written on My Heart

The Golf Courses of Stanley Thompson | Photoscape Publishing, 2007

Warmly, we called it "The Pit," and that's how those of us who played at the Uplands Golf and Country Club in Thornhill, Ontario, miss it: in the pit of our hearts. Thelma Coles was a member from 1957 to 1988, the last year the club operated as eighteen holes, and she said during a closing, teary party, "Uplands is written on my heart."

The funky old Stanley Thompson course offered uneven lies from start to finish, greens perched on headland across valleys, greens in bowls, and, always, a stern test of shotmaking. Yet Uplands, which opened in 1922, was only 6,000 yards long. Well, I'm wrong. The scorecard in front of me indicates Uplands was 6,019 yards when I played from the mid-1960s until its last days. It even reached 6,028 yards, as I see on another card.

We also called Uplands "the home of golf," and that it was. Five-time club champion Ted Durey said in a film about the treasured old place, "Everybody was equal," that millionaires and paupers belonged to the inexpensive club, and that they all got along. It was a place for golfers, not country clubbers, and it offered fun and simple, lively competition.

The Ontario amateur season effectively began with a tournament at Uplands called the Eager Beaver. I played the Beaver regularly, but never won it. The elite of Ontario amateur players did win it: Moe Norman and Nick Weslock, to name a couple. Meanwhile, Uplands members were proud to show off our tricky gem of a course.

The gem was never polished because that wasn't the Uplands way, but it didn't need to be. Uplands wasn't glamorous golf, just solid, good golf. The clubhouse fit the course. It was more like a humble, ramshackle home, and all the sweeter for it. Reg Acomb ran the club for many years, and later he built the Glen Abbey Golf Club with Jack Nicklaus. But Uplands showed Reggie, as we all knew him, at his best.

The small, two-level locker room included metal lockers and a collection of battered stools. Insolent teenager that I was, I'd put my feet up on a stool to tie my shoes. "Get your feet off that stool," Reggie would bellow. Each stool was so pockmarked it could hardly matter, but Reggie was the boss. Still, you could mess with him. Uplands had that down-home atmosphere.

I loved to joust with Reggie. I'd go out and hit four balls on a summer evening. When Reggie noticed, he'd give me one of those, "Rube, I told you. One ball only." I'd come back with impeccable logic: "Reggie, if you can tell me the difference between one guy playing four balls or four guys playing one ball, I'll go along with what you're saying."

Reggie knew I loved the place, and he'd often as not concede the point and let me play the four balls. Maybe his concessions helped me contend in the club championship from time to time. The competition was pure golf, seventy-two holes, stroke play. One year I shot 71–77–70 and was leading going into the last round.

The first hole at Uplands was 360 yards from the back tee, which was nearly up against the comfortable little pro shop. A creek crossed the fairway some 225 yards out, and the ground ran down to it. I laid up with my iron shot from the tee, and then, over the ball, had a million swing thoughts. I couldn't settle on one, chopped at the ball a few times before reaching the green, and double-bogeyed the hole. I shot 78 and finished down the line. Maybe Durey won. Or Bill Sheldon. Or Cal George. They all won club championships at the Pit. Me, I was destined to write about them.

So that's what I did. I poured out my Uplands anguish in a few pages. Later, it occurred to me that a magazine might be interested in my adventure. I sent the piece to *Golf Digest*, and an editor said he'd publish it. I contacted the magazine when I didn't hear from the editor for months. Apparently, his personal life had taken a dogleg into trouble, and he'd fled the magazine. The piece never did get published, but I got some confidence and kept writing.

That was a long time ago, but Uplands memories remain vivid. I see Moe Norman, a golfer so shy and isolated that he was never comfortable among anybody but his close friends. But there he is at Uplands on the first tee at the Eager Beaver, every year. A pro by then, Moe gave a clinic, and it was a must-see.

A hydro wire stretched across the first fairway about sixty yards out from the tee. Moe said he'd try to hit the wire, and you know how thin a hydro wire is. He'd hit it a couple of times out of ten tries. Clockwork Moe. He'd also take a wedge and hit it low, medium-low, medium, high, medium-high, really high. First floor, second floor, third floor, penthouse.

I sure do miss the old place. Uplands lasted as a private, eighteen-hole track until 1989, when it became a nine-hole public course as houses sprouted on the property. A few of the original holes remain, and, happily, the 232-yard, par-three seventeenth is one of them. It's one of the two or three best par-threes in North America. The hole plays down a corridor from an elevated tee to an elevated green, surrounded by trees to the right and behind, and a creek and trees to the left. The play was usually to go for the right side of the green, or to aim for the hillside there and wait for a carom down to the green.

I happened to be on the panel that selected *Golf Magazine*'s Top 500 holes in the world, and I insisted that this frightening beauty make the list. If I had my way, Heritage Canada would protect the hole, now playing as the eighth, from ever being lost.

I'd also protect the 103-yard thirteenth, called Dogmeat. The scorecard on my desk shows that I aced the hole on a summer day in 1983, playing with my great pals Craig Geleff, his dad Peter, and Tom Mitsui. I made five aces on the thirteenth, but I also made some big numbers when I whacked my wedge long or right into the trees, or hit the shot fat into the valley between the green and tee.

When Uplands closed we held a party at the club. Bill Towgood directed the film about Uplands that includes the party. I get choked up every time I watch it. So many long faces, voices breaking. The late Al Balding loved Uplands, and said, "It's too bad these things have to go." Jane Dixon, a member, pointed out that "Everybody says there'll never be another Uplands." That's true. I'd still be a member at Uplands, if Uplands as I knew it were still there. I'm sure everybody else would be as well. Uplands is written on my heart.

FIVE | Profiles

Stephen Ames

GolfObserver.com | April 4, 2006

You think you know Stephen Ames. You've decided he's a blowhard, noisemaker, politically incorrect, somebody who doesn't know how to keep his mouth shut even when the subject is Tiger Woods, and that the tipping point for you came when he said, on the heels of winning the Players Championship, that he might not play in this week's Masters.

You're right on one count, in that the forty-one-year-old Trinidad-born Ames, who lives in Calgary and is now a Canadian citizen, is often politically incorrect.

Well, good for him.

We in the media, and you who read us, often criticize golfers for saying nothing, even if takes them a lot of words to say nothing. Many in the media ripped David Duval for years because he hid behind his sunglasses and didn't say much. Then, when Duval did a dance around a green after making a putt at the Ryder Cup, some folks decided he looked foolish and unnatural. When he says something we don't like, we pout. We want him to be all things to all people. He's damned if he doesn't open up and damned if he does.

Then there's Tiger Woods. He said nothing when he could have said so much in a *60 Minutes* "interview" with Ed Bradley that aired March 26. Richard Sandomir called *60 Minutes* out on the silliness and he was on the money. You can't blame Woods and his people for wanting to control the show, but you can blame *60 Minutes* for taking whatever it was he would give them.

He gave them very little that he hadn't given before, which isn't much, because he likes to keep to himself, and fair enough there. So why did CBS agree to do the show? Ratings, of course. They did a double segment on Woods and their ratings were up 18 per cent.

All of this brings us back to Ames, in a manner of speaking. Or not speaking. He's opened up. He's let us in. That's a good thing. He also showed everybody he can play some golf when he smoked the best field in golf at the Players Championship, winning by six shots.

Sure, he fumbled somewhat when he talked to the media after he won. He implied he didn't care all that much about the Masters, and to tell the truth, it wouldn't be a surprise if he didn't. Ames could have simply said he wanted to discuss with his wife Jodi and their sons whether he would play, since they'd planned a vacation in Trinidad during the Masters. They'd rented a house, the whole bit. Instead, he thumbed his nose at Augusta, saying he preferred to go on vacation.

By the next morning he was telling a Toronto radio station he'd play the Masters. By late afternoon he was doing a lengthy conference call with Canadian media that his managers at the International Management Group in Toronto had arranged. He said something like why wouldn't anybody want to play the Masters, that it's the greatest place, yada, yada, yada.

He did want to play the Masters and that's where he is this week. But I've gotten to know Ames pretty well the last few years and I believe he does think the Masters is overblown, overhyped, and oversold. I admire his instinctive, shoot-from-the-lip response when he was asked about whether he would play so soon after he won the Players.

By the next morning and in the conference call he was on the politically correct track. He said he'd show up at Augusta; of course he would, etc., etc., now that he'd talked with his family. He said that, but he'd also told Canadian Press in February this year that getting back to the Masters after playing the first time last year is "not important to me at all." He wasn't crazy about the course changes he'd heard about.

Ames is an interesting character. He said a couple of years ago that he wasn't all that enthused about playing the 2005 Presidents Cup if he qualified, because he wasn't fond of team golf. He was speaking his mind. Ames didn't make the team, anyway. But he could well make the 2007 Presidents Cup that will be played at the Royal Montreal Golf Club.

Ames would get whipped and whupped if he didn't play. But why should golfers conform to our expectations? Maybe he'd be a burden to the team if he weren't all that keen about playing in the Presidents Cup.

But if he qualifies or is named to the team, he'll play. He's said so. He said before the 2005 Presidents Cup that he'd play if he made the team. PC: Presidents Cup. PC: Politically Correct. That's not Ames.

Meanwhile, anybody who has followed Ames knows the guy is passionate about things that matter to him. He started a foundation with $300,000 of his own money. He gave his name to the Stephen Ames Cup that the Canadian Junior Golf Association held last year just outside Toronto, and came up with the $25,000 to bring eight kids up from Trinidad and Tobago.

Ames also showed up in the summer of 2004 at a tournament that his fellow Canadian Tour pro Richard Zokol held for the Canadian Junior Golf Association in Toronto. He said at dinner, in front of everybody, "Whatever you want me to do for junior golf in Canada, I'll be there. You can count on me."

Ames means what he says. He missed the cut in the 2004 Bell Canadian Open at the Glen Abbey Golf Club in Oakville, Ontario. Asked about it, he said, "Ah, yes, wonderful Glen Abbey. It's not so much the design that I don't like, but the condition is never the way it should be."

But he also said he figured the tournament at the Shaughnessy course in Vancouver last September would be "awesome," and ditto for this year's Canadian Open at the Hamilton Golf and Country Club in Hamilton, Ontario. Hey, he's just being honest.

He's no fan of Glen Abbey. So be it. So he tells everybody. Fine.

You think John Daly grips it and rips it? Ames is the real gripper and ripper, when it comes to talking the talk, anyway. He'd finished third in the 1998 Nissan Open and the next week he was sitting in the locker room at Doral when an equipment representative walked by him. The guy said hi to Ames, how are you, what's doing, nice finish, and more. Ames wasn't all that warm to the fellow.

"That guy didn't have a second for me until last week," Ames sneered after the brief encounter. "He wouldn't say a word to me."

You get the edgy stuff from Ames. But at the Honda last month he did indicate Augusta was at least there, at the edge of his mind. "Two top-tens might get me in," he said. Instead he won the biggest tournament outside the majors.

By the way, Ames said at the Honda that Woods, who had won at Doral, played unbelievably against him at the Match Play Championship. "He was seven under par for ten holes," he said of the way Woods played to beat him 9 and 8. "I said that he's amazing, and it's true. He played amazing golf."

Ames also defended his earlier comments that Woods wasn't the most accurate driver of the ball, which made it even more amazing that he keeps winning. "Just like at Doral. He doesn't need to hit fairways, and he won."

Ames was killed in the media after Woods beat him 9 and 8. He wasn't killed after he said he might not play the Masters, but he did raise eyebrows. A quick search of articles about Ames shows the following words to describe him: "aloof, prickly, eccentric, blunt."

That's as it should be, because Stephen Ames is not PC. He's the Players Champion, but he's not PC.

Paul Bondeson: Promise Fulfilled

Golf World | March 14, 2003

He's confined to a wheelchair now, seventeen months after a car accident rendered him a quadriplegic, and four decades after he squandered a four-shot lead with seven holes left to lose the 1962 Doral Open. Paul Bondeson sits at the Palm Cove Golf and Yacht Club in Palm City, Florida, in late February, surrounded by friends who have organized a pro-am to raise funds that will help him and his wife, Shirley, cope with enormous medical costs. Chi Chi Rodriguez is hosting the event, called the Chi Chi & Friends for Bondo Pro-Am Invitational. Bruce Fleisher is here, a day after winning the Verizon Classic. Former major championship winners Gary Player, Orville Moody, and Bobby Nichols are here. Bondeson greets them all.

"Hey, Rocky," Bondeson says to Rocky Thompson, the Champions Tour player, "how did you get so much better looking?" J.C. Snead comes by. Bondeson, sixty-three, flashes a big smile, the same one that was all over newspapers when he was a teenager and winning many amateur tournaments, first in Michigan, where he grew up, and later in Ohio and Florida. "Hey, you son of a gun, this is fantastic. I may never run a hundred-yard dash again, but the heck with it."

Later, after the 125 or so amateurs and professionals have enjoyed a day's golf, they will give him a standing ovation. Those who know him well are aware of what he has been through – a world of woe – and that he was cursed with that heavily weighted word, "potential." He wasn't supposed to miss reaching the heights. But drinking and drugs beat him. And he beat himself.

Jack Nicklaus knows what might have been. He's not at Palm Cove because of a prior commitment in Mexico, but he donated generously to the event. Nicklaus and Bondeson met in 1957 at Scioto

Country Club in Columbus, Ohio. Nicklaus was a junior member. Bondeson was working for head professional Jack Grout, Nicklaus's instructor. He was there for two seasons, and the winter in between, because Grout wanted somebody on the premises to be in the pro shop in case anybody came in.

"We were seventeen," Nicklaus says of those long-ago days when Bondeson was young and strong – a blond bomber. "He was the only kid who could hit it as far as I did, and he was a very, very good player. I'd shoot 66 one day, and he'd shoot 67. The next day it would be the reverse. His game was very much a mirror image of mine. He hit it left to right, and very high, like I did. He was by far the best competition I had."

"There was no difference in talent between us," Bondeson remembers, "but there was a hell of a difference in motivation. The difference was between someone doing the right things and the wrong things. Jack had the focus, the ability to live the right way. He could put his clubs down for the winter and have a social life and play other sports. He wasn't compulsive."

Bondeson was. Born in Duluth, Minnesota, he was three when his family moved to Lansing, Michigan. Bondeson became a muscular, lean, six-foot-one, 185-pound kid in high school who excelled at several sports. He caddied at the private Country Club of Lansing and played at a local public course where green fees were a quarter. His father worked for General Motors, never making more than $100 a week. His parents divorced when he was fourteen, and at fifteen he drove his mother to St. Petersburg, Florida; he didn't even have a driver's licence. She worked as a waitress, and barely got by. Bondeson attended a local high school and worked on his golf. He won the city match- and medal-play amateur championships and a collection of other titles. The caddymaster from Scioto noticed his play and contacted Grout, who hired him to man the range in the summer of 1957.

He worked in the pro shop the second season but was let go for reasons that were never clear to him.

During his winter at Scioto, Bondeson took his first drink. He remembers it vividly. "Nobody was at the club but me, and I was staying in a little room there. I didn't have a car, and I had nowhere to go. There was snow on the course, and after closing the pro shop one day, I went into the men's grill and noticed a bottle of whisky. I wondered to myself what people saw in this and poured myself a glassful. Then I poured another glass. I drank nearly the whole bottle. The snow was swirling outside and I must have gone for a walk, because I woke up near a lake, passed out. I got pneumonia. You'd think you would never take another drink after that."

But Bondeson did. He needed a fresh rush after his two seasons at Scioto, from wherever he could get it. Having saved some money, he found himself trying to qualify for the L.A. Open. But he failed. He drank away his feeling of failure. This time it was beer.

"It went down real easy," Bondeson says. "I sat there and drank a few more, then turned to a guy and said, 'Can you live on this? Do I need to eat?' Something was lacking in me. The drinking made me feel so intense. I can see now that you drink like I did to fill a void, but I didn't know that then."

Bondeson took a four-day, cross-country trip to New York, where he pawned his clubs and suitcase and a trophy. His visions weren't of winning tournaments but of becoming an actor. At an actors' studio he and Robert Redford became friendly. Bondeson landed in the East Village at the time of the Beat writers and poets, including Jack Kerouac, Allen Ginsberg, and Gregory Corso.

"I got into peyote, then mescaline," Bondeson says. "My values went from wanting to do something in life to nothing. I spent a year there. I lived on the streets and slept in Central Park and in subways. I went to the movies on 42nd Street for ten cents in the morning, just to have a place to rest. I bottomed out. The way I was living was a fast way to nothing, but there was such passion on the way to self-destruction."

One June day in 1959, the bottomed-out Bondeson put on an old trench coat, bought himself a can of beans, and made his way by subway and train to Winged Foot Golf Club in suburban Mamaroneck, New York. The U.S. Open was on. Bondeson wanted to catch a practice round. Walking along one fairway, he spotted Nicklaus.

"I was feeling self-conscious, dressed like a Village guy," Bondeson says, "but I looked at Jack, and I thought I saw his head snap back, like he recognized me."

Bondeson skulked back to New York. After spending a year in the army, he returned to St. Petersburg. He'd lost fifty pounds, and his mother was shocked at his appearance and deterioration. She had her son committed to a state mental hospital. The institution had a nine-hole course. A kindly social worker took an interest in him and encouraged him to play. His game started to come back.

He got a job at the Twin Brooks driving range and par-three course after he was released from the hospital. Murle McKenzie Lindstrom, a friend from his high school in St. Petersburg who would go on to win the 1962 U.S. Women's Open, helped him land a job as a teaching pro at Green Acres Country Club in Northbrook, Illinois. There he met Shirley Limley, who was working as a receptionist. They were married in 1960. Some club members liked his game and offered to sponsor him on the tour. But he arrived at the inaugural Doral in 1962 having made only one cheque in fifteen tournaments, for $192.50.

At Doral, Bondeson was tied with Bob Goalby for the fifty-four-hole lead and a stroke ahead of Billy Casper, with whom he would play in a group including Ben Hogan the last day. He was leading the tournament by four shots, over Casper, with seven holes to play. But he made what he calls "the stupidest decision you could make," by trying to reach the green with a one-iron out of a bunker on the par-five twelfth hole. He buried the ball under the lip and made a double-bogey. Another double followed on the par-three thirteenth. He needed to hole a ten-foot birdie putt on the last hole to tie Casper.

"The ball went right down in the hole and came out," Bondeson says. Casper two-putted to win. Nicklaus, who had cashed his first check as a professional golfer a few weeks earlier at the L.A. Open, was third. Hogan, with whom Bondeson played a practice round in Miami, was fourth. "Paul didn't have as much patience then as he's exercising now," says Casper. "He sure had as much talent as any player out there. He could flat play."

He could also party. Bondeson's tour of duty at Doral included regular stops at one of the bars in his hotel, and he was up until 5:00 a.m. the night before the final round. His brush with victory would equal his best effort on the tour, a second-place finish at the 1964 Insurance City Open. He played in twenty tournaments in 1962, finishing sixtieth on the money list with $8,829. He averaged about twenty events a year through 1967. His best season was 1966, when he had five top-ten finishes and was fifty-fourth in earnings. He played nine tournaments in 1968, and that was pretty much it for his tour career. He "disappeared," says Nicklaus.

Bondeson worked at a McDonald's for six months, flipping burgers for sixty hours and $110 a week. "It was profitable," he says. "I learned I could work and do things. It gave me a lot of satisfaction."

But Bondeson was meant to work outdoors, and he began to bounce around the golf world. He did so for some twenty-five years. There was a stint as the golf director at East Lake in Atlanta. He played some mini-tour events in Tampa. He mowed grass at courses and came to know turfgrass. Bruce Devlin and Robert von Hagge hired him in 1969 to work at a course they designed in Orlando. Bondeson floated from job to job in Florida, Georgia, and Texas. In the mid-1960s Bondeson found some comfort in spirituality when fellow tour player Babe Hiskey introduced him to a Bible-study group. Though a committed Christian, he still had trouble with his self-destructive tendencies.

"Every time it looked like I would have some success," Bondeson says, "I'd do something to ruin it."

Meanwhile, Paul and Shirley were raising two sons and a daughter. They eventually moved to Hobe Sound, Florida, where they live in a quiet community. There is a stone in their front garden marked "Serenity." But serenity eluded them.

"'I was moving forward, although there were periods where I still struggled with the drinking and old habits," Bondeson says at his home.

There is a photo sequence of his phenomenal swing with a driver, framed on a wall, from the March 1964 issue of *Golfing* magazine. It's headlined, "Put a big turn in your status shot." The photographs show a man whose technique was flawless. The same swing sequence would turn up on a wall in the temporary clubhouse at the place where Bondeson eventually worked.

"I got the ultimate chance when Wayne Huizenga invited me to work at The Floridian," he says. "Wayne was phenomenal and still is." Huizenga is former CEO of Blockbuster Entertainment and owns the Miami Dolphins and Pro Player Stadium in Miami, as well as having many other wide-ranging business interests.

Bondeson started at The Floridian in 1994 and was instrumental in creating Huizenga's showpiece course. It gleamed. Nick Price showed up there one day and noticed the swing sequence. "I thought, 'Oh my goodness, who is that?'" Price says. "I had no idea who Paul was. John McNally, the pro at The Floridian, told me it was Paul Bondeson. I thought his swing was amazing and asked where this guy was. John told me he was right outside."

Price and Bondeson played a few holes together one day. Bondeson played in his work clothes. "He was so easy to talk to,"

Price says. "He was always eager to talk about the swing, which fascinates me. Paul is a good, all-around person. He has always been very friendly to me."

Things were looking up for Bondeson. He made money in the booming stock market. He hadn't taken a drink for a decade and was studying the Bible regularly with fellows who call themselves a band of brothers: Hiskey and his brother Jim, golf instructor Carl Lohren, former tour pro Marty Fleckman, amateur golfer Larry Fenster, and Billy Burke, the pro at North Shore Country Club on Long Island.

Then came the accident, on October 16, 2001.

"We'd bought a mountain home in Murphy, North Carolina, in the western part of the state in a corner near the Tennessee and Georgia state lines," Bondeson is saying in mid-February at his home. "We heard that a local school was trying to raise money and were just about to make the turn into the school when somebody making a U-turn hit us. Luckily, there were paramedics on duty at the school, and they got to us right away."

Their car rolled over four times. Shirley broke both her ankles and has a pin and three plates in her left leg. Bondeson broke his neck and was put on life support with a feeding tube and ventilator. He couldn't breathe on his own for five months, having suffered a spinal cord injury not unlike that which happened to actor Christopher Reeve. Yet here he sits, at home, at ease. He has found a peace he never knew when his body was intact and strong, when he could drive par-fours, as he did on the 380-yard eleventh hole during the final round at Doral in 1962.

"Bob Goetz [a former tour player] called and wondered why this happened to me," Bondeson says. "Then he answered for himself, 'Because you could handle it.' I think he's right."

Former major league pitcher Jim Kaat, an avid golfer who lives near Bondeson, spends a lot of time with him. Kaat often takes him to the Medalist Golf Club, where he is a member. Bondeson parks himself on the range and watches players swing, offering advice when asked. He can spend hours doing this, all the while telling stories of his days on the tour and of his life now. It's a rare moment when he's not smiling.

"Paul is very candid and open about his life," Kaat says. "I've gone out with other people to see him at his house, and we'll have tears in our eyes. You go there to cheer him up, and he tells you all these stories and cheers you up."

"You would think the accident would be the end of the line," Bondeson says. "But I started a phase of life where I had a peace that was so strong. Yes, I'd had this spiritual change in my life a long time before, but until the accident, I could get distracted. After the accident I realized how little awareness I had. I'd lived on such a superficial plane."

The event at Palm Cove is ending. Rodriguez has presented Bondeson with a flag from the day that his fellow professionals have signed. A cocktail party the night before at The Floridian raised $45,000 via a silent auction of memorabilia. Price, Tom Kite, and Tiger Woods, among other pros, contributed items for the auction. Bondeson's band of brothers estimate they'll be able to turn over $110,000 to him.

All day the pros and his friends have been telling Bondo stories. DeWitt Weaver remembers Bondeson hitting balls at an airplane that flew over during a tournament in Oklahoma, and that he had "a Sam Snead–like swing." Burke speaks of his "silky swing that had built-in 290-yard tee shots."

Bondeson has no illusions that he'll hit a golf ball again, or even walk. He's not deluding himself any more, about anything. It's a long time since a fellow sitting beside Bondeson at that bar the night before the last round at Doral told him that he was leading the tournament and should get to bed. Bondeson and his friends agree that he wanted to lose.

"He knew he didn't have the capacity to handle success," Fenster says. "But he can handle what he's going through now."

Paul Bondeson didn't win the 1962 Doral Open. He got lost for a long time. But he has found himself.

"What you guys did for me, well, I'm just so proud to be a golf professional," he says to his friends at Palm Cove as the proceedings conclude. He's smiling and crying at the same time. He's fulfilling – in the present and in a different way – that unlimited potential he so often squandered.

• • •

Bondo and Shirley now live in the mountains of North Carolina. Members of his band of brothers drop by regularly. He's always ready to go out to a range and watch as his pals and other fellow pros hit balls. He's also always ready to tell stories, and boy, can he tell them.

Jack Nicklaus

The Globe and Mail | July 16, 2005

In a most extraordinary gesture, but entirely in keeping with the gentleman and champion that he has been, Jack Nicklaus addressed the world's media at the end of his news conference at the Old Course yesterday.

He'd just completed his second round at the Open Championship, carding 72, which he said represented his best golf this year but not good enough to keep him playing competitively.

"As we finish up, just let me say that I want to thank you," the sixty-five-year-old said. "It's been absolutely a pleasure to be able to come in here and talk to you honestly and know that I'm going to get a good, honest, straight result."

But it is we who should thank Nicklaus. He's been an exemplary person on and off the course for the forty years he's played golf surpassingly well.

His golf was just fine yesterday, although he missed some putts that he would have made when he was winning everything, including eighteen majors. But the day wasn't all about golf. It was about something else entirely.

Any day a golfer spends at St. Andrews is special, but yesterday provided something extra.

The course and the town were all jacked up from morning until into the early evening as Nicklaus bid his favourite place in golf and his competitive career adieu, and as Tiger Woods, playing in the group two holes behind him, moved into a commanding position to win his second British Open here.

Nicklaus was greeted with standing ovations at every tee, down every crinkly fairway, and as he approached and walked onto each of the course's hallowed greens. The course became Carnegie Hall for him, and he was centre stage every step of the way at the Old Course, where he won the 1970 and 1978 Opens.

Nicklaus was grinding all afternoon as he tried to make the cut. He wore a sweater for the cool first few holes, designed to commemorate what he wore in 1978. He said he would have liked to have worn it today as well, but his scores of 75 on Thursday and 72 yesterday fell short by two strokes.

During that 1978 Open, Nicklaus was a stroke behind little-known New Zealander Simon Owen as they played the sixteenth hole. Owen had chipped in on the fifteenth. Nicklaus then birdied the sixteenth, while Owen bogeyed, and Nicklaus went on to collect his second win at the Old Course.

Nicklaus has said that the situation in that final round of 1978 was one in which intimidation might have been a factor.

Some players in the all-out interest of winning might have encouraged that atmosphere. Not Nicklaus. He instead tried to settle his opponent's nerves in an atmosphere of sportsmanship, not gamesmanship.

"The game we play is a game, nothing more," he said. "It's a wonderful game. It's a game I love. I think that the game needs to be played in that spirit."

Nicklaus isn't one to speak of a legacy. But he'll leave one because, being himself, he lived up to his high standards and those of his father, Charlie, who was fifty-six when he died, but left his own legacy – that of fair play.

In the Ryder Cup in 1969, Nicklaus conceded a short putt on the final hole of a match to Tony Jacklin, the Open champion that year. Nicklaus didn't expect Jacklin would miss the putt, but elected not to give him the chance. His stately gesture meant that the Ryder Cup ended in a tie.

Many of today's golfers have said they wouldn't do that.

"Then if they [decide not to concede such a putt], I feel sorry for them," Nicklaus said, his voice softening, emotions reaching the surface. "As I leave the game, hopefully if the example that I've set, if that's followed by some and it helps one young guy change what he's doing, then I'm successful."

Nicklaus and Jacklin are co-designing a course in Florida called Concession, which will mark an important moment in the game. Jacklin, who also played yesterday and missed the cut, spoke of his friend, partner, and foe for so many years.

"Jack's legacy is not just his eighteen majors, but the spirit with which he's played the game," he said.

Jack Nicklaus, golf colossus. As night fell yesterday on St. Andrews, his presence, and his example, lit up the auld grey toon by the sea.

Maybe sentiment and sport shouldn't collide. Yesterday, they did – and that was exactly right.

• • •

Nicklaus is on the road throughout the year to attend to his design business, which takes him all over the world. He captained the U.S. team to a win in the 2007 Presidents Cup at the Royal Montreal Golf Club. Nicklaus plays very little golf these days. The golf he does play is usually reserved for course openings. He never three-putts. "I pick up after two putts," he says.

Arnold Palmer
The Globe and Mail | June 1, 1996

LATROBE, PENNSYLVANIA

While his friends practise their putting near the first tee at the Latrobe Country Club, Arnold Palmer is talking on his cellphone at the edge of the practice green. He's holding the phone in his right hand and stroking putts with his left. The course he has owned since 1971, and where he grew up in a home beside the fifth tee, flows placidly out and around from this high point. Down beside the fifth tee is where his father, Deke, and mother, Doris, raised their first son, Arnold, his brother, Jerry, and sisters, Lois, Jean, and Sandy. Deke Palmer helped build this bucolic course, then became its superintendent and subsequently its professional.

Palmer, sixty-six, spends many afternoons golfing here from May through September, living in an unpretentious home across the street from the course. This day, one feels privileged to be joining him for a round; after a lifetime of following him and twenty years of writing about him, it's an honour to come to the place he loves to share a game with him. It's a pilgrimage of sorts, the chance to spend a few hours with the King, as he often is called, in the place where he is just a regular guy.

Now it is early in the afternoon, and Arnie – as his pals call him on the course, and as the golf world best knows this most popular of players – is off the phone and will not talk on it during the round. Bets are being made, a variety of wagers that set my head spinning, lots of action, although not for much money, thankfully. There is an overall skins game among twelve golfers in three foursomes: team bets group to group, team bets within foursomes, individual games. This writer also has a game with Arnie; we will play what he calls a walk-in, a straight match-play game over eighteen holes. Our game is for serious money – five bucks, Canadian.

As we roll our practice putts, club champion Jim Bryant tells a story. He will join us and Howdy Giles, Arnie's dentist and close friend from Wilmington, Delaware. Bryant went to high school with Arnie's daughter, Amy, and is remembering the time he shagged balls for the King at Statler's Golf Center, a range in the hills of central Pennsylvania near this course.

"That was one of the greatest thrills of my life," Bryant says. "I was shagging balls for Arnie during a clinic at Statler's. My responsibility was to shag the balls that went longer than 275 yards." Left unspoken is the fact that Arnie was regularly hitting his drives that long.

Arnie is in the middle of the green now, completing his wagers. I'm trying to negotiate an extra stroke or two from him. But he's tough and he won't let himself lose any bets on the first tee.

"What'd you say your handicap is, Lorne?" Arnie yells across the green.

"Four," I tell him, "but I'll be working, taking notes. Besides, you know this course."

"Four, huh? I'm scratch [zero], so I'll give you the four shots," Arnie says. No further discussion. Arnie is equally stern with everybody else. "Nobody gets any shots in the skins game," he announces. "We'll play $2 skins, so the most anybody can lose is $36. You don't want in, say so now."

Arnie winks at me, letting me know his toughness is a bit of an act but that he can get away with it here. And probably everywhere, I figure. This is Arnold Palmer, an icon in golf as Muhammad Ali is in boxing, as Joe DiMaggio is in baseball.

Lee Trevino puts it this way: "Arnie has more people watching him park the car than we do on the course." But not today, because this is just a guy who loves to golf and is about to go out for an afternoon round on his home track. His pals respect him enough not to bring a crowd of followers. Nobody is here but the golfers, and the first foursome scampers down the slope to the tee. Our group is up first. Arnie takes a ball from each of us and throws all four in the air. Mine and Bryant's fall near one another and so we will take on Arnie and Giles in a team game within our group.

The first hole is a 401-yard par-four. The tee is well-elevated above the fairway, with trees right and left. I'm calm, elevated by the company, camaraderie, and easy feelings that Arnie generates wherever he goes. It doesn't matter that we are part of Arnie's foursome today, not Arnie's Army. He's the same guy in a tournament or a casual round. He'll look you in the eye in the crowd at the Masters around a tee. He does the same here on the tee before you play. But first he rips one down the fairway, and then says, "Go ahead, your turn," pointing at me.

I zone in and nail a drive down the right side of the fairway with a slight fade. It just catches the right rough but it's down there, long and in play. Whew.

We walk down the hill to the fairway as his caddy, Scott, drives the cart. Arnie likes to walk and hates the trend toward forcing people to use carts. "I build walking paths on all my courses," he says of his work as a course architect. "I do ride from green to tee on some of these new developments, though, where they're two hundred to three hundred yards apart."

We talk about Latrobe, and this place he calls home. Arnie also has a house in Orlando and is a principal owner of the Bay Hill club there. But that's his winter home; it came later – after all this, and after his parents raised him in rolling farmland sixty-four kilometres east of Pittsburgh.

"Our accountants have told us that for tax reasons we should have our principal residence in Florida," Arnie says of advice that he and Winnie, his wife of forty-one years, have received. "But I love it here. We have made a very firm decision to stay right here."

His drive is twenty yards past mine, or a yard a year considering the difference in our ages. He's lost a yard a year since he was in his mid-forties, but he still can put it out there.

We're on our way. Life is good. This is Arnold Palmer country, all right. Sure, he is popular all over the world, but this is his place, his centre. He really is the King here, and you feel his influence from whatever direction you approach Latrobe. I've driven west from Baltimore for this game with Arnie, a couple of weeks before he will play the du Maurier Champions, a Senior PGA Tour event at the Hamilton Golf and Country Club in Ancaster, Ontario. He plans to arrive June 12, the day before the tournament. Arnie has good feelings about Canada: he won the 1955 Canadian Open at Weston in Toronto, his first victory as a professional. There's a grouping of photos and other material on the wall above the double doors of his office that testifies to that victory, including a nice message from Gordon Delaat, then the professional at Weston. That was a long time ago. Arnie has played many Canadian

Opens since then, and won the 1980 Canadian PGA Championship in Edmonton. He, Jack Nicklaus, and Gary Player also filmed a match for the old *Big Three* television show at the Royal Montreal Golf Club.

Driving to Latrobe, I get off Interstate 76 and head north on a country road. There's a sense that things don't change much here: U.S. flags fly in front of some of the clapboard houses; there's a chicken-and-biscuit dinner June 8 in a community centre; cabins are visible in the woods as men wade in streams, fly-fishing the languid afternoon away.

Up the two-lane blacktop, I notice the Ligonier Country Club and hit the brakes as I drive past. Backing up, I swing into the entrance and find my way to the pro shop. Arnie played matches here for his high school against the one in Ligonier when the schools were part of the same district fifty years ago. Club pro Lou Asti, Jr., is in the shop, arranging a club event for the Memorial Day weekend. In a minute, he's speaking about Arnie.

"He's my hero; he's my king," Asti, a friendly, middle-aged man, says. "Take a look at this photo here," he says of a black-and-white shot of Arnie that's signed, "To Lou, Best of luck and best regards. Arnold Palmer." Asti, who has other signed photos of Arnie at his home, wants to talk about Arnie's powerful – if less than orthodox – swing, about which *Los Angeles Times* writer Jim Murray once observed: "He had the ten-handicapper's swipe at the ball, finishing in the strange over-head power lock of a guy trying to block out the hook. The club looked like a Roman candle."

Asti knows it's a classic swing where it counts – at impact. Arnie wouldn't have won sixty-one PGA Tour events and seven major championships if he hit the ball like a ten-handicapper. Asti pulls out a photograph of Arnie's swing at impact to prove his point.

"If this isn't perfect, then I don't know perfect," he says of the position just through the ball, where Arnie's head is held still behind the ball and his right arm is extended well down the target line. "Hey, buddy, this will last," Asti says. "People say with his finish he couldn't play. Even his old high school coach told Arnie once that he should settle down because he could never make a living in golf. But he showed us, didn't he? Anybody denies he's the King has three weeks of 'shame on you.'"

• • •

Out on his course, Arnie starts with a couple of pars. He stands over a twenty-foot birdie putt on the first hole, his trademark knock-kneed stance still there as if it were yesterday and he was holing putts to birdie six of the first seven holes of the 1960 U.S. Open at Cherry Hills in Denver. He went on to erase a seven-shot deficit after three rounds to win the championship.

But the putt on the first green this day runs over the edge, dead weight and speed. Arnie swivels his head in agony as if to say, "How could that miss?" The guy wants every putt. He's got one objective: to rap that ball in the hole.

The second hole is a 126-yard downhiller, real estate for a hole-in-one. Arnie hunches over the ball and stares down the hole cut in the right rear portion of the green and, with an actor's sense of timing, looks up just before he starts to swing. He stares at his three companions and asks – no, declares – "You guys are in the whip-out, aren't you?"

I've no idea what he means and ask him. "You make an ace, the other guys whip out fifty bucks from their pockets," Arnie explains. Sure, I'm in. His pal Giles says, "He's done it. He's made us whip that cash out."

Arnie's punch shot is on the flag all the way but comes up short. Walking to the green, he tells of the time he, Nicklaus, and Player were in the same threesome at the Tradition tournament in Scottsdale, Arizona.

"Gary made a one on the seventh," Arnie relates, "and I asked him how many holes-in-one he had. He'd had seventeen. I said, 'That's interesting. I've also had seventeen.' Jack heard us talking and said, 'You're kidding. I've also made seventeen.' "

Arnie just misses his birdie putt again and gives me his "You're lucky" look. Then he points out Riley's Pond behind the second green. Riley was his golden retriever and liked to frolic in the pond. Now a plaque beside the pond honours him; Riley died three years ago, and Arnie's new dog is called Prince. He usually travels with the King: by car, in Arnie's private plane, and along the fields and country roads here around the course.

On to the third tee now. Doc Giffin, Arnie's ever-affable personal assistant of thirty years, is standing by a white fence at the side of the tee. He calls Arnie over to give him a quick update on a business matter. Arnie has a word with him, then gets back to the real business of the moment. He nails his drive down the fairway and walks down, talking about swimming with water snakes in the ponds on this property as a kid. As he walks, he takes a knife from his pocket and unwraps the leather grip from the driver he has just hit. There are two bags full of clubs on the cart. They hold fifty clubs, and Arnie will experiment with most of them today.

Down the course we go, up and down the rolling hills. On the fifth tee, Arnie points to a maintenance shed twenty-five yards away and an adjacent field with a few vehicles and says, "This is where I grew up. This is where our house was. And that's where I played football and baseball as a kid." He points to a playing field across the road.

This hole is also the site of a Palmer legend. A stream crosses the fairway 100 yards out from the tee, and when Arnie was five he would whack balls across the water for a nickel for some of the women who couldn't make the carry on their own. His father first made him a set of clubs when Arnie was three. The rest is history, history still being played out all around the golfing world. To spend time with Arnie on his home course in his home state in the landscape he loves is to appreciate that this is a man deeply connected to his past. One understands the influence of Deke Palmer on his son. Arnie jumps into his cart and invites me along for a ride; he wants to examine a turf nursery where his boyhood home stood and to speak for a moment about the past, one that lives with him every moment, even now.

"I remember playing here like it was yesterday," Arnie says. "My dad was a great person, but he was a strong man, very disciplined."

I mention a story I had read about how his dad would let him know in no uncertain terms if Arnie did something wrong, even into his thirties.

"Let me know it? Are you kidding?" Arnie says. "Yes, sir, he would let me know it."

Deke Palmer died in 1976, five years after his son bought the Latrobe Country Club. The scorecard has the name Arnold Palmer on it as club president, Bruce Rearick as club professional, and an entry about Arnie's dad. It reads simply, "M.J. (Deke) Palmer, LCC 1921–1976."

Deke Palmer's presence is felt everywhere here. His double locker remains the way it was when he died, with the same things in it. There's a revealing colour snapshot of him above the locker, showing a face lined by all the weather he faced in all the years he spent outdoors here. He looks much like the man his son would grow into.

There's another photo in Arnie's office in the pleasant, treed compound that contains his house and workshop. The black-and-white picture shows Arnie with his right hand on his dad's left shoulder. There is no mistaking the bond between them. "That's my favourite picture of the two of them," Giffin says.

Arnie is on the tenth tee, a killer par-three that is playing 228 yards to the hole cut to the right rear of the green, not far from a sand trap. He's shot an even-par 36 on the front side, missing a handful of putts by a whisker. He has a one-iron in his hand and aims between the bunker and the pin. It's a gutsy shot and he hits a beauty.

The ball turns slightly right to left, always working toward the hole. It's Arnie's famous "go for broke" philosophy, another aspect of the man that has not changed. His ball lands twenty-five feet short of the hole and starts rolling. "Go in," he yells like any golfer at any course: wishing, hoping, imploring, demanding.

The ball comes up short and Arnie soon holes it for birdie. He gives us the Palmer grin and pumps his right fist. Birdie with a one-iron in your hand: that's golfing your ball.

"I was thinking about the skin on that one," Arnie says, and no wonder. Nobody else is going to birdie this hole.

We stop for a cold drink and Arnie spots a young woman in the halfway house. She's a college golfer. Arnie engages her in conversation, encouraging her. Then we move on; I'm already three down to Arnie and soon will run out of holes. I'm hitting the ball well, but my swing is slightly out of sync. I'm hitting sand wedges fifty feet past the hole, three-putting. I guess I really am more anxious playing with Arnie than following him or writing about him. Surprise, surprise.

But Arnie has to give me a shot on the eleventh, so there's hope. I make par, as he does, and am only two down; maybe there's still a chance.

The twelfth is a 335-yard hole; a stream crosses the fairway 245 yards out. Arnie pulls out his driver and says, "This hole will determine my future in golf. When I can't carry the water any more, I quit."

Today, he carries the water, no problem. Walking down the fairway, he points out three covered bridges that give the course added character and mentions that his dad put them in. Walking on, we speak about the costs of time.

"One of the things I seem to have lost is the ability to score," Arnie says. "It's hard to put it down to any one thing. It's just that I always had a knack for getting the ball in the hole from whatever position I was in. Another thing is that in my best years I always felt if I wanted to move the ball out, I could always find another ten or twenty yards. It was there. Now, that's difficult."

As difficult as it might be, Arnie still is hitting the ball quite long. After his birdie on the tenth, he's been playing steadily, par after par. Then, on the final hole, he lets out some shaft and gets well up the steep hill on the way to the green in front of the modest but elegant clubhouse. In Latrobe language, he's "mamooed" his drive – long and straight, that is.

The hole is cut to the front right of the three-tiered green; there's not much room there at all to land a ball. No problem. Arnie shapes a shot about ten feet right of the cup, then holes the putt for a closing birdie and a two-under-par 34 on the back side. He shoots 70. I shoot 81, and he beats me 3 and 2. It's a privilege to lose to the King. Well, hell, that's only partly true. I would have liked to beat him.

The Golf Channel is on all the time in the grill room; Arnie is chairman of the twenty-four-hour network and says it's going to succeed. He drinks a Jack Daniels while the rest of us tote up the wagers. Arnie is a man in his element, full of good humour.

Giles catches me looking at a famous illustration that artist Leroy Neiman did of Arnie; it hangs on the wall above the fireplace. Giles tells me it's based on a photo he took of Arnie; he's always snapping pictures, a man bent on documenting Arnie's life whenever he can. Arnie overhears Giles telling me of the photo and ribs his friend.

"The painting isn't so famous," Arnie says. "But the photo sure is."

Arnie is going over one of his matches, by memory, with one of the golfers. He's also looking at a log of the day's phone calls provided by Giffin, while glancing at the tournament on the television and sipping his drink. I reach over to give him the five dollars that he won from me.

"Nah, I won't take that," Arnie says. "But I'll tell you what. I'd take one of those new coins you've got, a two-dollar coin, isn't it? I'll use it as a ball marker in Canada."

I haven't got one in my pocket, but there's one somewhere in my car. We walk to the parking lot and I find the coin and give it to him. Then he and Giles get in Arnie's Cadillac and drive off into the Pennsylvania early evening.

But Arnie will come back across the street to his club on the weekend; he'll participate in some way in Memorial Day weekend festivities. Somehow, despite his fame, Arnie has remained, as Giffin observes, "the common man with the common touch."

Giles certainly knows this, and had told a story of the time he asked actor Jack Lemmon about a round he had with Arnie. Lemmon made a pertinent observation about Arnie, of whom it is often said: "He made golf what it is today." That is, a game that people of all ages and from all walks of life enjoy.

"People say Arnie has charisma," Lemmon told Giles. "But there's another word, too. He has grace. Think about what that word means to you. I'll bet you can't say that about five friends that you have."

Arnie's grace and common touch must derive from his connections to this place. That a man of such fame, influence, and wealth should remain essentially unmarked by all that can corrupt and separate, even isolate, is interesting in itself. This is not to say that Arnie has not had his reversals on and off the course – he has, but he has dealt with them squarely. Through it all, he somehow seems to have not travelled very far at all from Latrobe.

As I drive back to Toronto, I think about this aspect of the man – the way he has anchored himself by choice to Latrobe. To travel as far as he has and to remain in the same place, to accomplish so much in his chosen field and yet remain as if he had stayed at home working on the course, making the grass grow, Deke's boy. This, I think, is Arnold Palmer's accomplishment: with all his success, in a few hours around the place where he grew up he still can show a visitor the critical importance of home and of remaining constant and consistent.

"I love it here." Arnie's words, as we walked down the first fairway, rumble around in my mind as I drive through the night. Home is who we are, and Arnold Palmer knows who he is.

● ● ●

Palmer was diagnosed with prostate cancer in 1997, and made an excellent recovery. His wife Winnie died in 1999, and he remarried in 2005. Palmer will turn eighty on September 29, 2009. He continues to fly his own plane, and to tee it up with his pals. He assumed the role of honorary starter at the Masters in 2008.

Marlene Streit

Golf Journal | July 1994

"It's the house with the yellow mailbox in front, between the row of big pine trees," Marlene had advised. There it was, at the end of a long and winding entrance, Marlene Streit's Magnolia Lane: a ranch-style home on fifty acres that bespeaks this magnificent but unaffected golfer's appreciation of the outdoors.

Marlene Streit has made much of her feeling for outdoor life, especially on golf courses. She turned sixty in March, having established a golden tournament record of victories: the 1953 British Ladies' Amateur, the 1956 U.S. Women's Amateur, the 1963 Australian Ladies', eleven Canadian Ladies' Amateur Opens, four Canadian Senior championships (her most recent last summer), the 1985 U.S. Senior Women's championship. She has beaten the best and, of course, lost to the best.

For winning the 1953 British Amateur, Marlene, then nineteen, received a heroine's welcome in Toronto. Fifteen thousand people cheered as she drove by in an open convertible. She took the 1956 U.S. Women's Amateur when she defeated JoAnne Carner, then the Great Gundy (for her maiden name Gunderson), 2 and 1.

Today she is respected throughout the golf world as perhaps Canada's finest amateur ever, male or female. There is talk about a campaign to pick her as Canadian athlete of the half century. She has already won two awards as Canada's athlete of the year, male or female. She's come a long way from the small farming community of Cereal, Alberta, where she was born in 1934, but looking out over the open spaces she shares with her husband, Doug, it is easy to see that this is a woman who still thrives on a Canadian prairie sort of landscape – wide, free, and roaming, just like her golf swing.

The Stewart family – Marlene, her parents, and her sister Dolly – lived in Alberta until World War II. Marlene's father, Harold, who had farmed in Cereal, was sent by the Royal Canadian Air Force to help the war effort by working in an Ontario factory. At twelve, Marlene took to golf when an older friend asked her to caddy. She hooked up with Gordon McInnis, Sr., the professional at the Lookout Point Golf Club, in Fonthill, Ontario, an attractive town in the southwestern region of the province. McInnis was a gifted instructor who established a lifelong relationship with Marlene. He helped her develop a swing steeped in the basics of grip, stance, and posture, knitted into a unit by rhythm.

That rhythm is still evident in Marlene's swing. She was a medallist in the Doherty Invitational senior division at Coral Ridge Country Club last January in Fort Lauderdale. Writers said Streit reminded them of Ben Hogan. Some called her "Little Ben" for her "impassivity, deliberation, and stillness in assessing a shot." Her handicap today? One.

"I think it was the mental state I was in when I was playing my best that made the difference," Marlene said. "I would get myself into this *que sera, sera* attitude. The idea was not to make something happen, but just to let it happen. It was all rhythm. I got myself in a tunnel. I was aware of what was going on outside, but I didn't pay attention. People would talk to me and I would hear them, but I had no notion of replying. Not that I was being discourteous, but I just wasn't involved that way.

"I always played my own game," Marlene continues. "I was into my own game, not my opponent's. When I play alone, even today, I have a little game with myself against par. It makes me laugh when people say that the best champion is determined by medal play. I think it's the other way 'round. Look at what happened to the U.S. Ryder Cup players after their matches last year. Corey Pavin and Jim Gallagher have both won since then on the PGA Tour. Match play did so much for their confidence."

Marlene's temperament suited match play. It is easy to understand why, sitting with her in her combined kitchen–living room on a cold Ontario winter's day, gazing out at the snow-covered fields all the way to the horizon. Marlene is attracted to solitary activities: going for an energetic ski run, hitting balls for hours on the long lawn that sweeps away in front of the gracious home she shares with her husband. Her directness is appealing, as is her appreciation of the moment. Marlene lives for today.

"It's funny, I can't even remember who I played in so many of my tournaments," Marlene said, laughing and even slightly embarrassed. "I think that's because I don't dwell on those things. Somebody will come up to me and tell me I beat so and so. Well, I really have to think about it to remember anything about the match."

This quality of focusing on the moment may be the bedrock ingredient that has made Marlene a winner. How else does one explain a nineteen-year-old's ability to compete in her first British Ladies' Amateur, during her first visit to the U.K., and win her final match against Philomena Garvey, a six-time Irish champion? Sure, Marlene had at seventeen won the 1951 Canadian Ladies' Amateur, and had progressed wonderfully under the tutelage of McInnis. He had stressed fundamentals and only fundamentals. "Smoothness, rhythm, and balance," he would repeat to his protégé as an incantation. "Smoothness, rhythm, and balance, Marlene. That's all you need."

Over the years she came to be called "Little Miss Murder," "Little Miss Robot," "Canada's Queen of the Fairway," "Little Train." The reference to Marlene as "Little" became somewhat trite, even if she is but five feet tall. Marlene turned out to be a giant of the game, recognized for her achievements wherever she travels. A golfer of international standing, she is Canadian through and through. A friend, amateur golfer Pauline Kelly, said that Marlene "has become a role model" for her and her fellow golfers. "You wanted to be like Marlene Streit. She's sort of the Gordie Howe of golf." Both are children of the vast Canadian prairie.

Marlene loves her home. Her golf club, York Downs, is only a few miles away. She and Doug also have a home in Florida, where they visit periodically during the winter. But then, as was the case last February, she needs to return to Canada to ski.

"Skiing is very rhythmic, just like golf," Marlene pointed out. "I'm not a bust-down-the-hill kind of skier. I just go down to get up.

I call myself a terminal intermediate. It's the feeling I like, such a free feeling."

When Marlene is on the slopes, or competing against herself on the course these days, sometimes her thoughts go to two people she lost last year. Her teacher, McInnis, without whom Marlene has often said she would not have succeeded, died in May 1993. Her mother died in November.

Marlene won the Canadian Seniors last summer for McInnis's memory. She stood over a five-foot putt on the final green for the win, and thought of her teacher. The putt went in. "Smoothness, rhythm, and balance, Marlene. That's all you need."

She also needed those qualities of equability to cope with her mother's year-long illness. They were very close, as Marlene and Doug are to their daughters, Darlene and Lynn. Marlene has reacted to the deaths of her teacher/friend and her mother as one would expect her to: straightforwardly, not sentimentally, and yet with deep feeling. Maybe she learned something about fate on December 17, 1954. That day Marlene was one of twenty-three passengers aboard an airplane when it undershot a runway at Toronto's Malton Airport by nine miles and crash-landed in a field. All twenty-three passengers scrambled out of the plane just before it exploded and burned. "God spared us," Marlene, pictured near the wreckage, was quoted as saying the next day on the front page of *The Toronto Star*.

Now it was almost forty years later, and Marlene was thinking about that day, her mother, and McInnis. "You just have to go on," Marlene said. "But you sure do miss them, don't you? Not being able to pick up the phone and talk to them."

Winter was coming to an end in Ontario, and Marlene was anticipating another competitive season. Marlene Streit, Canada's "Queen of the Fairway," was looking forward to the new season. She believes there is more to accomplish. There is no profit in thinking this extraordinary amateur could be wrong.

• • •

Marlene won the 2003 U.S. Senior Women's Amateur Championship. She was sixty-nine and became the oldest golfer to hold a USGA title. A year later she was the first Canadian inducted into the World Golf Hall of Fame, in St. Augustine, Florida. She was inducted via the Lifetime Achievement category. Smoothness, rhythm, and balance had taken her to the highest levels of amateur golf. She still competes, and she still wins.

SIX | Gone Now

Al Balding

The Globe and Mail | January 23, 1993

One of Canada's finest golfers is clearly also one of its most under-appreciated players. Toronto's Al Balding turns sixty-nine in April. That is the season of the Masters and, for Balding, the season, he hopes, of his return to top-flight golf.

"I'm getting better and better as I'm getting older," Balding says on a wintry afternoon at his home in Etobicoke, Ontario, not a hundred yards from where, in the mid-1950s, he and his wife Moreen ran the pro shop in a trailer at the Credit Valley Golf Club. "You know, I'd like to leave some kind of mark in the game. It's a funny thing, but after all kinds of troubles, here I am at my age enjoying the game more than ever. It's something I can do for the rest of my life so I better enjoy it."

Look out any rear window in the Baldings' comfortable home and you can see the driving range at Credit Valley. It's a pastoral scene. But, as Balding says, troubles lurk in the background. The problems include a diagnosis of cancer in the mid-1970s, recurrent shoulder problems, an often uneasy relationship with the Canadian golf establishment, swing problems, and, more than anything, quarrels with his own sensitive nature. No wonder, then, that he has not always enjoyed his chosen career.

Balding is the first to admit he has not enjoyed his golf all the time. Never mind that it's a game, or that Balding's swing is so smooth that even Sam Snead sought him out for practice rounds. Balding has taken his knocks. The game has beaten up on him even as it has rewarded him with luminous moments.

Balding, or "the Silver Fox," as he is known for his full head of grey hair, reflects on these matters while seated by a crackling fire in his home, a glass of red wine on a table, a cigar in his mouth. He's thinking about the beginnings of a career that is not yet over, not by any means, he feels.

"I did some caddying as a kid at Islington [in Toronto]," Balding recalls. "But then I left school early, enlisted in the Marines, and got discharged because I hurt my arm. I drove transport, and got a job as a starter at Oakdale in 1949 on weekends while I was still driving."

Golfers who knew Balding in his early days remember a hard worker whose silky swing seemed natural, but was the result of constant practice, application, and refinement. Paul Williams, vice-president of Telemedia Broadcasting Systems and an accomplished amateur golfer, remembers when Balding used to pray for rain so that he could hit balls in the inclement conditions for hours.

Such effort eventually led Balding to Les Franks, his mentor and one of Canada's finest teachers. Franks taught sixty to ninety lessons a week at Islington.

"I would pick up balls on the range," Balding says, "fifteen cents a lesson. Les would whack a player's left knee to make sure it worked properly on the backswing, and insist he finish the swing with his elbows together."

Balding learned to swing the golf club gracefully and efficiently. He soon became the professional at Credit Valley and in the off-season made his way south for competition. In December 1955, Balding won the Mayfair Inn Open in Sanford, Florida, over Snead, Tommy Bolt, Doug Ford, and Dow Finsterwald, all of whom had won or would win major championships.

That was the start. In 1957, Balding and Moreen – his strength, he says – set out for the U.S. tour full-time with savings of $10,000 and a stake of $8,000 from a backer. Balding had met a young George Knudson by then; Knudson caddied for him from time to time and liked to tell of when they saw the legendary Ben Hogan at a tournament in Los Angeles.

Knudson noticed Hogan first and suggested to Balding that they watch Hogan. Hogan had the crowd that round, as he did most days.

"To hell with that," Balding said. "Let them watch me."

Those who chose to watch Balding savoured his style. A tall player, he stood up to the ball and swung with a rhythm most players envied. Such form could not be denied, and in 1957 Balding finished eighth in official earnings on the tour. He continued to earn a decent living on the tour for some years while winning four times all told. He and Knudson won the 1968 World Cup in Rome for Canada. Balding also won the individual trophy as low scorer over the seventy-two holes.

But it is commonly agreed that Balding did not get, nor has yet received, the recognition in Canada that his play warranted. He is the only Canadian to finish in the top ten for a season on the PGA Tour. His World Cup win with Knudson was a significant accomplishment at a time when that tournament was very important. And from 1955 to 1970 he won four Canadian Professional Golfers' Association championships. Balding and Knudson were the two golfers a Canadian follower of the game had to see.

But not until 1985 did the Royal Canadian Golf Association admit Balding to its Hall of Fame. Balding spoke emotionally at the presentation, and it was clear that he had been hurt by what amounted to a serious error on the part of the Hall of Fame's selectors.

"I never knew why it took so long," Balding says, shaking his head. "After all, only a few Canadians won tournaments in the United States, I was the only one to finish in the top ten on the tour, and George and I were the first to win the World Cup for Canada."

People who have followed Balding's career agree that he has not been granted the attention he deserved.

"He should have gotten more recognition," Williams said. "Look, we're talking about somebody who Gary Player said had one of the ten best swings in the game."

"His swing was always marvellous," Sandra Post, Canada's most successful LPGA player, said. "The lines are there. He's been a beautiful striker of the golf ball. I really respect his game and ability, but I think he has not gotten enough credit for what he did and how well he still plays."

Jamie Kavanaugh, a thirty-five-year-old competitive amateur who is taking lessons from Balding, is aware of how little recognition Balding received. He offers an explanation. It is an explanation often heard.

"Al will give you the world once he knows you. But he can also be gruff and hard on you. He's stubborn and he's been misunderstood. A lot of people rub him the wrong way, and he rubs them the wrong way."

But Kavanaugh watched Balding play nine breathtaking holes during a howling wind in the CPGA Seniors' last summer at Blue Springs in Acton, Ontario. He has sat on the bag at the edge of the range and watched Balding paint pictures in the sky with the ball. He senses a change in Balding, that he is softening, warming to the simple pleasures of trying to play. Kavanaugh, like those in Balding's inner circle, thinks he knows why.

In 1975, Balding was told he had multiple myeloma, a cancer of the blood. He learned that most people with the disease live two or three years, and that many die within a year. Balding was diagnosed the day after he became director of golf at the then-new National Golf Club in Woodbridge, Ontario.

"You try and prepare for what might happen," Balding says, surrounded by photos of his golf life – he and Knudson holding a cocktail at the airport after arriving home from their World Cup win in Rome;

a painting inscribed to him by Gene Sarazen; Balding with Snead and Jimmy Demaret in Tokyo.

"It's there," Balding says, "and you worry about what you are doing for yourself and for your family." The Baldings have a son, Al, Jr., and a daughter, Erin. "You do get run down at times."

That is an understatement. Balding took sixteen pills a day for years. He has annual bone marrow tests and has had to revert to medication a few times in order to balance his white and red blood cells.

"The doctors tell me that the cancer is in slumber," Balding explains. "But it's always there. I have it and it's been controlled. I was lucky, maybe because it was caught early."

But there has also been understandable stress – from the diagnosis of cancer, from a series of shoulder operations, from too many missed short putts, from financial reversals, from feeling ignored. Balding has had to face the consequences of a life soaked in tension.

So it was that he found himself under the treatment of a therapist. The fellow asked Balding to lie down and soon he was feeling all kinds of pain in his head. He was asked to imagine that he had a hole in his head. Maybe then the pain would emerge.

"I told him I was seeing black stuff in my head with some red in it. I was in a big city, New York, I think, and going through a black tunnel, the Holland Tunnel. I never saw such garbage, then I realized it was all my garbage, that I had to let it go."

Balding is animated as he speaks, rising to mimic a swing. He speaks of his experience with the therapist as an epiphany, and now, as he prepares for another golf season, he thinks only of relaxation, of playing the game subconsciously, of not getting caught up in swing mechanics. That's what he's working on with Kavanaugh. It's what he would like to work on with golfers young and old. It's the focus of the work he does on himself.

"I can relax at will now most of the time," Balding says. "I relax my eyes and get a warm sensation from the eyelids down. The feeling goes right through my whole body. I still can't do it with my putting as well as I would like, but it's coming. I probably try too hard."

Does knowledge lead to awareness? Does awareness lead to change, and hence to lower scores induced by a relaxed state? These are the questions Balding finds fascinating today. Laughing, he jingles a few coins in a pocket, swings his arms, elbows finishing together, as Les Franks advocated. In early December, he tied for third in Phoenix in a tournament billed as golf's field of dreams, against twenty-seven other seniors. Balding won $8,500, feeling good all the way.

"I don't know," Balding says. "Maybe this good feeling will only last a year. Who knows? Tomorrow you may be gone, so I've learned just to worry about today. Not that it's always easy on the course. Golfers worry about what's behind, what's ahead, not what they're doing now."

Just now Balding is humming a tune. He practises humming through his swing, a gentle, "Hmm, hmm, hmm."

"That's the way to play," says Balding. "Not that hard 'HMM, HMM, HMM' that people use to hit the ball."

Humming for better golf seems appropriate for a man who, at sixty-eight, is still in search of what makes him tick, on and off the course. Bobby Jones used the technique. Nick Faldo has music in his mind as he swings.

But Balding also wishes that golfers would accompany him in his quest. Kavanaugh and Williams believe he could do much for Canadian golf. Inside Al Balding lies a teacher.

"It would be nice to see Canadian golf recognize this man," Williams says. Golfers who follow the game know Balding, though. They know he's a player. There's no higher compliment.

• • •

The Silver Fox was seventy-six when he shot 70–70–70 to win the 2000 Canadian PGA Seniors' Championship. He'd undergone quadruple bypass surgery a couple of years before. The win was Balding's first in the CPGA Senior, and a testament to his ability to swing the club so well even at his advanced age. His feat was noted around the golf world.

Balding died in August 2006. A Who's Who of Canadian golf attended his funeral at the Islington United Church, not far from his beloved Credit Valley club. Windsor, Ontario, pro Bob Panasik remembered when Balding watched him hit balls when he was starting out on the Canadian Tour. Balding helped him and said that nobody could beat him on the tour. "I felt like a winner when I went out," Panasik recalled. "I won a few tournaments and led the money list."

Balding's fellow Hall of Famer Marlene Streit attended the funeral. She wiped away tears as his casket was carried out of the church on a beautiful summer afternoon. She wasn't the only one.

Jack Grout
Golf World | May 6, 2006

Few people referred to Jack Grout as "Jack Nicklaus's teacher," fewer still called him his "coach," and nobody spoke of him as his "guru." Grout wasn't a celebrity. Far from it. "Jack Grout never set one foot on a practice tee at a major championship," Nicklaus says of the man who taught him until Grout's death in 1989. "He might be there, but he'd be back in the bleachers. If I was doing something I didn't like, I'd go back and ask him."

In a season in which Nicklaus's finest hour, his 1986 Masters triumph, is being celebrated, it also is appropriate to recall the modest man who moulded the immensely talented Nicklaus in ways that helped the Hall of Famer separate himself from other golfers of his time.

It is part of Nicklaus lore that his father, Charlie, signed him up for Grout's two-hour Friday junior clinics at Scioto Country Club in Columbus, Ohio, in 1950. Nicklaus was ten years old, and Grout was the head professional. Pandel Savic, a long-time friend of the Nicklauses who was close with Grout, says: "Jack Grout recognized quickly that Jack was ahead of others in terms of intensity and ability. He told me that Jack's power impressed him. He always taught him to hit it hard, even if he hit it all over the world."

As Grout's son Dick, a courtly golf pro who lives in South Carolina, puts it: "Dad was a big aficionado of the idea of hitting it as hard as you can. He said that young muscles need to be stretched and that accuracy can come later. You didn't want Dad to say, 'Let's go get a lemonade or iced tea.' The only reason he'd be saying that is because he didn't think you were hitting it hard enough, and so the lesson was over. He'd say, 'Don't let's try to be pretty. Let's not lollygag out here.'"

Nicklaus was his star pupil from the start. Grout would ask the boy he called "Jackie B." or "Jackie Buck" to demonstrate to the other kids in the clinic, gave him a free private lesson every two or three weeks, and provided him with the fundamentals that helped Nicklaus forge golf's finest record. Moreover, he was a friend and confidant. "I'm much better off for having known Jack Grout," Nicklaus says, and he means on and off the course.

On the course, Grout gave his charge the knowledge to correct his own swing. "I never called him once from a tournament," Nicklaus says. "I didn't need to call him every five minutes. I had to learn how to correct myself, which is the antithesis of the way it is today. For me it was more like the way it was with Bobby Jones. Jones told me that he became a good player when he didn't have to run back to [his teacher] Stewart Maiden."

Grout let Nicklaus be, even when that meant Nicklaus letting out a little shaft with his emotions as well as the club. "One time we were out on the course and I was trying to hit two-irons," Nicklaus says, "and I wasn't doing what I wanted to do. I was so frustrated that I took the shaft and broke it. Jack said, 'Good boy, Jackie. You got to get that out sometimes.' We went over to the shop, replaced the shaft, and went back at it. I only did that the one time, but I could do it with Jack. He'd tell me [it was] fine, that I [had] to get rid of how I was feeling."

Aware that young Nicklaus was a powerhouse in the making, Grout wasn't about to make radical changes in the way the child wanted to go after the ball. He taught him how to use the clubhead while swinging hard and to stay centred over the ball with a steady head, rolling his left ankle toward his right in the backswing and his right toward his left in the downswing. "Most guys today teach by positions. I don't agree with this way of teaching," Nicklaus says. "Jack taught you what to do with the clubhead, not with your body. I think you should be playing with the golf club."

A family of words comes up when people speak of Grout. One is "gentleman," another is "humble," and a third is "quiet." Dick calls his father "a quiet, proud man." Nicklaus's wife, Barbara, says: "He was the kindest and sweetest man there ever was. He never raised his voice or said an unkind word. He didn't know how."

One of eight children, Grout was born in Oklahoma City in 1910. When he noticed some of his older brothers had extra money during golf season, he wondered about the source. Grout followed them to Oklahoma City Country Club, where he learned they were caddies. He started to caddy as well, and by fifteen he was a pro at Edgemere Country Club under his older brother, Dick, the head pro. When Jack was twenty, he followed Dick to Glen Garden Golf Club in Fort Worth, where he became an assistant to his brother, and was soon playing with junior members Ben Hogan and Byron Nelson, respectively seventeen and eighteen at the time. The threesome practised most mornings and played a few times a week in the afternoons. The Grout brothers noticed that Hogan's equipment included only seven clubs, three left-handed and four right-handed. Hogan hit hooks from either side. Grout's brother gave Hogan three hickory-shafted right-hand clubs, and they soon convinced him to play exclusively from the right side.

Grout and his wife, Bonnie, were married in 1942 and had two sons, Dick and John, and two daughters, Ronnie and Debbie. Grout delivered Debbie in a taxicab in front of the hospital. Bonnie Grout lives in Stuart, Florida, with Debbie. She suffers from Parkinson's and osteoporosis, and, Debbie says, "is in constant pain, just getting by." Of her father, she says, "He was my best friend. I just felt comfortable when he was around."

From Glen Garden, Grout moved to Hershey (Pennsylvania) Country Club, where he worked as an assistant under legendary teacher and player Henry Picard. There Grout learned the value of footwork, which Picard had assimilated from the instruction that renowned teacher Alex Morrison had given him. Grout later wrote that Nicklaus had better footwork than anybody, including Bobby Jones, Walter Hagen, Nelson, and Hogan.

Grout came to Scioto in 1950 and worked there until 1961, when he went to La Gorce Country Club in Miami Beach. He retired in 1975 after Nicklaus made him professional emeritus at the newly formed Muirfield Village Golf Club in Dublin, Ohio, north of Columbus. He had a similar role at the Loxahatchee Club when the Nicklaus-designed course opened in 1985, and also taught at Frenchman's Creek and, during the winters of 1977 and 1978, at a Nicklaus-designed nine-holer at the Cheeca Lodge in the Florida Keys, where Ted Williams liked to fish for tarpon and bonefish in the flats.

While working as a club professional, Grout played in five U.S. Opens and three PGA Championships. He frequently roomed and travelled on the tour with Picard. According to Dick Grout, his father had thirty-five top-ten finishes. In the PGA Championship, then a match-play event, he knocked off Jimmy Demaret in the first round in 1941 at Cherry Hills Country Club in Denver, defending champion Bob Hamilton in 1945 at Moraine Country Club in Dayton, Ohio, and medallist Johnny Palmer in 1953 at Birmingham (Michigan) Country Club.

Grout succeeded as a player despite severe nearsightedness – he was one of the rare pros who wore glasses – and a mild manner. Hogan told writer Ken Bowden, who has collaborated with Nicklaus on eleven books, that Grout could have won plenty of tournaments with his graceful swing and ball-striking. "Ben said he could have been a great player if he had a different personality," Bowden says. "I think he was implying that he didn't have the killer instinct."

Bowden first met Grout during the 1965 PGA Championship at Laurel Valley Golf Club in Ligonier, Pennsylvania, when British writer Pat Ward Thomas introduced them. Along with some sixty pros, they were watching Hogan stamp out four-wood shots on the range when Grout asked Bowden if he would like to meet Hogan. Bowden certainly would.

"I'll never forget how warm Ben was to Jack," Bowden says. "He softened right up when he saw it was Grout. He wouldn't talk to anybody else on the range, but it was like they were relatives. It was a very different Hogan."

As gentle as Grout was, he was firm in his views. But he provided advice only when he had something to contribute. One year, Hall of Famer Ray Floyd was having a terrible time when he sought out Grout at La Gorce. "I was laid off and short, and it's hard to play golf that way," Floyd says. "He gave me a move with my right elbow that solved the problem. He told me to get my right elbow up going back, which got the elbow and my right thumb under the shaft. Jack was an incredible guy. He dealt with what you had, and he kept it simple. He was very much a positive influence. Jack would tell you how good you were."

After Charlie Nicklaus died at age fifty-six in 1970, Grout became even more of a father figure to the Golden Bear. "We would go out on the driving range," Nicklaus says of the time he spent with Grout at Loxahatchee, "go down there and hit balls at the other end, and talk about everything but golf and my golf swing. We did that day after day, and finally, maybe after four or five days, we would be hitting balls and he would finally say, 'Hey, you know, I would like to see your hands in a little different position at the top.' 'Oh, really? What do you think that would do?' He said, 'It will make you hit it better.' 'Okay, we'll do that.' But that would be the only comment he would make for a week. We weren't talking about golf. We were talking about being friends and the relationship between two people."

Away from golf, Grout loved horse racing and often slipped out with Floyd to one of the Florida tracks. He made small wagers on college football, and at Loxahatchee, club co-founder Gordon Gray and his pals taught Grout a card game called "Oh, Hell," an offshoot of Hearts for which they made their own rules. One of Loxahatchee's formal dining rooms is named after Grout, which is both an honour and an irony given that he wasn't much for formality.

Grout was comfortable in his own skin. He didn't need to go to parties although he knew how to have a good time. He didn't need to promote himself as the man who taught Jack Nicklaus. "Never in a hundred or a thousand years would he do that," Nicklaus says. And he was even reluctant to write a foreword to Nicklaus's book *Golf My Way*, for fear of drawing attention to himself and away from the golfer he loved. But, as Bowden points out, Grout did finally agree to write the foreword, "and he was glad he did."

Nicklaus was about to tee off in the third round of the 1989 Memorial Tournament when a siren went off to stop play because of storms. Barbara presently received a call that Grout had died. "It was very weird," Barbara says. "I think he died within a minute or two of when Jack was supposed to tee off." Nicklaus had last seen his teacher, mentor, and friend a month earlier, just after the Masters, where Nicklaus had missed the last green. Grout was in bed at his home and asked Nicklaus to make a swing. He watched and, Nicklaus says, "He told me why I hit the ball to the right. He was still teaching, and he couldn't even get out of bed."

Item 6 of Grout's Last Will and Testament included observations he had made about his relationship with Nicklaus. Grout felt he had been given far too much credit; at the same time, he acknowledged that he had helped him with the fundamentals. Grout had written, "There is not the slightest doubt in my mind that Jack Nicklaus is the finest golfer ever to swing a club in the entire history of the game. It has been a distinct honor and great privilege for me to have played some part in his career. And that brings me to my final bequest. To you, Jack Nicklaus, I give my thanks."

Humble to the end.

Peter Gzowski

The Globe and Mail | January 26, 2002

JUPITER, FLORIDA

When I heard the news yesterday about Peter Gzowski's death, the memories of various experiences with him came flooding back. Writing from 2,500 kilometres away, I see him in many places and many ways.

There was the letter, a few lines scrawled on CBC notepaper. This was about fifteen years ago, after I'd written a *Globe and Mail* column on golf in November. I played the Glen Abbey Golf Club on my own while carrying my clubs. This is golf at its best – walking and playing a fine course quickly, in bracing air, and I'd written my column about the round.

A couple of days later a letter arrived from Gzowski. An avid listener of *Morningside* on CBC Radio, I'd been taken with Gzowski's love of reading and feeling for sport. He wasn't afraid to think of sports writing as real writing. To him, good sports writing belonged as much on the books and cultural pages as the sports pages.

"I've been thinking about writing a book on golf," Gzowski wrote. "But I read your column this morning. You write the book."

When he started his tournaments to raise money for literacy in Canada in 1986, he invited me to play. Maestro ball-striker George Knudson also played. Knudson, like Gzowski, succumbed to the ravages of lifelong smoking in 1989.

Gzowski appreciated the way Knudson hit the ball – pure, without a hitch, flowing through to his target in balance. He liked Knudson's simple feelings for golf as play and recreation. (Oddly enough, both Gzowski and Knudson died on January 24, and that morning two days ago, Knudson's wife Shirley welcomed the birth of her second granddaughter, Georgia.)

Knudson, to Gzowski, embodied the principles of golf. He tried to help Gzowski swing better. Gzowski knew the game, having played it as a kid with family at the Briars Golf and Country Club in Jackson's Point, Ontario, on Lake Simcoe, where he and his companion, the gracious Gill Howard, now had a cottage.

Gzowski had returned to golf at what was truly his home course, to raise money for literacy – his well-known Peter Gzowski Invitationals started at the Briars. He said at the first PGI that he had committed to raising a million dollars for literacy through golf.

"I wrote the promise down on a Scotch-stained napkin," Gzowski would always say. John O'Leary, the president of Frontier College and the man who first asked Gzowski to help out with literacy issues in Canada, is glad he did, as are communities across Canada.

The PGIs soon played across the country and have raised $7 million; they constitute a true Canadian tour. Gzowski travelled to the tournaments and ensured there were Canadian connections at each one – actors, comedians, writers, musicians.

The tournaments were boisterous fun. I played with Jack McClelland, the long-time president of McClelland & Stewart, who played with vintage clubs circa 1940 and rattled the ball around the Briars with gusto. There were memorable rounds with the first-class sportswriters – and Canadian treasures – Scott Young and Trent Frayne. Friendships that endure were formed.

The PGIs were creative acts, and Gzowski always credited members of his team, especially his assistant, Shelley Ambrose. Consider one event in Yellowknife on a frozen lake in April in the early 1990s. It represented an impressive feat of organization. Ken Dryden was there, as was the gifted actress Cynthia Dale. We walked out onto the frozen lake to watch the Northern Lights the night before the tournament, teed it up with orange golf balls on the ice the next day where holes three feet square had been cut, warmed ourselves with tea and stronger liquids on each tee, ate toasty bannock, the local bread, and had a blast. Gzowski and others read to kids at a local school one afternoon.

By then, Gzowski had established the Knudson Award at the PGIs. A silver tee was given in Knudson's name to the person who Gzowski deemed had the most fun during his or her round. To heck with the score. The Knudson was the most important award at each PGI. Still is.

Meanwhile, I had taken up Gzowski's suggestion in his letter two decades earlier that I write books. He provided a foreword to my collection *Touring Prose*, and, recalling one of our rounds at the Briars, wrote, "We had our usual pleasant time." We sure did.

On *Morningside*, a salon for writers, Gzowski had me on a couple of times to talk golf writing. He generously made me the first writer-in-residence for the Briars PGI. Later, he made Canadian golf writer John Gordon the writer-in-residence. Gzowski championed our work.

As writer-in-residence, my only responsibility was to write an essay about golf and writing and the ways in which they link with each other, which I did, and called it "In Peaceful Communion." It sounds corny just as a title, but together on an evening playing golf at the Briars, Gzowski and I knew that the game did offer a peaceful communion – with friends, with nature, with our quiet selves, at play.

Now Gzowski is gone, at sixty-seven. He would probably have cracked that it's a good number, at least in golf. Knudson is gone. But their influence remains, firm, encouraging. Gzowski connected with Canadians, and he helped us connect, on and off the course.

• • •

The Peter Gzowski Invitationals have raised more than $10 million for literacy programs across Canada.

Ben Hogan

The Globe and Mail | July 26, 1997

When it comes to big names in golf, none was bigger than Ben Hogan, who died yesterday at his home in Fort Worth, Texas. Hogan, eighty-four, underwent surgery two years ago for colon cancer, and he had Alzheimer's disease. He had been ill for some time, though his secretary, Pat Martin, said she did not know the exact cause of death.

Hogan pursued an ideal – the absolute understanding of the golf swing. He devoted his life to the task, and in the end he won sixty-three professional tournaments. The list included four U.S. Opens, two Masters, two PGA Championships, and one British Open.

Hogan's lone British Open win was in 1953, when he also won the U.S. Open and the Masters. He didn't enter the PGA Championship because of scheduling problems. But his three wins in majors in one year qualify that season as one of the best ever.

How good was Hogan? Gene Sarazen, a man of many majors himself, said, "Nobody covered the flag like he did." That says plenty.

Yet golf didn't come easily to Hogan, who was born August 13, 1912, in Dublin, Texas, a small town about 125 kilometres southwest of Fort Worth. His father, Chester, was a blacksmith; his mother, Clara, had grown up in a family that bought cotton.

Chester Hogan was by all accounts a quiet man, prone to depression. He killed himself in front of his son when Ben was nine years old. By then the family had moved to Fort Worth, where Hogan would live for the rest of his life.

Hogan began to caddy at the Glen Garden club, eleven kilometres from his home, and he walked there. He won his way into the caddying ranks by beating an older, bigger caddy in a fistfight. Such was the way of the caddy yard then.

Hogan took to golf, and as all the sports world knows, he eventually reached the game's highest levels. Curt Sampson has told his life story in a recent biography called, simply, *Hogan*. Hogan learned the game by means of practice akin to devotion.

That practice, and the rigours of tournament golf, precluded his and his wife Valerie's having children. It is a matter of record – apocryphal record, perhaps – that their home had but one bedroom. It has been said this was the case so as to discourage guests, though writer Dan Jenkins and golfer Mark O'Meara have said Hogan was simply a shy man, a modest man who did give time to friends.

Hogan's main efforts were reserved for the practice range. He said all he wanted to say about the swing in his classic 1957 book, *Five Lessons: The Modern Fundamentals of Golf*. Some people believe Hogan had more to say, but chose not to. That may not have been the case.

"I would write it the same way I did in 1957," he told *Golf Digest's* Nick Seitz nearly thirty years later, when the magazine was preparing a new edition of *Five Lessons*. "Everything I know about the full swing is in here. I don't think the fundamentals will ever change."

Hogan came to understand the fundamentals after a car accident in February of 1949 in which he was nearly killed. He and his wife were driving in Texas during a ground mist when a bus rose from the fog as it tried to pass a car and slammed their vehicle head-on. Hogan, who was driving, threw himself in front of his wife to save her.

Doctors thought his extensive injuries would keep him from tournament golf, but he came back and won the 1950 and 1951 U.S. Opens. Then he won his three majors in 1953. It was apparent that Hogan knew something about the game not given to many, or any, others.

The late Canadian great George Knudson was a Hogan aficionado, and went in the late 1950s in search of him on the tournament trail. Hogan birdied the first four holes Knudson saw him play, at Cypress Point on the Monterey Peninsula in California.

"Ben Hogan was involved in that horrible automobile accident which almost took his life in 1949," Knudson told CBC's Bob Moir. "I don't believe he really thought about how he had to go about becoming the world's greatest golfer. I think it was after the accident, when his life was spared, that he came to the proper realization [of what the game was all about]."

Hogan won six of the nine majors he played after the accident. That is an astonishing statistic. Equally astonishing is the volume of stories that have built up around him. Nobody who has met him or seen him hit a golf ball forgets Hogan.

I saw him hit but one shot, late in a round during a tournament at Oakland Hills near Detroit. Hogan watched Arnold Palmer and another golfer, whose name I forget, hit very good shots to the green. He then stared down the flag, took a drag on his cigarette before flipping it to the ground, pulled an iron from the bag, and ripped a shot all over the flag. The ball settled a couple of feet from the hole. So be it.

"Hogan's ball has its own channel in the sky," somebody once remarked.

"When Hogan was around I just stood and watched," Knudson said. "I used to tell my caddy, 'Watch, this guy is really going to hit a shot here.'"

Hogan's friend Dave Marr, the 1965 PGA Championship winner who is now battling cancer himself, once told me that the golfing legend "was nonpareil. I never saw anybody do what he did, the sound he made when he hit the ball. We played a lot together at Seminole. I might shoot a good score, but it wasn't anything like the picture he painted. Mine sounded like the 'Anvil Chorus' and his was 'Moon River.' I mean that seriously. The ball would come off the club face and you would think, 'How do you do that?'"

Hogan hit many tremendous golf shots, shots unique to him. It wouldn't be far-fetched to assemble a catalogue of his shots; they would define what is possible in the game.

Now the man in the grey cashmere sweater who didn't see anything startling about shooting one 68 after another is gone. The consummate golfer known as "The Hawk," or to the Scots when he won that 1953 British Open at Carnoustie as "the Wee Ice Mon," is no longer with us.

Or is he? Hogan leaves a legacy born of the way he approached the game, his disdain for commercialism in the sport, his belief that the swing could be understood, and the exemplary shots he played. It's a legacy, surely, that will endure, one that he recognized but did not seek to create.

But because Hogan was who he was, he could not help but create it. It is a legacy of which he would quite rightly be proud, and one for which all golfers can be grateful. To study Hogan is to penetrate to the core of the game, and to come away fascinated.

George Knudson

Senior Golfer | January 1999

They were taking the roses in for the winter at the Mount Pleasant Cemetery in Toronto when I visited George Knudson's last resting place recently with his wife, Shirley. It was hard to believe that it had been ten years since the golfer whom Jack Nicklaus described as having "a million-dollar swing" passed away, in January 1989. Knudson was a maestro when it came to hitting the golf ball with precision. Players who watched him used to say he was closer to Ben Hogan than Hogan himself. Ten years? He'd been on my mind often.

Shirley and I stood by the headstone for a quiet moment. Knudson was buried under the spreading limbs of a white oak tree, and many of us who were fortunate to call Knudson a close friend used to joke – and still do – that this was the first time he found himself under a tree. It was unthinkable that this perfectionist of the golf swing should hit a shot into that sort of trouble.

Ten years had gone by? George was only fifty-one when he died from lung cancer, and had he lived, he would now be enjoying the

Senior PGA Tour. He had all but left competitive golf when he was in his mid-thirties because he didn't enjoy the travel; George missed Shirley and their three sons, Kevin, Paul, and Dean. Now the boys were men – Kevin a commercial pilot, Paul a club professional, Dean an economist. He and Shirley would have been out there with Bob Charles, Miller Barber, Lee Trevino – they would have been enjoying the game at which he toiled while trying to find a better way to strike the golf ball.

Knudson had found that way while winning eight PGA Tour events. He tied for second in the 1969 Masters, a shot behind George Archer, when he didn't make a putt over ten feet until the seventieth hole. He liked to tell a story of how he was feeling when he reached the twelfth tee on the last round. As it happened, Knudson had encountered Arnold Palmer in the locker room after the round, and told him the story first. It became a central story in the Knudsonian archives that many golfers – and not only Canadians – carry around in their memories.

"I walked onto the twelfth tee and I was so excited that I couldn't settle my feet down," Knudson, a member of the Canadian Golf Hall of Fame, would say. "But I had to hit the shot. How was I going to hit that shot over Rae's Creek if I couldn't settle down? So I just tried to hit it between the bounces of my feet."

Knudson related his experience to Palmer, who shot back: "What else is new? I feel that way every time I'm in the hunt at Augusta." Knudson laughed. If you were going to contend in a major, well, you had better get used to the bounces – mental and otherwise.

The guy was really something – simple as that. George had one of those temperaments that seemed placid on the outside, but inside, hidden behind dark glasses he wore to protect his eyes from the sun, he felt plenty. He smoked two or three packs a day to ward off anxiety, and he was on friendly terms with more than a few hotel bars in tour stops across America.

When he was diagnosed with lung cancer in 1987 Knudson said, not holding back – he never did hold back – "Who was I to think I wouldn't get lung cancer from smoking? It's a filthy, stinking habit." He quit then and there, but the damage had been done.

I had gone off to the U.S. Open at the Olympic Club in San Francisco that June. We had started work on a book a week earlier, sitting by the pool at the Knudsons' home in north Toronto, where their backyard sloped down to a wooded ravine. He wanted to tell the story of how he came to leave cold Winnipeg, Manitoba, where he had been born, and how he had struck out to study Hogan; how he had come to believe that the golf swing was subject to the laws of nature – centrifugal force, inertia. Hence the name of his book: *The Natural Golf Swing*.

When I returned home from Olympic there was a message from a friend on my answering machine. "Have you heard about George?" the fellow asked. I didn't know what he meant, but found out right away. George had been diagnosed with lung cancer. I called him, and the first thing he said was, "I'm going to have my bad days and my good days. But we'll work on the good days when I'm not tired from the chemo. We'll get the book done."

We did get the book done. Many a night George would call me because he had found a better way to say something. He became an enthusiast of the English language, examining the nuances of words the way he liked to examine the nuances of the golf swing. Does a golfer "transfer" his weight from the forward foot to the back foot, or does he "shift" his weight? Of such details was his book born. I loved every minute of working on the book with him. It was a privi-lege to do so.

The book came out in 1988, and George was proud of it. He was helping people through words, and even while he was undergoing treatment he never refused a phone call from somebody who wanted to talk about his book, his ideas. He answered letters, elaborated on the pleasures of the game. Cypress Point on the Monterey Peninsula was his favourite course in all the world; he liked nothing better than playing a practice round early in the morning for what was then the Bing Crosby Pro-Am, setting out in the fog and watching it lift over the sea and then feeling the sun on his back as he played along. Knudson had studied art as a young man; he had become an artist of the game, of the swing, of the better ways of playing it.

"Never do anything at the expense of balance." That was one of his favourite sayings. "You have to give up control to gain control." That was another. George meant that that the golfer who tries to control the club becomes tense, and doesn't let the club travel on an uninterrupted path. Control is compromised in this way. The idea is to let things happen by setting the club in motion during the backswing motion, the "loading" motion, as he called it. "The purpose of the loading motion is to gather energy," he wrote. "We do so by transferring weight to the right foot while rotating the body around the trunk."

"You have to give up control to gain control." I keep thinking of that. It's a Zen koan, in a way. Let go to go. Lose to gain. The message was implicit in something else George liked to say: "You don't play golf to relax, you relax to play golf."

George was a teacher. I'm sure that the wonderful, late golf writer Charles Price would have agreed that he was one of those individuals he called "golf people." He spoke softly but carried weight, transferred golfing wisdom, even life wisdom, to people he encountered. I didn't know him very well when I wrote my first article in a major magazine. That was in 1979, when I wrote an essay on golf for the magazine *Toronto Life*. George left a message for me after he read the piece.

"Okay, Rube, you've got your foot in the door now," George said. "Just keep writing and good things will happen."

I've met some wonderful people in golf – teachers, wise men and women who have learned from their experiences in the game. Knudson was one of those wonderful golf people – the best friend a young man trying to make his own way in the game could have.

I was at home on January 24, 1989, when word came through that George had died. He had often projected mental images of Cypress Point onto the wall of his hospital room so that he could relax. Only a couple of months before, George had finished a short videotape that he was sending to the PGA's teaching conference in Dallas. He couldn't be there; his ideas, his words, could. In the spring of 1988, he had played the Legends of Golf tournament in Austin, Texas, although he had been unable to practise and felt quite weak. But he wanted to see Sam Snead and Tommy Bolt and Johnny Pott, his partner. Hogan showed up at the tournament and told George his swing looked as good as ever.

George birdied the first hole he played, but he wouldn't play any more competitive golf after the Legends. A legend in golf would soon pass from the scene.

The Knudson family asked if I would deliver the eulogy at George's funeral, which I of course considered an honour. I'd called Dale Douglass, one of George's contemporaries and by then already a five-time winner on the Senior PGA Tour. He said, "Everybody still comments on what a fine player George was and how many shots he could hit that the rest of us couldn't." Art Wall said, simply, "He had class. The players respected George. They knew how great he was. That's not a word we use too much, but it applies in his case."

Now it's ten years later. I've been rereading letters that continue to come in about George. Here's a beautifully expressed sentiment. "Let's hear it once more for George and the principle of balance," one John Federitz writes.

I also think of an e-mail I received recently from Jim Kaat, who won sixteen Golden Gloves while pitching professional baseball.

Kaat's an avid golfer, and I played with him this winter at the Medalist Golf Club in Hobe Sound, Florida. "Stand tall and finish in balance," Kaat advised me. He'd read the Knudson book long ago and believed what the maestro said. So yes, let's hear it once more for George and the principle of balance.

"We can get so much out of golf," George wrote. "I know I have, and I'd like to see the same for you. Golf is the game of a lifetime, one in which you can get better and better."

I'm learning to give up control to gain control. It's a powerfully liberating idea. George Knudson was a powerfully liberating human being – a gift to the game, and to more people than he ever knew, or can ever know. I'd wager, in fact, that his name comes up on the Senior PGA Tour week after week: George was that good. A good person, a good player. Amend that: a great person, a great player, and a great teacher.

Moe Norman

The Globe and Mail | August 28, 1993

In the middle of a summer's day, golfing wizard Moe Norman is giving a clinic to fifty people at the National Golf Club in Woodbridge, Ontario. His left hand is heavily callused from fifty years of providing the main connection to his clubs while he hit more than 3 million balls. His patter is folksy but insightful – "long and low, stretch it; shake hands with the flagstick; swing easy, hit hard" – these are some of Moe's pearls of wisdom. (Everybody calls him Moe.) His listeners are getting a fast read on a man whom the late George Knudson described as "the most sensitive player in the game," whom Tom Watson said may be the most commanding ball-striker in the game, ever.

Now the ball soars on its private Moe Norman trajectory. "Fill the hole in the sky, fill up that hole in the sky," Moe likes to say. It drops out of the sky like a steamed tomato. Moe has spent his life thinking about golf; he's a loner in a loner's game. Maybe he was meant for the game.

John Czarny is one of the handful of people in whose company Moe, a notoriously withdrawn person, can relax. Czarny was seventeen when he played a round with Moe, then fifteen, at a nine-hole course in Walkerton, Ontario. Moe had been golfing for about a year.

"I put eight Coke bottles down on a tee, and a ball on each," Czarny recalls with pleasure. "There was a tree in mid-fairway. Moe asked what kind of shots I wanted, draws, fades, big slices. He hit every shot exactly as I called it. Those Coke bottles went down like bowling pins."

Moe had clipped the ball precisely from each bottle, and moved it every which way but straight. However, Moe's usual shot is dead straight, the hardest shot, according to Watson. At sixty-four, Moe still dazzles anybody who watches him stand far from the ball, arms fully extended, humming before he swings. He's an impish genius of golf, flicking his way across the channels of the game.

Moe won the 1955 and 1956 Canadian Amateurs, has won some fifty tournaments of more than two days, including seven Canadian Seniors pro championships, and shot 59 three times. "Nice to break 60," he says. But Moe never made it in the big time, and never really tried to. He has shown his game around Canada and in Florida, where he spends the winters. Yet one cannot travel anywhere in the golf world without hearing tales about Moe Norman. He has attained legendary status.

Rock singer Neil Young was once playing golf on an exotic island with a French professional who didn't speak English. Young accidentally hit a ball straight up in the air. "Only Moe Norman could do that," Young exclaimed. The Frenchman who couldn't speak English dropped his club in amazement. "You know Moe Norman?" he blurted in a feat of spontaneous English.

Lloyd Tucker, a golf teacher, knows Moe. He first encountered him when Moe was fourteen, a .610 hitter in softball who could knock down singles anywhere he wanted. He liked to jump from hills thirty feet down to riverbanks, and was blessed with a raw physicality. In school he cared little for any subject but math, and could rattle off the answers to multiplication questions without thinking. Today it seems he can recall shots he hit at every course he played.

Moe was in Grade 9 when he discovered golf while caddying at the Rockway club in Kitchener. There he met Tucker, who also taught Gary Cowan. Tucker wouldn't allow Cowan, Moe, or his other pupils to work together. He recognized that golf is an individual game and that idiosyncrasies should be encouraged.

Tucker let him be for the most part, although Moe says he helped him cure a tendency to hook the ball. Moe, Tucker says, was one of the first people to strengthen his hands, by squeezing a couple of tennis balls that he kept beside his bed. Hence his ability to hit millions of balls. "Scratch it [his left hand] all you want," Moe says. "It doesn't hurt. It's like sandpaper."

Forty years after Tucker encountered Moe, he addressed a gathering at the Westmount club in Kitchener. Moe had caddied there as a kid. His friends wanted to acknowledge his accomplishments and to help him out financially. This was in the mid-1980s, when Moe was short of cash.

"If you've seen [Fred] Astaire, you've seen the best dancer," Tucker said, his voice breaking. "If you've seen Peggy Fleming, you've seen the best skater. And when you see Moe hit a golf ball, you know you've seen the best that ever hit a golf ball."

Tucker isn't the only person who feels this way. Lee Trevino told the CBC television show *Fifth Estate* in 1988 that "when you talk about Moe Norman you're talking about a legend, and I'm talking about a living legend, because the public doesn't know Moe Norman . . . ask any golf professional, whether you're in Australia, or whether you're in the U.S., or whether you're in Great Britain, and you say, 'That's the Canadian guy that hits it so damn good, isn't it,' and I say, 'That's him.' He's a legend with the professionals."

PGA Championship winner Paul Azinger agrees. "When I first really learned how to play, in '78–'79," Azinger recalls, "my teacher John Redman had a practice range in Titusville [in Florida]. He told me this guy had shown up who was the greatest ball-striker who ever lived. I walked over and there was this guy in a long-sleeved turtleneck. It was 100 degrees. He watched us hit balls for an hour and a half and didn't say a thing. John asked him to hit balls for us. He hit three buckets out to a patch of the range where the grass was pretty long. Moe would call how many times the ball would bounce."

Then there's Nick Price, the 1991 Canadian Open champion who has won four times on the PGA Tour this year. Says Price: "I've seen him hit balls at Glen Abbey and in Florida. It's amazing. He's incredibly talented."

These assessments suggest the question: why did Moe not succeed at the highest levels of the game? Knudson's comment about Moe's sensitivity offers an important clue. As Moe himself says of the brief appearance he made during the late 1950s on the U.S. circuit, "I felt everybody was smarter than me. I only went to Grade 9. I just couldn't mix with people. They'd come up with these big words that I couldn't understand. I didn't feel at home. I always felt they were gods [in the United States], and that I was their servant."

Moe withdrew from the U.S. tour after being embarrassed there. He visited his Kitchener friend Gus Maue at a rented home beside the Riviera Golf Club in Daytona Beach after playing a tournament.

Maue says that Moe told him he would never play the U.S. tour again.

"Two days later Bert Weaver [a touring pro] came to Riviera," Maue elaborates. "I asked him what happened. He said that Moe put the ball on a big tee, and hit it so good. Moe was playing to the gallery, carrying his own bag. A player in his group called him aside and told Moe to fix his teeth, to get new clothes. He was insulted and said he would never play the U.S. tour again."

That was thirty-five years ago, and Moe never did play the U.S. tour again. But the stories continue to play, years later. Moe still makes narrow holes wide. One is still tempted to theorize about why Moe plays so quickly – he calls himself "the 747 of golf, miss 'em quick, that's always been my theme song."

Why does Moe stand so far from the ball, placing his clubhead a foot behind it? Why does he often repeat himself – "People laughed at me because I made it look so easy, they laughed at me. Sure they did, sure they did." Who is Moe? Why is Moe?

Moe's childhood pal Ernie Hauser has one theory about Moe's rapid speech. "When he was younger you could hardly understand him, he spoke so quickly," Hauser explains. "You'd always have to say pardon me, and he'd repeat himself. I think that's where the repetition comes from."

There are other theories about this golfer whom many people consider the game's number-one enigma. He was still a child when he was hit by a car while sleigh-riding in front of his home and sustained a head injury. Moe walked away from the accident, apparently unhurt. But his mother later regretted that her son wasn't examined for possible head injuries. It's impossible to know whether the accident accounts for Moe's unusual double-time speech and motion.

But here is one theory, a personal one after following Moe for years. He was the one person I wanted to watch when I was a youngster. Night after night Moe enthralled onlookers at the De Haviland

Golf Centre in Toronto while he spot-painted the night sky with golf balls. His speech was rapid-fire, his swings came rat-a-tat-tat one after the other. How could he be understood?

One way is to understand him on his own terms. Understand Moe as a person whose powerful insecurities may be the source of his singular talent. He might not move as quickly or swing as rapidly were he not so shy that he needs to remove himself from the public eye as quickly as possible. His quirky set-up and swing may account in no small measure for his precision.

Moe has turned golf into a reaction sport, thereby neutralizing the elements in the game that make it psychologically complex. Golf is played slowly with a stationary ball; the player initiates the motion rather than responding to, say, a thrown ball.

But Moe simply looks at his target and swings. His glance ignites his swing. Moe's vulnerability may have interlocked so effectively with the demands of the game that he can play exquisitely. But that same vulnerability may have prevented him from reaching his potential as a competitor. He would have had to deal with too many people, from journalists to fans, had he succeeded. "Let your body memorize your swing," Moe advises at his clinics. He is giving seventy clinics this year across Canada at $800 each. Some clubs pay his expenses, some don't. He drives from club to club, and covers vast distances in doing so.

Moe is delivering to the crowd. He might say, "Golf: it's hitting an object to a defined area with the least amount of effort and an alert attitude of indifference." Or, "Imagination plus vividness equals reality in your mind." Or, "Two things you got to finish in this game, your backswing and your follow-through." Ask Moe a question, and his deep, blue eyes almost go wild. He's intense, a spinning top of direct response, words like trains pouring forth.

The guests at the clinic are listening to Moe, who is finally getting real respect in the golf world after decades of being laughed at.

A prominent western Canadian paper, when checked recently, still referred to him in its files as "Moe Norman, clown prince of golf," while the reference to Knudson was, simply, "golfer."

This contrast reflects another theme of Moe's story: professional golf really does remain the purview of the upper-middle-class. The rough-hewn Moe – his lack of concern for social niceties, his snaggled teeth – mark him as a person not to the clubhouse born. And yet the enormous talent. His story also involves a measure of tragedy based in the divisiveness of social class.

But Moe began to attract serious media attention a decade ago. The focus on his golf as opposed to his mannerisms has intensified. A consensus is growing that Moe is a Canadian legend who has too long been what pro golfer Jim Nelford called "the country's plaything."

The respected British writer Peter Dobereiner wrote in 1984 in *The Observer*, a British newspaper, that Moe was the greatest of the golfers who chose not to become champions. Articles have since appeared on Moe in major Canadian and U.S. golf magazines, and in mainstream non-golf publications. Chapters about Moe have appeared in books. CBC Radio is preparing a segment of its show *Inside Track* on Moe. A new video is on the market, Moe's first. The rehabilitation and reclamation of Moe is in full flight.

Perhaps the most significant piece of late was an editorial Bob Weeks wrote last fall in *Score* magazine. Weeks argued sharply that Moe belongs in the Canadian Golf Hall of Fame, which the Royal Canadian Golf Association runs. The RCGA answered that it had never received a nomination for Moe. It has since, and will deal with the nomination prior to its annual meeting in February, where an induction would occur. Many people feel it should have happened long ago.

"We were playing in a little deal in the fall of 1984," Knudson, who felt for Moe, once recalled. "The news had just been released that I'd been inducted into the Hall of Fame. People were congratulating me. Moe said about himself, 'I'll never make it.' I said, 'You mean you're not there?' Why wouldn't he be in, of all people? He's in my Hall of Fame."

"You tell me about the Hall of Fame," Moe says when the possibility of his being inducted is raised. "I haven't heard a word, just people talking, not a word, not a bloody word from the RCGA, just talk. They haven't done it yet, why would they do it now? It would make them look dumb if they did. You don't put somebody in when they're sixty-four. Why would they wait until now?"

Moe lives in a motel room in Kitchener, for which he pays $400 a month. His long-time friend Nick Weslock speaks of Moe's generosity with his time and his money, though by no means has he ever been wealthy. Moe could well turn up this weekend at the Canadian PGA Championship at Credit Valley in Toronto or the du Maurier Ltd. Classic at London Hunt. He could hit golf balls for the players, as he often does at the Canadian Open. One year he held Ben Crenshaw and Larry Mize spellbound as he flung shots far down the range at Glen Abbey on a string.

Is Moe content?

"Why sure, sure I am. I very much enjoy the clinics now. I feel comfortable with the people, so much more than twenty years ago."

But Moe's increased sense of comfort with others has not eradicated his feeling of being estranged from the world outside the boundaries of a golf course. That would be difficult for one whose alignment to his golf target is so precise but whose alignment to the world is somewhat askew, as others perceive it.

"I still feel misunderstood," Moe said. "I think I always will, because my story is so different. But I don't let things bother me so much now. I know that I have something that people want, to hit the ball in a repetitious way. What a good feeling, even in countries I've never been they've heard of this guy Moe Norman."

That's the feeling Moe takes to his motel room every night after making his rounds of courses in and around southern Ontario. His home is only that one room, but it's enough. Golf courses and his car are his real homes. He carries a veritable library of books on the mind in the trunk of his car, so that he can study popular psychology.

"It's nice," Moe says of his motel room home. "I park right against the door. That's what I like. It's beautiful. There's a pop machine right outside, you put a loonie in. No elevator, a nice colour TV. I need very little as long as I'm doing what I want to do. I'm the happiest guy on two feet."

• • •

Moe was finally inducted into the Canadian Golf Hall of Fame on August 24, 1995, during a ceremony at the Foxwood Golf Club near Kitchener, Ontario. A small group of family and friends gathered at this public course in the countryside where he felt comfortable. He wasn't far from the Rockway course where he grew up and learned the game, and which later filled a room with some of his memorabilia and designated it the Moe Norman Room.

"This club is working people like myself," Moe said at Foxwood. "It's like Rockway. I know I'm not an outsider, that people here grew up like I did. Being here brings good memories."

By then Moe was receiving $5,000 a month from Titleist, whose golf balls he had played for years without compensation. The company had decided to recognize Moe, for life, in this simple way, another gesture that made him feel good. Tim O'Connor had written a biography of Moe, called The Feeling of Greatness. He was on the cover of Golf Digest in its December 1995 issue, under the words, "Moe knows what nobody else knows." As 1995 ended, Moe mentioned how many balls he had hit during his lifetime. "I keep track. Four hundred one day, six hundred the next. I mark it down every day. Now I'm up to 5,131,000."

It wasn't accurate any more to refer to Moe as "little-known." CBC did a film about him for its Life and Times *series. It wasn't long before Tiger Woods said that only two people in the history of golf had "owned" their swings: Ben Hogan and Moe. Woods wanted that feeling.*

But Moe was ill. He'd had a heart attack on September 27, 1997, passing out while driving. He had double-bypass surgery, and later was diagnosed with congestive heart failure. His condition deteriorated to the point that doctors insisted he move in the fall of 2003 from his motel room into a retirement home. He couldn't go to Florida during the winter. Moe died of heart failure on September 4, 2004, on the eve of the 100th Canadian Open. Four hundred people attended his funeral in Kitchener. Flags flew at half-mast at the Glen Abbey Golf Club during the Canadian Open. Players told stories about Moe. They missed him on the practice range, where he would always show up on the Tuesday of Canadian Open week, and, in his street shoes and using a player's clubs, dazzle the pros with his ability to control the flight of the ball.

George Knudson once said of Moe's swing: "It's good today, it's good a hundred years from now. It's not an issue. That's what's called quality."

Moe Norman was quality.

Gene Sarazen

The Globe and Mail | May 1, 1999

When a golfer for the ages dies – and in his case, Gene Sarazen lived nearly a century, 1902–1999 – it's reasonable to ask whether he left anything other than his tournament record for the game and for people who care about it. Sarazen, who died on Thursday in Naples, Florida, of complications from double pneumonia, left a lot.

It would only be proper, mind you, to acknowledge his sterling record. Sarazen won seven majors: two U.S. Opens, three PGA

Championships, one British Open, and one Masters. He was the first of only four players to win all four Grand Slam titles in a career, the others being Ben Hogan, Gary Player, and Jack Nicklaus.

But he also made significant contributions beyond his record. Here are a few ways we might remember him.

First, Sarazen played the game in a lively, swift manner. He was walking, and often nearly jogging, proof that it was possible to play championship golf quickly. He didn't like to play with well-known amateur Frank Stranahan, an agonizingly slow player.

"Suppose you sat down to your dinner and ate like that?" Sarazen once admonished Stranahan. "It isn't natural. You'd drive everyone nuts."

Sarazen was a joy to watch, and to picture him is to cure swing confusion. English writer and fine player Henry Longhurst was once asked what he thought about when he got messed up by swing theory.

"Whenever I get fouled up in the mechanics of the game," Longhurst wrote, "I just think of Sarazen." Why not? He stood up to the ball and swung back and through it. Just like that. Sarazen believed that the grip is 75 per cent of golf and that a player ruined himself or herself by focusing on the body rather than the swinging of the club with the hands. End of story. End of instruction for all but special shots.

If fast play and clear thinking about the swing were hallmarks of his approach, he also was canny enough to know that equipment could make a difference. Sarazen had been having trouble with his sand play, "scalping the ball or digging down so deep that I fluffed the shot," he wrote in his 1950 autobiography *Thirty Years of Championship Golf*, with Herbert Warren Wind. It's the best book of its kind.

Sarazen's solution was the sand wedge. He is credited with inventing the club and wrote that it was born in a small machine shop at his home in New Port Richey, Florida, late in 1931. He had become interested in flying and realized that a pilot taking off doesn't raise the tail of the plane, but lowers it. Sarazen had an equipment epiphany.

He went to work, trying to make a club whose face would come up while the sole contacted the sand. He soldered lead along the sole of his niblick – the deepest-faced iron in his bag, equivalent in loft to today's nine-iron – and came up with a club that had what he called "an exceptionally heavy, abrupt, wide curving flange."

The sand wedge was born. Sarazen fiddled with it and experimented with the most functional way of using the club. He decided it was most effective when he took the club away slightly outside the target line, and that became the standard way of playing the greenside explosion shot from sand. He began to carry the club in 1932, when he won the PGA and Open championships. "The year," he wrote, "I had been waiting for for ten long years."

Next time you're in a sand trap beside the green, with a high lip in front of you, use your nine-iron. You'll appreciate what Sarazen's invention has meant to making sand play easier.

Sarazen also influenced course design, although he hasn't received the proper recognition for doing so. His most important contribution, in my opinion, was his belief that the green on a par-five that is reachable in two shots should be relatively small. He felt that the golfer who was going for the green on his second shot should be asked to hit a very good one.

There are many examples of this at fine courses. The par-five eighteenth hole at the Glen Abbey Golf Club in Oakville, Ontario, is one with which Canadians are familiar. The green hides, scrunched up, behind a lake, and is very narrow, back to front. The golfer hitting a long iron or fairway wood has to stop the ball in a confined area. Miss just short and the ball is in the lake. Miss long and face a very tricky shot from the rough or from the bunker – even with a sand wedge.

Of course, the fifteenth green at the Augusta National Golf Club, where Sarazen holed out his four-wood during the last round of the 1935 Masters, is also fairly small. Sure, it has substantial square footage, but the green appears small from the fairway. And its front part slopes back to the water. The effective hitting area is quite small for anything other than a mid-to-short iron.

None of this affected Sarazen when he holed his Turfrider, the name of the four-wood. He was three shots behind Craig Wood, the leader of the tournament. Wood had finished his round. Sarazen's double eagle made up the three shots and put him into a playoff with Wood. Sarazen won the eighteen-hole playoff. The double eagle became "the shot heard round the world" and put the tournament on the sporting map forever.

"His swing into the ball was so perfect and so free, one knew immediately that it was a gorgeous shot," said Bobby Jones, the Masters co-founder, who was watching from a mound fifty yards away.

Jones also remarked on what kept Sarazen so young even as he neared the century mark. Every April, including this year, Sarazen would hit a ceremonial ball off the first tee to start the Masters. It was always a treat to get out there for the early-morning starting time.

The answer to Sarazen's agelessness, as Jones termed his longevity, was in "his unconcealed and undiminished zest for the game and for competition."

Sarazen, of course, hadn't competed for years before his death. But he retained his zest for the game. I was fortunate to find him on the Tuesday evening at the 1985 Masters on the clubhouse veranda at Augusta. We chatted for thirty minutes or so while we looked out over the course. I wrote a column about the encounter.

"There is a touch of George Burns in Sarazen," I wrote then. "He spoke with feeling when asked about anything to do with golf, always droll, always smiling."

Today, after honouring this sweet man, we should smile. He left us plenty. Sarazen smiled on golf and golfers. Golf and golfers should smile back.

Sam Snead

The Globe and Mail | May 24, 2002

Has anybody swung a golf club more eloquently than Sam Snead, who died yesterday, four days before his ninetieth birthday? Sweet-swinging Sam Snead, Slammin' Sam, he was all rhythm, grace, and tempo.

But Snead was also much more than his swing. He won the 1949, 1952, and 1954 Masters, 1942, 1949, and 1951 PGA Championships, and the 1946 British Open. But he never won the U.S. Open, finishing second four times. That bothered him.

Snead's best chance to win the U.S. Open was probably in 1939, in Philadelphia. But there weren't many scoreboards on the course. Snead didn't know where he stood on the last hole and made a triple-bogey eight after taking a chance with his second shot that led to trouble. A par would have won the championship for him. He often talked about the experience, with a uniquely Sneadian snarl.

Then there was the matter of how many official PGA Tour events he had won. Tour officials some years ago got in the habit of declaring some of these events unofficial.

"That Jack Nicklaus is going to pass me without winning another tournament," Snead said, snarling again.

But he needn't have worried. His record of eighty-one official tour wins remains the gold standard. A man of many golfing decades, Snead played with the best golfers from the whole of the twentieth century, and lived long enough to see the dawning of and still maturing Tiger Woods age. Woods admired Snead's swing and loved to hear him tell stories at the annual dinners for Masters champions.

Snead liked to help players who sought him out, too. He was generous with his knowledge – and what knowledge he had. Tom Watson, in particular, took his advice whenever necessary.

As a player, Snead was part of what could be termed the great American triumvirate that included him, the late Ben Hogan, and Byron Nelson, who won the aforementioned 1939 U.S. Open. They were every bit as good, and perhaps better as a group, than Gary Player, Jack Nicklaus, and Arnold Palmer.

Snead had all the shots, all over the world. When he first saw the Old Course in St. Andrews, Scotland, from a train, he thought it was a pasture, not a golf course. But soon, grudgingly, he came to appreciate the humps and bumps and unkempt seaside turf. Snead that very year, 1946, won the British Open over the Old Course. Away from the actual action, Snead was captain of the winning 1951 and 1959 U.S. Ryder Cup teams. He also was captain of the 1969 Ryder Cup team at Royal Birkdale in Southport, England, that the United States and Britain tied.

Nicklaus conceded a short putt to Tony Jacklin of the British team on the last green of the last match that year. Nicklaus elected not to give Jacklin the chance to miss the putt, so the match was halved.

Nicklaus's gesture was a singular act of sportsmanship. It was gutsy for Nicklaus, then twenty-nine, to concede the putt, given his captain's ferocious desire to win. Snead was a tough man from a hardscrabble background from the backwoods of Western Virginia, and winning meant just about everything.

He showed that far from the world of pro golf. I might mention a personal experience. I played with Snead at the Upper Cascades course in Hot Springs, Virginia, almost exactly eleven years ago. He made it obvious on the first tee that he wanted to play for a few bucks. I just wanted to take notes and hear his stories, but as we walked down the first fairway I said to myself, "What the heck, it's Sam Snead. He likes to play for money, and who am I to say no?"

So I told Snead that I would play for $100 – my donation, I was sure, in the interests of the story I would write.

"Never mind," Snead growled. "We don't have to play for anything. I'll tell you all the stories."

Snead told stories, followed by his golden retriever, Meister. He gave me a tip on one hole, something about letting the club shaft come through impact at the same angle I set it at address. I was under par the rest of the way. But Snead, about to turn seventy-nine, would still have won the $100.

A few days later my wife and I called Snead from the road to wish him a happy birthday. He had an eye for the ladies, so I wasn't surprised when he asked, "How's your pretty lady?"

That was vintage Snead. He left anybody who met him with stories and memories and images of his syrupy swing. His eyes were failing in recent years and his health was deteriorating. Recently he was suffering from something that was described as stroke-like symptoms, and as the honorary starter at the Masters last month he hit a spectator with his ceremonial drive off the first tee.

Yet he somehow maintained the rhythm of his swing even then. To watch him was to absorb some of his smoothness. He always sent golfers to the driving range, dreaming of swinging sweetly.

We who think of golf as a high art were lucky to follow Snead. Golf was lucky to have him.

Payne Stewart

The Globe and Mail | October 27, 1999

In a spare, disquieting memoir, a mother writes of how she felt when she got the call informing her that her two young daughters had been killed in a car accident. "I immediately felt how impossible it was to raise myself to the scale of this event," Genevieve Jurgensen, a Parisian woman, writes in her recently published book *The Disappearance*. "The terror mounted in me out of all proportion to my own dimensions."

Anybody who has lost a loved one without warning is in a separate world others cannot know, imprisoned there by unspeakable grief and shock. It is impossible to imagine how horrible it must have been for Tracey Stewart, watching on CNN Monday as news was being transmitted of trouble on the plane in which her husband Payne was a passenger. It must have been equally desperate for the families of the other five people who were aboard the ill-fated Learjet. All six people aboard were killed.

Inevitably, an outsider's thoughts fix on memories. There's no making sense of the tragedy, of how it happened, or why. The mind reels, and goes to images of the person one remembers or knew, to whatever degree one knew him.

Stewart did let people know him. He always spoke his mind and stood up for what he believed. I could discern no difference between the public golfer and the private man. Many examples come to mind of a person who spoke up, who tried to make a difference.

During the 1998 U.S. Open at the Olympic Club in San Francisco, for instance, Stewart didn't think it fair that a shot he hit the last round into the middle of the twelfth fairway landed in a spot that the grounds crew had filled with sand. Stewart felt such a spot should be considered ground under repair, and that a free lift was warranted.

Many observers criticized Stewart, who bogeyed that hole and lost the championship by one shot to Lee Janzen. They felt the bad break he got constituted "rub of the green," or part of the game. They mistook Stewart's comments as complaints, and selfish. But he was speaking logically. The sand was put in to repair a hole left by a divot. He had a point in maintaining that it was ground under repair.

Then there was the time Stewart spoke about the Canadian Open, which he played nine times. He played around the world and first established himself twenty years ago at tournaments in Asia and Australia. He once said any golfer who aspires to being considered a world-class player has to play around the world.

But that didn't mean Stewart was going to play the Canadian Open every year. He tired of the tournament being played year after year at the Glen Abbey Golf Club in Oakville, Ontario, then owned by the Royal Canadian Golf Association.

"I've told them the Canadian Open should move around," Stewart said. "There are so many great courses in Canada and the one they have the tournament on is not one of the best."

Stewart backed up his comments. He did want to play in Canada, and participated in the 1997 Bell Canadian Open at the Royal Montreal Golf Club's Blue Course, where he tied for eighth. He didn't play the tournament the last two years, when it was back at Glen Abbey.

But you can bet that Stewart, had he lived, would be back at the Canadian Open down the road when the RCGA moves it around. You knew where you stood with him. He was a man of his word.

People who speak their minds aren't always well liked, especially when they are highly successful, public figures. Stewart recognized that he wasn't always diplomatic in what he said, and he paid the price from time to time. He was quoted in 1990 as saying that the issue of racial discrimination was a joke when it came up at the Shoal Creek club in Birmingham, Alabama, during the PGA Championship.

Stewart was the defending champion there. The club president, Hall Thompson, had said that blacks weren't members at Shoal Creek, and so the comments Stewart was alleged to have made were considered inappropriate. And last week some people thought he was being racist when he did his imitation of a Chinese person in response to a comment the British television analyst Peter Alliss had made. Alliss had said that Americans know Europe about as well as Chinese people – a strange comment, to be sure.

Whatever Stewart said in the above situations, I certainly never noticed in him a lack of compassion for, and understanding of, other people. We spoke at length during the 1991 Irish Open in Killarney, having arranged the meeting some time before. Stewart had won the U.S. Open the week before, and was very busy in Ireland. But he kept our meeting.

"I got letters saying that I'm a racist," Stewart said. "I got so many I decided I wouldn't talk to the media beyond yes and no if I was going to catch the heat from something I didn't say. Suddenly I was Mr. Racist. That's the farthest thing from my mind."

This discussion occurred one early morning at the Hotel Europe, in Killarney. I was supposed to meet Stewart for breakfast but first came upon him swimming in the hotel pool. We sat at poolside for an hour and then had breakfast. Stewart was forthright, as always.

"You need arrogance on the golf course," Stewart said, in response to my observation that many people felt he was cocky. "I just have to believe in myself. If that's arrogance, so be it. But I enjoy meeting people, talking to people. I'm a nice guy."

Stewart chuckled when he made that last comment. One evening that week I accidentally came upon evidence that supported his self-analysis.

The scene was a small restaurant in the busy downtown area of Killarney. Kids walking by the restaurant noticed that Stewart was in there, and stopped to look. He smiled at them, and waved. Soon he was signing autographs, patting kids on the head, chatting with them.

There he was, showing the man, not only the golfer. So what if he was arrogant on the course? Elite athletes wouldn't achieve what they do without some arrogance. Golfers stare anxiety down every time they stand over a golf ball. It doesn't take many swings for a golfer to lose confidence. Golf is a private affair played in the most public of arenas – a course where players are truly up close and personal.

In such an arena Stewart distinguished himself in a singular way. He conceded a putt to Colin Montgomerie on the last green of their singles match the final day of the Ryder Cup last month. The U.S. team had already won the Ryder Cup – the one, the only, objective. The conceded putt meant that Montgomerie won the match.

That was the right thing to do, and Stewart had the presence of mind to do it. He also had the presence of mind to do the right thing on the last green of the U.S. Open last June. Stewart holed a fifteen-foot par putt to win his second U.S. Open, defeating Phil Mickelson, with whom he was playing. Stewart went directly to Mickelson and consoled him. Mickelson's wife Amy was soon to give birth to their first child, and Stewart told his opponent – his friend – that he was about to experience something wonderful.

Stewart also distinguished himself on the course in other ways. Sure, he dressed differently with his plus-fours and tam-o'-shanter. But consider, finally, his swing.

Stewart's was lucid.

I use the word "lucid" because it means expressing something clearly. Stewart's extended, graceful swing expressed a particular beauty. If you want to think of the golf swing as art, then Stewart's represented a modern apotheosis of the art. Most modern golfers' swings are tight, even wiry. Stewart's was curvy, slow, easy to follow.

"The swing has to be a natural act, at least for me," Stewart said that morning in the Hotel Europe in Ireland. "You should swing and allow your natural ability to come through. If you start manufacturing things you run into problems."

Stewart didn't manufacture things – not his words, not his actions, not his golf swing. He was a pure golfer who, when he donated $500,000 to the First Baptist Church of Orlando's building campaign recently, said, "The thing about dreams is sometimes you get to live them out."

Stewart lived out his dream of being a successful professional golfer. Then, on Monday, aboard a disabled airplane, he was suddenly in a nightmare. His family, and the families of the other people on board, are living that nightmare now. We should think of them, and remind ourselves that Stewart was a classy golfer.

Payne Stewart graced the game wherever he played it. He wanted to make a difference, and he did.

Nick Weslock

The Globe and Mail | November 1, 2007

He was called "Nick the Wedge" because of what he could do with that club, but Nick Weslock could make the ball dance with any club in his bag. Weslock, who died on Saturday, six weeks shy of what would have been his ninetieth birthday, was simply a marvellous golfer.

The four-time Canadian Amateur champion was all about the game. To visit him in his charming home on a hillside a couple of hundred yards from a small green at the Burlington (Ontario) Golf and Country Club, where he practised daily, was to become immersed in all things golf.

Here, in one of his many scrapbooks, was a photo of his friend and fellow Canadian Golf Hall of Fame member Gordon Brydson, the congenial and accomplished professional at the Mississauga Golf and Country Club from 1932 until he retired in 1971. Brydson and Weslock helped each other with their games for years. For decades.

Then there was a photo of Lloyd Tucker, the pro at the Rockway club in Kitchener, who taught the late Moe Norman. The Ontario Golf Hall of Fame will induct Tucker next spring. Weslock had a deep respect for Tucker and for Norman, one of his closest friends. Weslock and Norman met for breakfast regularly before Norman died in September of 2004.

Weslock was such a keen student of golf that it was constitutionally impossible for him, even in recent years, to believe a better game wasn't around the corner. He tried everything he read and heard. Weslock had forever asked the best golfers for tips, and recorded them in a series of black books. In 1985 he compiled them into his book *Your Golf Bag Pro: Nick Weslock's Little Black Book of Key Golf Secrets.*

They weren't secrets, though, because Weslock shared what he had gleaned. At home, he'd grab a club, assume his address position, and say, "When I'm playing my best, I feel my shoulders are hanging." At a practice range, he'd point to a ball on the ground and mention something he'd learned from Irv Schloss, a well-known teaching pro.

"He always said to aim at the inside dimples on the ball," Weslock would say. "That way you get a nice draw on the ball." His keys were incantations. "Keep staring at a blade of grass right behind the ball after you hit it," or, "I like to kick my right knee in at the start of my backswing, like Gary Player does."

Weslock knew everybody in golf. His four Canadian Amateur wins got him invitations to four Masters. He and Ben Hogan met for breakfast at the Augusta National Golf Club, promptly at 7:30. Weslock asked Hogan if he might film his swing. Hogan consented.

"Do you have enough?" Hogan asked Weslock after he'd shot 175 feet of film. "Or would you like my fingerprints, too?"

Weslock loved to examine the positions used by golfers who had won majors so he could help golfers trying to win a dollar skins at their club, or a local amateur tournament. He played national events, but also all around Ontario. He played the Early Bird at the St. Thomas Golf and Country Club, the Eager Beaver at Uplands in Thornhill, the Willie Park at Weston in Toronto, which he won seven times, and events in London, Windsor, and elsewhere.

"He was one of the classic, great Canadians," Richard Zokol said yesterday from Vancouver. "He had knowledge, and he wanted to share it."

Zokol recalled some remarks Weslock made just after the 1981 Canadian Amateur. Zokol had won the tournament, and Weslock said, "This kid will make it."

"I was so flattered," Zokol said. "I was shocked. Nobody had ever said that." Zokol went on to win twice on the PGA Tour.

A fierce competitor, Weslock still liked to see others reach their potential. "He was quite a guy, and always so nice to me," Marlene Streit, his fellow Canadian Golf Hall of Fame member, said yesterday.

Given his nature, Weslock would probably have wanted any column about his life and legacy to end with a couple of tips. They're from his book's "Final Reminders" section.

"Keep your composure," Weslock advised. And his final reminder in the section? "Feel relaxed in the neck area."

There you go, a couple of nuggets from a man who was golfing gold, a couple of pearls to think about and practise, courtesy of the late, truly great Nick Weslock.

SEVEN | Mike Weir

KING CITY, ONTARIO

There were at least two impressive aspects to the Canadian Tour's Tournament Players Championship that ended yesterday at the King Valley Golf Club. One was the exceptional composure that Mike Weir of Brights Grove, Ontario, showed to win his first tournament since turning pro less than a year ago. Second was the atmosphere of the tournament, which Weir and others said made it feel like a real championship.

The Canadian Tour should benefit from the TPC. It certainly can use a new winner like Weir, who at twenty-three is attracting attention because of his thoughtful approach to golf and his creative play. Weir plays left-handed, and said that one of his main goals is to try for his PGA Tour card for the 1994 season. It's not out of the realm of possibility that this Brigham Young University graduate could meet up with lefty Phil Mickelson one day in a final group on the PGA Tour. He's got that much potential.

"I'm very happy with this young man," Richard Zokol said after his disappointing finish yesterday to tie for second at three under par, a shot behind Weir with Remi Bouchard of Lasalle, Quebec, and Steve Stricker of Edgerton, Wisconsin. "He's a class guy."

Weir's play during the back nine yesterday, when the tournament was decided, indicated that he is beginning to reach some of his potential. He eagled the par-five fourteenth after hitting a big drive and a five-iron near the hole. Then, after driving into a hazard on the fifteenth, he "three-quartered" a three-wood within twelve feet of the hole. He was three under par for the tournament at the time, and needed that par putt to stay in touch with the leaders.

"I got over the putt and said to myself, 'You're on the practice green at Huron Oaks.' That's my home course," Weir said.

The greens at Huron Oaks must be good greens, because Weir rolled his par putt home. He then hit a six-iron within a couple of feet on the sixteenth hole for birdie to reach four-under. That turned out to be the winning score when none of Zokol, Bouchard, or Stricker could birdie the par-five last hole to tie him.

Zokol and Bouchard had the most reason to be frustrated. Zokol had gotten to five-under through fourteen holes, but then missed the fifteenth and sixteenth greens, which led to bogeys. And Bouchard led heading to the ninth green, but three-putted there for bogey and followed with three consecutive bogeys before making a comeback through the middle of the back nine to stay near the lead.

"Up to fifteen I was happy with the way things were going," Zokol said. "I'm disappointed with the way things turned out for me, but I loved the excitement of having to birdie the last hole to tie."

Bouchard didn't share Zokol's excitement. The smooth-swinging golfer was hurting too much.

"I'm very, very disappointed," he said quietly. "I really thought I was going to win when I started out [in the last round]."

If Bouchard can take only small consolation from how close he came to winning the first prize of $18,000, perhaps he can take some good feeling away from the tournament itself. There may not have been as many people as at the Skins Game across the city at the Devil's Pulpit in Caledon, Ontario, but the good-sized crowd was enthusiastic while walking King Valley, a strong course where the TPC will be held the next two years.

"It was big, a lot more people for Toronto," Bouchard said. "The Canadian Tour is getting some recognition. A lot of guys can play out here."

Zokol felt that the atmosphere of the tournament developed over the course of the event's four days.

"I was really excited about this tournament," Zokol said. "It's the best atmosphere I've seen on the Canadian Tour since the Canadian PGA at Quilchena."

That was in 1990, in Richmond, British Columbia. Now the Canadian Tour has a new commissioner in Richard Grimm, building on the work that Bob Beauchemin did during his seven-year tenure as commissioner. And it also has a new home for the TPC, and a gifted young man as its latest winner.

Weir finished second in the 1991 and 1992 Canadian Amateurs, and took *Score* magazine's award as Canada's top amateur in 1992. He comes from the same Brigham Young University background as Zokol, Jim Nelford, Bobby Clampett, Keith Clearwater, and Johnny Miller. Weir spoke Saturday night to his long-time coach at BYU, Karl Tucker. He let him know he and Zokol were contending for the TPC.

"It feels unbelievable," Weir said after his win. "It felt real good to pull out the shots as I did the last few holes. That gives me a lot of confidence."

Weir will take that confidence to the Ontario Open this week at the Bridgewater Country Club near Fort Erie, Ontario. The Canadian Tour can take with it some positive feelings that it took a big step forward with a well-run TPC that produced a disciplined champion. More will be heard from him in coming years.

The Globe and Mail | April 14, 2003

AUGUSTA, GEORGIA

Out on the prettiest course in the world, Mike Weir was moving through the back nine, resolute. He was following the prescription that George Knudson once gave for success in golf: Get the job done, any way. Stay strong. Make it happen.

So it was that Weir got mentally stronger as the day wore on, and as he worked his way toward becoming the first Canadian to win a men's professional major championship.

Weir was a study in discipline. He didn't vary his routine while shooting a four-under-par 68, not when he needed a precise wedge to set up a birdie at the par-five fifteenth hole, not when he needed to hole a six-foot par putt on the last hole to get into a playoff with Len Mattiace. Not once all afternoon.

There were so many challenges for Weir, who has come so far in his few years on the PGA Tour. He said Saturday night, after he had shot 75 to fall two shots behind third-round leader Jeff Maggert, that there are challenges when a golfer shoots that number, or a 66. Weir looked forward to the challenge.

He also showed a lighter side when he was facing the heaviest of pressure. Weir had driven into the left rough on the par-five fifteenth, a hole he had hoped to reach in two shots. Mattiace was at eight-under at the time and Weir needed a birdie, no doubt about it.

Walking to his ball, which was down in the grass, Weir said to the people massed around him, "This is Augusta National. They're not supposed to have rough."

Weir had provided a light moment in a tense situation. He then hit a perfect layup and then the most beautiful little shot across the water, right at the hole cut in the back right of the green. His brother Jim was nearly in tears.

"That's awesome," he said. It was.

Weir was at six under par as he walked up to the green in front of a huge spectator stand to the left, receiving a well-deserved standing ovation. As Weir walked onto the green a roar was heard. Mattiace, who had been playing tremendous golf himself, had bogeyed the final hole to finish at seven under par.

Weir made his short putt to get to that number, and then parred the sixteenth and seventeenth holes. He had to par the last hole to get into a playoff, and made a seven-foot par putt to do that. Weir ripped his tee shot on the tenth – the first playoff hole – and put his second shot into perfect position on the green, below the hole. Mattiace hit a poor second shot left of the green and double-bogeyed the hole. Weir had two putts from a few feet out to win. He missed his par putt, tapped in, and the Masters was his.

All day he had been a study in tenacity. He said during the closing ceremony that he hoped some young kid in Canada would be inspired by his performance, and someday win his own green jacket. That young kid, and any golfer, would do well to study Weir's grit. That's not to underestimate his precise swing, but to stress that he hates a bogey just about as much as Tiger Woods does.

There were so many gripping moments yesterday. Weir hit his third shot close to the hole on the par-five second. How close was it? The crowd around the green made a fair bit of noise, and it looked close. But who of us from 100 yards back in the gallery could be sure?

Weir's wife Bricia was in that gallery, having flown in yesterday from their home in Draper, Utah. When he was over the ball on the green she wondered if this was his first putt, because he was standing so close to the hole. He made the little putt and was on his way to a 68 when he needed exactly that.

Later, on the seventh, Weir hooked a low shot from a mucky area right of the fairway around some tree limbs and into a bunker in front of the green. That was all he could do from there, and it was a lot. Weir hit a sweet bunker shot to within tap-in distance and saved his par that way.

So much was asked of him yesterday, and he responded every time. Jeff Maggert, with whom he was playing, ran into a mess of trouble on both the third and twelfth holes, making a triple bogey and then a quintuple-bogey. Weir had to wait a long time at each hole, first to play a tricky second shot on the third hole, and then to try to make a five- or six-foot par putt on the twelfth. He came through each time.

That's what the best players do, of course. Years ago somebody complained to Knudson that Canadian golfers don't get much financial support when they're starting. Knudson, a hard but kind man who cared about people, said that golf was a game in which a player could reach the top alone, without financial support. Only the numbers count – that is, the numbers a golfer posts – and that necessary condition of tenacity.

"It's an unbelievable progression that I've gotten here," Weir said, looking dapper in the green jacket that Woods, who had won the past two Masters, helped him don. But, he added, he always felt he would reach the highest levels of the game.

There's no higher level than winning a major. Mike Weir, Masters champion. It sounds good, doesn't it? Let the party begin, right across Canada, for a golfer who never forgets where he's from, and who thanked his Canadian supporters yesterday at every opportunity.

Canadians should also thank him for providing a huge sporting highlight, and an example of how to play the game, whether in the Ontario Amateur, which he once won, the Canadian Tour, where he won, or the Masters, which he has now won and richly deserves.

The Globe and Mail | September 14, 2004

On Sunday, September 12, Weir took a two-shot lead over Vijay Singh to the sixteenth hole in the Bell Canadian Open, but he three-putted the green there from ten feet above the hole and eventually lost his lead. Singh beat him in their sudden-death playoff. Weir was shell-shocked, as were all his supporters gathered at the Glen Abbey Golf Club in Oakville, Ontario, and watching on television across Canada. They were hoping Weir could become the first Canadian to win the country's national championship since Pat Fletcher did so fifty years earlier.

Weir's family didn't say a thing to him about the surprising reversal of his fortunes when he showed up to get something to eat after his press conference. Weir flew home the next day. We spoke that day, and this column appeared on the following Tuesday.

• • •

Mike Weir had been home in Draper, Utah, for only an hour yesterday and he sounded somehow tired and energized at the same time. It wasn't twenty-four hours after his extraordinary and disappointing day at the Bell Canadian Open, and he'd done some thinking about what had happened.

"I didn't get much sleep [Sunday] night," Weir said. "But I watched a tape of some of the round, and I can look back at so many things that I can't believe happened."

Among the events Sunday afternoon was the wild reception Weir received down the back nine and the playoff. His fans had welcomed him with great enthusiasm from his first hole Thursday, but even he couldn't have anticipated the noise level as the tournament wound down, with Vijay Singh winning on the third extra hole of their sudden-death playoff.

"It's a totally different thing for me at the Canadian Open than any player on tour faces at any tournament," Weir said. "I'm in a unique situation. It's just a different animal. You hear 'Go, Tiger, go' on tour, not 'Go U.S.A.' It was like a hockey game out there."

That it was. Fans offered multiple choruses of "Go, Mikey, go" as he made his way toward what looked like victory. Weir was moved by the crowd's response. But the enthusiasm might have been in his way a couple of times.

The first instance occurred on the tee at the par-three seventh hole. A writer who doesn't normally cover golf had situated himself on the left rear of the tee, three yards from the spot Weir chose to play from. The fellow was allowed there, but he was very close to Weir.

"I was in my routine and walking into my set-up when he stood up, trying to get a little closer, I guess," Weir said. Weir noticed the movement, and pulled his shot into a greenside bunker. He gently tapped the fellow on the shoulder and whispered, "Please stay still when I'm getting ready to play."

Later, somebody grabbed Weir around the neck after he'd left the tenth green. Weir wouldn't blame the incident on the seventh tee for his shot there or this fellow for the drive he hit into a bunker to the right, which led to another bogey. But now he was well aware he was dealing with the different animal to which he referred yesterday.

"Everybody was getting excited," Weir said. "I understand that."

It might have been the extreme excitement of the afternoon and the fact that Weir had never been in a similar situation that contributed to mistakes he made. He will surely learn from what happened.

Weir learned about how to deal with the pressure of a final round in a major when he shot 80 that Sunday at the 1999 PGA Championship. Weir was tied for the lead starting out and was in the final twosome with Tiger Woods.

Many people thought Weir choked that day, and believed he wouldn't recover; many people said the same thing yesterday. But Weir absorbed the experience, learned from it, and won the Air Canada Championship in Vancouver three weeks later. That was his first PGA Tour win.

"I'll learn from Sunday this time, too," Weir said. "That was my first time in contention at the Canadian Open. Now, I know how everybody will react. And sure, I had some butterflies. Who wouldn't? But I don't buy the idea that the situation got to me so that I couldn't play. I think I handled it very well."

Weir had already moved on to thinking about how he can improve off his Sunday Bloody Sunday. He noticed when he watched the telecast that his alignment was off on his putting. Weir really hadn't putted well from the start of the tournament.

"But my putting got worse as the pressure increased Sunday," Weir said. He was still surprised, however, at some of the putts he missed, and spoke first of the eight-foot, downhill birdie putt on the sixteenth hole in regulation play.

"I misjudged the speed for sure," Weir said. "I was talking to Dean Wilson [a friend and a fellow tour pro] and he told me he was playing with Hunter Mahan, who had the same putt and rolled it five feet by." Weir's putt slipped four feet by and he missed the par putt.

Weir needed to birdie the par-five last hole of regulation play to win, and had only an eight-iron in after he nailed his drive down the fairway. But the ball went into a bunker behind the green.

"I was trying to hit the shot five yards right of where it went, to where the green opens up," he said. "I pushed it just a bit and it went into the bunker. It was perfect distance but just not quite on the right line."

Weir's bunker shot came out to eight feet. He had that putt to win.

"I felt the most confident over that putt of any all week," Weir said.

He hit the putt on the line he chose, but it didn't fall. Was it his alignment? Nerves? Who knows?

"I can't believe that putt didn't go in," Weir said. "That was disappointing, not making birdie with an eight-iron in."

Weir then missed an eagle putt on the first playoff hole (number eighteen) that would have won. He missed a four-foot par putt on the next hole (the seventeenth) that would have won. It's hard to win tournaments without a putter, and Weir's putter wasn't on.

Still, maybe he could win on the third extra hole, the eighteenth again. But things fell apart there. "I aimed down the right side and tried to hit a hard slider to ride the wind," Weir said. "But I pulled it and hacked it out of the rough down the fairway."

He had one last chance, to birdie the hole off a wedge from 130 yards. Singh was just through the green in two. But it wasn't to be.

"I aimed five yards left of the pin and tried to draw it in there, but I pulled it five yards," Weir said. The ball caught the bank on the other side of the green and rolled into the water. The tournament was all but over.

Misjudged and mis-hit critical putts. A pulled drive. Short irons that were off a few yards. Anxiety? The unprecedented circumstances to which his precision ball-striking had brought him? Hard to say.

Joseph Heller once wrote a novel with the title *Something Happened*. Something, and some things, happened to Weir Sunday afternoon. He'll figure it out. He's already figuring it out.

"I'll probably fly my coach [Mike Wilson] in this week to work on a few things," Weir said. He didn't sound like a guy who was in a state of shock. Well, he wasn't, nor did he sound like a fellow who wasn't already moving forward.

On to the next tournament. The Canadian Open is history. Not the history Weir or Canadians wanted, but history nonetheless. What happened Sunday?

Golf happened, that's what.

U.S. Presidents Cup captain Jack Nicklaus calls Mike Weir "sort of the hero darling of Canada." Gary Player calls him "a hero in his country, deservedly so." Weir, one of Player's two captain's picks for the International team at the Presidents Cup – New Zealander Nick O'Hern is the other – is used to such accolades. He's carried the Canadian flag almost alone on the PGA Tour since he arrived there in 1998, and especially since he won the 2003 Masters.

"Nobody on tour is in my situation," Weir says. "People say 'Go Tiger,' not 'Go U.S.A.' Wherever I play, it's 'Go Canada.'"

Weir, thirty-seven, has borne the burden of being the golfer Canadians follow microscopically, and often myopically, with distinction. He's won that Masters and six other PGA Tour events, including the 2001 Tour Championship. He qualified for the last three Presidents Cups and has a winning record of 8–6–0. Weir lobbied for the competition to come to Canada. His presence will mean Canadians, in rooting for the International squad, will be rooting for the home team.

But Weir, who was recently elected to the Order of Canada, his country's highest civil honour, hasn't won since the 2004 Nissan Open. Later that year, Weir was on course to becoming the first Canadian to win the national championship since Pat Fletcher did so in 1954. The enormous crowds at the Glen Abbey Golf Club in Oakville, Ontario, were beside themselves with excitement as he played the sixteenth hole the last day with a two-shot lead over Vijay Singh. But Weir three-putted the sixteenth green from eight feet and couldn't maintain his lead. He and Singh headed for a sudden-death playoff. As Weir approached the eighteenth tee for the first playoff hole, the spectators gathered started singing Canada's national anthem.

Singh won the playoff, and Weir appeared nearly shell-shocked as they shook hands on the green. Many Canadians think he hasn't been the same golfer since the 2004 Canadian Open. Weir has said countless times that's far in the past. He gives no credence to the theory.

Still, Weir's results have certainly declined since 2004, when he finished 14th on the money list. They've declined dramatically since his banner 2003 season, when he won three times, was 5th on the money list, 85th in greens in regulation, 11th in putting, 12th in last-round scoring average, and sixth in overall scoring average. Through the Deutsche Bank Championship earlier this month, he was 82nd on the money list, 156th in greens in regulation, 73rd in putting, 93rd in last-round average, and 114th in overall average.

Weir was looking for better results when he changed coaches near the end of 2006 to work with Andy Plummer and Mike Bennett, the advocates of the hot new approach dubbed "Stack and Tilt." He said he was using smoke and mirrors even when he finished sixth in the 2006 PGA Championship. "I didn't feel comfortable over any shots," he says, and that's when he decided he needed more consistency and, perhaps, a change of coaches. Weir also revamped his swing because he couldn't stop himself from moving off the ball on the backswing, which, he felt, was putting too much stress on his back and neck. He couldn't hit as many balls as he likes during practice, and he wanted to be able to play for a long time yet, injury-free.

Last July, Weir tied for eighth at the AT&T National in Bethesda, Maryland, and followed that up with another tie for eighth in the British Open at the Carnoustie Golf Club. He tied for thirty-fourth the next week at the Canadian Open. He then withdrew from the Bridgestone Invitational in Akron, Ohio, after hurting his neck while trying to escape from the high rough, and he missed the cut in the next week's PGA Championship before tying for forty-first at The Barclays, the first tournament in the FedEx Cup playoffs. By the time of the Deutsche Bank the following week, Weir was eighty-eighth on the FedEx Cup points list. He figured he had to finish seventh or better to move into the top seventy and advance to the BMW Championship. Weir opened with a six-under-par 65, and backed it up with a 68 to tie for the halfway lead. But he shot 74–73 on the weekend to tie for thirtieth and finish eighty-seventh on the FedEx Cup list. That meant a three-week layoff before the Presidents Cup, something he didn't want.

Notwithstanding his results this year, Weir maintains that he feels comfortable with his altered swing. "I don't even think about my swing when I'm out there any more," he says. "I'm just playing golf. That's nice."

The day before the first round of the Deutsche Bank, Weir had visited Royal Montreal, thereby signalling how important the Presidents Cup is to him. He wanted to see the changes Rees Jones had made to the course since the 2001 Canadian Open. Weir liked what he saw, did a small media scrum immediately after his round – he can't come to Canada without the media wanting to grill him – and flew back to Boston. The bulletin boards at mikeweir.com were humming during the tournament.

"If I could ask Mike one question," one regular wrote when Weir fell from contention during the third round, "I would say, 'Mike, how does it feel to know that you will never win again, and that you are tagged a choker?'" Bulletin boards are ferociously intense and can verge on the malicious. Still, that post, while extreme, is a measure of how personally Canadians take Weir's career.

"What bothers me more than anything," Weir's brother Jim says, "is when people say that Mike's resting on his laurels, that he sits on his couch at home when he's not playing. They say he's doing too much away from the course, that he's set financially and that he doesn't care. There's nothing wrong with people having opinions if they get their facts right, but they're dead wrong. He's working harder than ever."

Weir has continued to work hard during his layoff. He'll be in a pressure-packed situation during the Presidents Cup, and he welcomes the opportunity. Weir would happily take on Tiger Woods in the Sunday singles were Player to put him there.

"Absolutely, I'd be ready for that," Weir says. "He's the best player. You want to play the best player. It would be great if it pans out that way."

Whether or not Weir plays Woods, his presence in Montreal will fire up his team and the spectators. As Player said when he announced Weir as one of his picks, "If we didn't have a Canadian in the team, I can assure you, in my opinion only, the series would be quite flat amongst the Canadian people. And I'm sure the Canadian people are going to be relieved, because I continuously had questions every week: 'Are you putting Mike, are you putting him in?'"

Canadians were indeed relieved, although there was plenty of controversy about Player's choice. He'd said earlier that it was his responsibility to field the best team, and that he wouldn't pick Weir only because he was a Canadian. Weir was twentieth on the points list of players eligible for the International team when the period for qualifying based on performance ended August 12th with the PGA Championship. His fellow Canadian Stephen Ames was in sixteenth position. Seven other players were ahead of Weir. Still, Player picked Weir, the player Canadians love. They respect Ames, who became a Canadian citizen in December 2003, but they adore Weir. And they expect him to perform. They certainly don't hold it against him that he's been a long-time U.S. resident. Weir and his wife Bricia and their two daughters live near Provo, Utah, where they graduated from Brigham Young University.

"When I won at Augusta, maybe that's the way Canadians thought it had always been for me, that I was always winning," Weir says. "But it took me a long time to get to the PGA Tour. I had to go through Q-school six times before I made it. I felt like I had some talent, but it took a lot of hard work. I still feel I'm doing well, even if I haven't won in a few years. But that's the nature of the game. One small thing can happen and things change. Your confidence and your swing can erode quickly."

At Royal Montreal, Weir will have to concern himself only with beating his opponents. Score won't matter as much as it does on the PGA Tour. With all eyes on him, though, he'll still need all the concentration he can muster. He won't be able to avoid the spotlight on him, not that he'd want to. Besides, he's learned how to cope.

"I don't play for Canada," Weir says. "Sure, I realize how closely people are watching me, but it's not like I'm out there thinking about that when I'm over the ball, or even at other times. I couldn't play if I did that."

There are no precedents for what Weir faces as the Canadian, although Richard Zokol has some sense of what he's experiencing. Zokol was tied for the lead going into the last round of the 1987 Canadian Open, but shot 75 as Curtis Strange won. Zokol won the 1992 Greater Milwaukee Open, and for a time was the main Canadian his fellow countrymen looked to on the PGA Tour.

"Mike's a big fish in a small pond in Canada," Zokol, forty-nine, says. "If he were an American, he'd be like a Mark O'Meara or a Zach Johnson, a very good player who won a major and some other tournaments. But in Canada he's in a different stratosphere. He's the only guy who's ever won a major. Canadians expect so much of him, and he also has high expectations. Meanwhile, the interest in golf has exploded exponentially in Canada since I was out there, too. There's no way Mike can enjoy the anonymity that I had, and before me, [George] Knudson, [Dave] Barr, [Dan] Halldorson, and [Jim] Nelford."

Surveying his career, Weir says, "If I think about where I was ten years ago and where I am now, I'd have taken it in a heartbeat back then. But that doesn't mean I'm satisfied. I want to get back to where I was in 2003. It felt so easy then. I think I can get back there, but it doesn't get any easier."

Maybe he'll find inspiration at Royal Montreal. "We'll have tremendous support there," he says. He looks forward to coming up with the goods. He knows that he'll feel emotionally engaged when he gets to Royal Montreal, and that he'll get the proverbial chills up his spine when he hears "O Canada," the country's national anthem, played during the opening ceremonies.

"I realize that the microscope is on me," Weir says. "But it's not a concern of mine. I don't play to get nice articles written about me. I play for the challenge of the game. I like the hard work."

Jim Weir will be at the Presidents Cup. He sometimes finds himself thinking about the competition, and the possibility of his brother playing Woods in the Sunday singles, in, perhaps, the decisive match.

"Mike could leave quite a legacy for golf in Canada if that happens," Weir's brother says.

There's another way to look at Weir's career, and it's equally valid. Simply, no matter what happens in Montreal, Weir has already left quite a legacy for golf in Canada. He can only enhance it at Royal Montreal. If he can find the game he knows he can play, and that he's played, he'll do just that.

• • •

Weir was the International team's leading performer in the Presidents Cup, taking 3.5 out of a possible 5 points. The highlight of his performance was his win over Tiger Woods in their Sunday singles match. The U.S. team handily defeated the International side in the overall competition, but there wasn't a Canadian who cared about that. Weir had come up big against the best player in the world, and they were nearly as excited as when he won the 2003 Masters.

Was Mike Weir's strong play in the Presidents Cup and, especially, his win in the Sunday singles over Tiger Woods an indication of better things to come for the 2003 Masters champion?

Weir will begin to answer that question for himself and Canadians in particular who watch him closely when he returns to the PGA Tour in this week's Frys.com Open in Las Vegas, and next week's Fry's Electronics Open in Scottsdale, Arizona. He certainly answered Gary Player's call at the Presidents Cup. The International team captain took Weir along with Nick O'Hern as his captain's picks. Some critics assailed Player for taking Weir over players ahead of him in the world ranking. But Weir justified the captain's choice.

Meanwhile, one fact remains. Weir hasn't won since the 2004 Nissan Open in Los Angeles, almost four years ago. He changed swing coaches a year ago when he elected to get into the "Stack and Tilt" approach that Mike Bennett and Andy Plummer teach, and which has become both popular and controversial on tour. Weir said all year that his ball-striking has been improving, that he can practise harder because he's less prone to neck and back problems that had affected him, and that he was on the cusp of good results again.

The results came during the Presidents Cup at the Royal Montreal Golf Club, where Weir was the International team's leading point-getter. He won three and a half of a possible five points. The U.S. team smoked the International side by five points, not that any of the 35,000 people on hand during the singles matches cared. For the Canadians, it was all about Weir against Woods.

Weir took a three-up lead over Woods through ten holes. He was hitting fairways with his driver time after time, something that has been missing from his game. His iron play was sharp, as were his short game and putting. Weir was playing his best, while Woods wasn't playing his best. Still, Woods stiffed an iron shot on the eleventh to win the hole, and took the twelfth, fourteenth, and fifteenth holes to go one-up over Weir.

All across the course, Weir's supporters started to fear the worst. Sure, they thought, their favourite golfer had showed well for a while. But now they were getting a sickening feeling. The majority was convinced it was all over. Nice try, but no scalp.

Still, it wasn't as if the landscape, painted all colours on a gorgeous autumn afternoon, had suddenly gone grey. Something festive was still in the air. It was a feeling only Canadians could grasp. Maybe it has something to do with living next door to the United States, but many Canadians have always had something of an inferiority complex when it comes to where they rate compared to Americans. Golf-watchers around the world can't possibly appreciate what it means to Canadians to have somebody like Weir on the world scene. They can't possibly appreciate what it meant to Canadians when Weir won the Masters, and how excited they were to see him against Woods at Royal Montreal. They felt down, but not quite out, as Woods took the lead.

Maybe Weir could yet pull it off, get a half, anyway. The noise level did seem to diminish, if only for a few minutes.

The volume had been turned up all day. Eleven other matches were in progress, but very few people were following them. U.S. captain Jack Nicklaus had said early in the week, "It will be great if Mike Weir played Tiger this time. I think that would be a great match. I think it's the logical thing to do." Player liked what he'd seen in Weir. He'd told Weir he'd been reverse-pivoting. Weir decided he'd overdone "Stack and Tilt" and eased up on it during his backswing.

The Weir-watchers liked what they were seeing that Sunday at Royal Montreal, at least until Woods made his move, accompanied by a couple of mistakes that Weir made on the fourteenth and fifteenth holes. The best moment had come when both golfers were circling their putts on the eighth green. Weir had received a stand-ing ovation when he approached the green, and it had finally died down. The sounds of silence filled the space while Weir and Woods surveyed their birdie putts.

Suddenly a voice cut the silence.

"Great to see you too, Tiger," somebody said from the bleachers behind the green.

Woods couldn't help but smile. Weir, facing in an opposite direc-tion, also couldn't suppress a smile. Each golfer then two-putted, and Weir maintained the three-up lead he had at the time.

But then, ninety minutes later, he was a hole down. Still, Weir is nothing if not mentally tough. He's always said he aspires to playing a Ben Hogan–type game, putting the ball in play and getting it on the greens in the right places. Weir knows he's not a super-power player, although his new swing and his rigorous workout under the guidance of his trainer Jeff Handler have helped him add distance. He was within ten or fifteen yards of Woods most of their singles match.

Now Weir hit two solid shots on the fifteenth hole, and halved it with Woods. Still one-down, his shot to the par-three seventeenth took the slope of the green and finished about twelve feet behind the hole. Woods missed from fifteen feet left. Weir made his putt. All square.

Weir drove perfectly into the left centre of the fairway on the last hole. Woods drove into the water left of the fairway, took a drop, and ripped a shot from 247 yards right at the flag in the rear right corner of the green, on a plateau. But it came up short in some rough. Weir's iron was on the money, about twenty feet right of the hole. Woods hit a superb pitch that finished about a foot left of the hole, walked briskly on the green as he took off his cap, and conceded the hole and the match to Weir. They embraced. It had been quite a match. The fans went crazy, screaming, "Mikey, Mikey, Mikey."

This wasn't the Masters, as some people tried to make it out as after the win. Weir was asked whether the win over Woods meant as much as his win at Augusta. In the flush of victory over the world number one, Weir said, "It's right there, but obviously, winning the Masters," and then his voice trailed off. Clearly, Weir knew that his Masters win ranked higher. That was a win in a major, his first win in a major, his only win in a major. This was one round, one match.

Weir acknowledged that he had to play his best to beat the world's best player, and that Woods hadn't displayed his top form. He expected Woods to chip in on the last hole, and that he would have to make his birdie putt to win. Weir added of Woods, who was so gracious in losing, "He's a class act."

The important thing that came out of the match was that Weir was calm, from the first tee. He didn't panic when Woods pulled ahead, and remembered that he had lost his focus over the last few holes during the 2004 Canadian Open at the Glen Abbey Golf Club in Oakville, Ontario. Weir had a two-shot lead there over Vijay Singh with three holes to play, but three-putted from eight feet on the sixteenth green and lost in a playoff. The situation and the support overwhelmed him.

Lesson learned. Three years later, Weir didn't let the crowd get into his head. He was aware of the support, and moved by it. He was stirred, but not shaken. It was in that regard that Weir said that one day far down the road when he looks back on his career, he might feel the win was more special than the Masters. That's because he showed up so well against Woods in front of Canadians. It was very emotional for him.

"Maybe I'll feed off this week," Weir said of how he might perform when he returned to the PGA Tour. "I'd like to finish off the year well. I was determined to battle back. This gives me a lot of confidence for the rest of the year."

At the same time, Weir confessed that he should be feeling a lot better than he was. He meant that his team had lost. He'd played on his fourth Presidents Cup team, and the International team had only one tie, in 2003 in South Africa, to show for those four events. "It's a downer," Weir said.

As for his game, Weir added, "When you finally start hitting it good, it settles everything down." That's why he was calm. He'd shown that calmness when he holed a seven-foot par putt on the seventy-second green at the Augusta National Golf Club to get into a playoff against Len Mattiace. That putt went in dead centre. Weir heard from thousands of Canadians soon after his Masters win.

He heard from tens of thousands right there at Royal Montreal, all week, and never more loudly than when the match ended. He's continued to hear from them via his website. "I'm lucky to have this kind of support," Weir said. "Playing for your home fans, I'll remember this for the rest of my life."

He might also remember it as a turning point in his already impressive career.

• • •

Weir won the Fry's Electronics Open in Scottsdale, Arizona, three weeks later. It was his first PGA Tour win since early 2004, when he took the Nissan Open. He had played eighty-seven PGA Tour events since his last win.

In 2008, Weir finished 14th on the PGA Tour money list with US$3,020,035, and 21st on the official world ranking. He'd finished 35th on both the money list and ranking the year before. Weir didn't win in 2008, but he was playing the consistently sharp golf that he seeks.

EIGHT | Tiger Woods

The Globe and Mail | June 17, 1995

Just outside the forbiddingly deep rough that borders the fifth fairway at Shinnecock Hills, a man was waiting on a seat-stick for his son to play a shot. The man was Earl Woods and his son is Tiger Woods, a golfing prodigy if ever there was one. This nineteen-year-old freshman at Stanford University has stardom written all over him.

But this time, during the second round of the U.S. Open, the teenager was undergoing a harsh education in the company of defending champion Ernie Els and British Open and PGA Championship winner Nick Price. Woods had just bogeyed the second through the fourth holes and was already eight over par in his first U.S. Open. Moreover, he had just driven far into the deep rough, just beyond his philosophically minded but anguished father.

"He's not ready," Tiger's dad told a passerby who inquired after his son's mood. "He's a walking zombie. He hadn't hit a ball for nine days before coming here because of final exams, and he had two hours of sleep a night for five days. But that's all right. He's a student first. This is a good learning experience, playing with Price and Els."

The learning was about to come to a sudden and painful end. Woods took a ferocious slash at his ball, just trying to extricate it from the knee-high grass and back to the fairway. He had a similar slash at the ball on the third hole, when he nearly let go of the club through the ball.

This time, Woods did let go of the club as he tore through the steel-wool rough. The ball knuckleballed across the fairway, while Woods looked at his left wrist as if he had injured it. He had. Maybe it was no surprise that, as he walked to his ball, Woods had his head down. "He looks very depressed, doesn't he?" a woman who was watching said.

Woods went on to bogey the fifth hole, and on the sixth tee asked for a doctor. He tried to hit his drive on the sixth, but again found the hay. It was over for Woods. He walked to his ball, then to Price and Els on the fairway. He shook their hands, having withdrawn from the U.S. Open because of injury.

"I really couldn't make a grip on the club and couldn't really swing," Woods said after coming off the course. He could not apply normal grip pressure and so decided to quit rather than risk further damage to his left wrist.

The spectators didn't know that Woods had pulled out. Down the fairways and around each green, they asked, "Where's the Tiger? Where's the Tiger?" Upon learning of his untimely departure, many of his fans also left. Meanwhile, Price and Els soldiered on, their pace and rhythm broken as they often had to wait on the three-some ahead.

It all turned out wrong for Woods, known simply as "Tiger." That's what everybody calls him, just as they call Moe Norman "Moe." People feel something for him, think they know him, perhaps.

That was the case right from the start at Shinnecock. Woods was in the feature group with Price and Els and he was the big apple of the New Yorkers' eyes. The folks knew that this phenom has more shots on offer than a bartender serving drinks, even if his promise was not to be fulfilled this time.

Still, there was plenty to admire: enormous drives, soft flop shots around the greens, youthful exuberance, even teenage impatience that must mature into a waiting attitude while not neutralizing deep desire. Woods will be in the golfing news for years.

But let's not forget that he is still a college freshman and plans to complete his education. To many blacks, Woods is a symbol of hope and even triumph, although he would like to be seen just for his golf and not his background, which is part Asian and part black.

This U.S. Open was even more a coming-out party for him than was the Masters. It is, after all, the national championship of his country. Should Woods ever win it, his effort will be celebrated widely.

But Woods will not win this year's U.S. Open. Does it matter? Not now, anyway. As a Long Island policeman who was following Woods and providing security said during a lull in play, "I didn't know anything about this kid until I came here. Just the fact that he's here at nineteen is incredible."

Exactly. And Woods will be in the U.S. Open at twenty-one and thirty-one and forty-one. He's for real. Woods is one of those golfers who make watching the sport such a pleasure. One hopes he can handle the glare that will be on him everywhere. Woods deserves our patience while he works on his.

The Globe and Mail | April 16, 1997

What makes Masters champion Tiger Woods a breakthrough golfer, if it's all too early to lionize him as somebody who will bring minorities into golf? That's a huge responsibility he may or may not accept. It's more sensible to consider his fabulous talents on the course.

It would have been impressive if the twenty-one-year-old had won the Masters in his first appearance by a single shot. But he won by twelve shots with an eighteen-under-par 270, beating the Masters record of 271 that Jack Nicklaus and Ray Floyd held. This is more than impressive. This is mind-boggling.

For an introductory thought about what sets Woods apart from all other golfers, we turn to Nicklaus.

"I think the day will come when an athletic golfer arrives who is tall and strong and can hit the ball miles," Nicklaus had often said when asked if somebody could dominate golf as he once did. "He'll also have fantastic touch around the greens and be able to putt the eyes out of the hole. He'll be smart and he'll also have a deep desire to win."

That golfer has arrived. Woods demonstrated convincingly that he is the golfer of whom Nicklaus spoke. He had already won three tournaments in fourteen events on the PGA Tour since turning professional last August, but because he won the Masters at Augusta National, "on this kind of stage and with this kind [extent] of media," as he said, his victory was there for all the world to see.

But it wasn't the win alone that has made Tiger the talk of the town. People have been talking about him in restaurants, motels, gas stations. He was on the front pages of newspapers from Georgia through Tennessee, Kentucky, Ohio, Michigan, into Ontario.

More than by his win alone, people have been taken by how Woods assumed absolute command of the course and swept aside his fellow competitors as if they were B-flight players. It seemed that Greg Norman and Nick Faldo didn't exist any more; they didn't make the cut, and nobody missed them on the weekend.

Woods, as always, responded supremely well to pressure. Last August, he came from five holes down after the first eighteen holes of their scheduled thirty-six-hole final match to win the U.S. Amateur over Steve Scott, for example. But the Masters was different, and showed another aspect of Woods's talents.

Woods had to impose the pressure on himself, given that he had opened a nine-shot lead after three rounds. When he could have coasted to victory, he still went out and shot 69 to set the Masters scoring record.

The short-but-testing par putts Woods made the last few holes were as indicative of his powers of concentration as his many birdies and eagles were of his sheer power. They helped define the final round as one for the books, because it showed that Woods can make things happen all by himself.

Athletes for the ages respond not only to outside pressure and stimulation, but generate a tension within themselves and then release it through their performance. That could be the ultimate expression of what they have inside them. Think about Bobby Orr when he dominated hockey while playing for the Boston Bruins. It is still said that he could control the pace of a game like nobody then or since. He could turn it up or slow it down. And he could make these things happen, seemingly, on his own.

That is one of the things Woods can do, and that helps set him apart. He has an uncanny ability to focus intensely on one shot at a time. This faculty is part of him, as is his winning smile, his powerful swing.

That swing is awesome, and averaged 328 yards a drive at the Masters. Woods can launch a nine-iron 190 yards if he has to. His power transformed Augusta National into a much shorter course than for the other golfers.

"Tiger has the ability to do that [overpower the course]," Nicklaus said at Augusta. "That's why this young man is so special. He makes the golf course into nothing."

Yet Nicklaus's observation suggests the question, from where does Woods get his power? Other golfers are as tall (six-foot-two), as young and as lithe, maybe even as flexible. And Woods weighs only 160 pounds. Many golfers are in that range.

David Leadbetter, who teaches Faldo, Norman, and Nick Price, has observed Woods closely. He believes Woods may be golf's best pure athlete ever.

"Tiger is so strong and flexible," Leadbetter said. "He has a huge arc and also manages to keep his lower body almost still on the backswing while rotating his upper body so far. You'd think he is going to hurt his back one day, but maybe he's just so athletic that won't happen. And then on the downswing he spins his hips so fast that he generates tremendous clubhead speed."

Leadbetter was saying that Woods epitomizes the modern swing, yet elevates it to a nearly ultimate level. His huge swing arc allows him to accelerate the clubhead over a much longer distance than most players. An analogy would be that he is accelerating his car over two blocks rather than one, and therefore can reach a higher speed.

At the same time, Woods's swing is efficient in the extreme, although he says that he swings at about 70 per cent of his available power. He maintains his rhythm and balance while crushing the ball.

Leadbetter said he had never heard a sound between club face and ball such as the one Woods made at the eighth hole during Saturday's third round when he hit a 256-yard, two-iron uphill at the flag on the par-five. It was a sound that nobody else makes, like the report from a rifle.

But Woods has still more going for him. Arnold Palmer observed that his posture over the ball is exceptional. Leadbetter said that most golfers who hit the ball a long way do so with some funny things in their set-up or swing. Not Woods, who is a picture of elegance from start to finish.

Then there is his focus. He has been groomed for championship golf since he watched as his father, Earl, swung a club for his infant son's absorption. Now, Earl Woods calls his son an "assassin" on the course. He also has the composure of a finely tuned assassin; he is just taking care of business. Emotion, if felt, is controlled.

Who's to argue with the father's description of his son? Sweden's Jesper Parnevik said at the Masters that he would prefer not to face Woods in match play during September's Ryder Cup in Spain; he thinks Woods will start with a five-hole advantage, he's so intimidating a competitor.

All of this is impressive, but what was most notable at the Masters was Woods's ability to adjust to the super-fast greens. His stroke for short putts on fast greens had been suspect. He tended to drive the ball rather than roll it smoothly.

"We worked on his putting all year with a view to this week," Woods's teacher Butch Harmon said while standing near the sixth green last Sunday. "That's why he probably didn't putt as well at some tournaments coming in as he might have. We worked on a slower pace to his stroke, because Tiger is usually an aggressive, harder putter. But it really paid off because he has putted beautifully here."

Harmon added that Woods has room to improve.

"He needs to learn more short shots," Harmon said, "and to become a better bunker player. He's not a good bunker player."

Woods found three greenside bunkers during the Masters and did not get up and down once, a measure of a flaw that Harmon means to change. He also said that Woods has learned to drive the ball lower without as much curvature. That more piercing flight should help him keep the ball in the narrower fairways of the Congressional Country Club near Washington during the U.S. Open in June.

"I think that at his age and at his level of competitiveness and maturity, he could almost win anywhere," Palmer said before the Masters. "I don't think there is anything to stop him from winning right here or anywhere else."

Nobody could stop Woods from winning the Masters while demolishing record after record. Can anybody stop him from winning the U.S. Open, the British Open, the PGA Championship? He makes the Grand Slam of four major wins in one year thinkable, if still highly improbable.

Woods will not win every tournament, but surely nobody would suggest that he lacks the physical talent and the strength of mind to blow the field away any particular week. Not after the Masters, not after what Woods did in one magnificent four-day stretch to stamp himself as golf's superstar.

Right now, nobody else is close. Augusta wind blew across the Masters last week, in the person of a welcome breeze named Tiger Woods. Except it wasn't a breeze, it was a hurricane, and it left everybody reeling.

The Globe and Mail | December 23, 1997

ORLANDO, FLORIDA

It's always possible to run into a golf legend at the Bay Hill Club and Lodge because Arnold Palmer spends his winters there. Palmer was there recently on a grey December day. He planned to play in a multi-group shootout around noon, with each golfer throwing in some money before the golf and needling was to begin. The shootout is a fixture at Bay Hill in the winter.

There was a second legend at Bay Hill that day, although "legend" seems absurd when the subject is twenty-one. But Tiger Woods was the PGA Tour's leading money-winner in 1997, the Masters champion by twelve shots, and winner of four events on the Tour. He was at Bay Hill for a three-hour roundtable discussion with twelve writers, followed by some golf.

The event was organized by the International Management Group, which has looked after Woods's business affairs since he turned pro little more than a year ago after winning his third consecutive U.S. Amateur. Woods won two PGA Tour events at the end of 1996, and followed with this fantastic 1997 season, even if he did tail off in the last half. Woods, who turns twenty-two on December 30, was the golf story of the year.

He is already "Tiger" to everybody, a measure of how familiar he is to golf fans. It took the public years to feel comfortable calling Jack Nicklaus by his first name, and many fans still don't. Even Palmer wasn't "Arnie" to everybody as quickly as Woods has become "Tiger."

Woods acknowledges that things have not always gone smoothly between him and the press, and the recent meeting was a chance for him to meet writers in a setting more relaxed than a tournament.

"It's been kind of a whirlwind and I haven't gotten to know you," Woods says to begin his talk. The group is seated at a long table with Woods at the head of one end; Bay Hill's big practice putting green is just outside the room, with the course spreading beyond. "I've known some of you guys since college days, but some of you I've only met in passing. I really don't know you very well and you don't know me."

Woods's pro career has been well chronicled: the way he dominated the game after turning pro; how he went twenty-two under par the last sixty-three holes after opening with a four-over-par 40 on the front nine of the Masters last April.

The result was that Woods found himself in the middle of a golf world gone crazy. The PGA Tour assigned extra security staff to him at every tournament, and when he won the Masters there was talk of a Grand Slam. Pundits thought it possible that he could follow up with wins in the U.S. Open, British Open, and PGA Championship. But he faltered in the last half of the season, when he felt exhausted. He had won four times on the PGA Tour by early July, but would not win again in 1997.

"People don't understand that you have to be intense for four hours on the course," Woods said. "Physically you're fine. I've never had a problem with being tired physically after a round. I'm used to playing thirty-six holes a day in college, carrying my own sticks, so this [playing eighteen holes a day on the PGA Tour, with a caddy] is easy for me.

"But the fatigue factor is definitely something people don't understand, especially when you're dealing with the things that come with being who I am, what I have to deal with on the golf course. And then, if I go into town, I'm not left alone at dinner, so then that kind of wears on you. Then people will follow me home to hotels and wait in the lobbies for autographs and pictures. That starts to add up. So if you look at that from the moment I get up to the moment I come home, that's a busy day."

He is speaking evenly, not arrogantly, and there is consternation in his face.

At the same time, Woods is well aware that the tradeoff has hardly been all that bad. Sure, he misses spending time with his college buddies, and will sometimes fly them in to tournaments. Many an evening he and his pals will play ping-pong for four hours at a time. That was the case during the Masters and also during the British Open, where Woods arranged for a ping-pong table to be brought to the house where he was staying.

The trappings of fame are stupendous. Woods is all smiles when he says that he enjoys hanging out with his pals Michael Jordan and Charles Barkley, whom he calls "M.J." and "C.B." What twenty-one-year-old sports fan wouldn't enjoy that?

Woods's friendship with Mark O'Meara, his neighbour at the exclusive Isleworth community in Orlando, is also important to him; he calls O'Meara "Marco." O'Meara is nineteen years older than Tiger but has helped him deal with Tour life, while Jordan and Barkley have chatted with him about fame and celebrity. Woods has been on the cover of *The National Enquirer*, and as he said, "How many PGA Tour players can say that?" But he'd rather follow his basketball friends in their exploits, anytime. And he particularly enjoys getting free tickets to Orlando Magic or Chicago Bulls games.

Still, Woods has been affected by some of the more difficult aspects of celebrity in our culture. The topic of maintaining a personal life comes up often; he wishes he could draw a line about what is permissible, and what is not.

"The hard part of the year was that after a while the public didn't want to hear about how good I hit a five-iron," he said. "They don't want to hear that any more. They want to know what I do off the course, things I do with people . . . that part of it, my dad calls it 'going horizontal' because you're no longer in the game but you're spread out. It's been more difficult than I thought it would be."

But haven't Palmer and Nicklaus accepted celebrity's burdens along with its rewards? A tableau presents itself outside the window, where Palmer, under a darkening sky, is putting on the practice green and chatting with people, always gracious, always smiling.

"I watched Arnold walk from here to the practice range [during the Bay Hill Classic last March] and not one person was going to knock him down," Tiger recalled. "It's because of the respect level for an older person. I mean, I have grandmas grabbing me, saying, 'Sign this for me now, you're the same age as my grandkid.' You don't see that kind of reaction toward a Jack Nicklaus or an Arnold Palmer because they're much older than me. People respect them."

Woods pointed out that his generation "is a little more aggressive. We naturally are. Then you bring all of them to a golf course, they don't know how to react, they have that football, basketball mentality, screaming and yelling, 'Oh God, I can get his autograph, he's right there in front of me' . . . When you get a crush the way I do, that many people fighting and knocking each other over, kids get hurt sometimes. That's when I have a problem, and when I stop signing, when adults trample kids. I've seen that. One little kid was crying his heart out at the Australian Open, because he was getting crushed up against this fence. Guys were pushing this kid away, knocking him down trying to get my autograph."

But then it can all stop, just like that. This happens when Woods reaches the practice range. He has a powerful, sinuous swing that unleashes with such controlled power at the ball.

"I look forward to playing more than I ever have," Woods says. "It's evolved into more of a love than I had before. I thought that was impossible, but I love playing golf more than I ever have. No one can get to me out there. You can't wait to get on there, to warm up. Ah, peace at last."

A season of following Woods produces memories. There was the Saturday evening at Royal Troon, site of the British Open, when he was practising alone on the range; Woods was eight shots behind leader Jesper Parnevik but believed he could win. And so he was pounding drivers into the soft summer sky, while behind him Scottish golf fans filled the bleachers. Tiger was all business, but when he was done he took a baseball stance and batted a few balls with his driver. The crowd loved it. So did Woods, who was in his element, doing his thing.

Then there was a shot that Woods elected to play during the U.S. Open at Congressional in June. He chipped a three-wood ten yards up a closely mowed slope to the hole cut in the rear left portion of the eleventh green. The ball scooted up the slope, on to the green, and into the hole. Nobody can teach that shot. And only a few gifted players have the touch to get the ball anywhere near the hole, let alone make the shot. This was more than luck; this was golfing grace.

At the same time, Woods hit plenty of shots that went awry during the season, especially during the last half. He tried to cut the corner at the par-five thirteenth hole at Royal Montreal during the second round of the Canadian Open, but went too far left into rough so thick he could not see his ball until he was on top of it. Woods could only whack a sand wedge out.

Woods missed the cut at Royal Montreal, the only cut he has missed as a pro. He showed he is human, something we should not forget even as we question his judgment on some shots where he tries to be too aggressive.

Back at Bay Hill, he said he learned a lot this year; perhaps he'll introduce a more conservative element into his game as required. That would make him only more competitive on courses with deep rough and narrow fairways, such as at the U.S. Open and the PGA Championship, in particular.

Woods moves to the range to hit some balls. He's simply swinging away, a pure golfer hitting pure shots. He loosens up with a few irons, then hits rocket after rocket down the range.

Woods can do much more than hit the ball a long way. He would not have won three U.S. Junior championships in a row and then his three consecutive U.S. Amateurs, or the six Tour events so far, without being strong mentally; he said he really believes he can will the ball in the hole sometimes, and that Nicklaus and all the great players are able to do this. But the will fades as the mind tires. That, Woods said, was one effect of the fatigue he felt from July on. There's so much to the mental game, though. Woods warms to speaking about it. At one point, he is asked if he can smell fear in another player.

"Oh yeah, you can," he answered, his face lighting up. "You just look at their eyes, they can't hide their feelings behind their eyes. This area here [he points to the upper half of the eyes] tells the whole story, the way they're squinting, if the eyes are wide open, bulging, if they're looking around. You can always tell."

Woods spoke about how players sometimes change under pressure, and tells of how Greg Norman seemed different that fateful early afternoon of the final round of the 1996 Masters. Norman held a six-shot lead over Nick Faldo after three rounds.

"Before the round, it was the first time all year Greg was actually laughing and joking with Butch [Harmon, Norman's teacher then and Woods's teacher]," Woods remembered. "He's never done that. He was so nervous he had to release it somehow."

This isn't to say that Woods won't admit to being nervous when in contention. But he monitors his feelings closely. For one thing, he often doesn't speak even to his housemates before a round, and certainly not to the press.

"I hate to say it, but I'd say, the guys who are doing well on tour, they don't talk before a round because they're already focused on what they have to do. You can judge a lot by a person in the locker room, you can judge a lot about a guy before he plays, whether he's talking to somebody or is not talking to somebody, how he's acting. You just watch him, and that [his behaviour] usually determines how he's going to play."

So far, Woods has been quite a player.

The Globe and Mail | September 6, 2000

Think Bobby Jones in 1930, coming to Merion near Philadelphia to try to add the U.S. Amateur to the U.S. Open, British Open, and British Amateur titles he had won that year. Think Ben Hogan in 1953, coming to Carnoustie in Scotland to try to add the British Open to the Masters and U.S. Open he had won that season. Think Jack Nicklaus in 1972, arriving at Muirfield in Gullane, Scotland, and trying to add the British Open to his Masters and U.S. Open wins that season.

Now think Tiger Woods in the waning days of the summer of 2000, this week coming to the Glen Abbey Golf Club in Oakville, Ontario, to try to win the Bell Canadian Open. Think Tiger Woods not so much because he has a chance to add that to the U.S. Open, British Open, and PGA Championship that he has won in his radiant season – the Canadian Open is not in the class of these majors. But think Tiger Woods because, like the aforementioned golfers, he is an authentic champion of the game and probably for the ages, and primarily because he comes to Glen Abbey standing alone among his colleagues as one who has command of the game.

Jones, Hogan, and Nicklaus arrived at the aforementioned events at the top of their games, although they, like Woods, felt they could still improve. They had by their play drawn a distinct, deeply etched line in the fairway between themselves and other players. Woods is on one side of that line. Everybody else is on the other.

Woods isn't a sure thing to win the Canadian Open. It would be absurd to suggest that. There are many superb players in the field, and golf doesn't allow one golfer to win every time he tees it up – not Jones, Hogan, and Nicklaus, and not Woods. It never has and it never will.

At the same time there is something wonderful about watching an athlete who plays a game surpassingly well, as Woods has been doing. Woods is only twenty-four and one must always guard against being too exuberant about him – there is always a danger to exaggerate his place in the game. Let his record over time decide that. But everybody who cares must realize he is a special golfer.

"I am not surprised that all these things are coming his way," Angelo Dundee, who trained Muhammad Ali, has said of Woods and what he has done. "He has those qualities that Ali had, the same supreme confidence and killer instinct. All the great ones have it. It is not an ego thing. They just know."

That says it, doesn't it? They just know. Woods does not think about records, or at least he does not mention them publicly. There isn't any reason to believe he thinks about them privately either, except, perhaps, for Nicklaus's record of winning eighteen professional major championships. Woods has already won five.

He may or he may not match or surpass Nicklaus's major record. If Woods does pass Nicklaus in this way, it won't be because he has dwelled on it. It will be because he hasn't. He can set aside history and the pursuit of records even while he creates history and new records. His interest is in golf shots, one by one by one.

Woods tipped his tough-minded approach six years ago, and probably earlier. It was the summer of 1994, when he came from six holes down in the U.S. Amateur to defeat Trip Kuehne two-up at the Tournament Players Club in Sawgrass, Florida. Woods holed a birdie putt from the fringe of the seventeenth green to take the lead for the first time in their thirty-six-hole final match, and then won the last hole.

Woods was asked about records prior to his final match. He had already won three consecutive U.S. Junior Championships, and was on track to win four U.S. national championships in a row. A record? So what?

"That's the product of playing good golf," Woods, then eighteen, said before he and Kuehne went out for their match. "The first thing you've got to do is take care of business. If the record falls, whatever."

Woods dismissed the idea of records then and he dismisses it now. He is a golfer, pure and simple. He covets pure golf shots, and he hopes to make them simple golf shots.

He has a huge, instinctive talent for the game, onto which has been grafted a technical mastery born of relentless application to the task of improvement. His best shots don't so much fly toward the hole. They coast toward it.

Woods is hardly the first golfer to have been gifted an instinct for the game. There must be many other golfers who, when they were infants, could whack a ball along a narrow corridor in their homes without touching the walls on either side. It is said that Woods could do this, and whether the story is apocryphal or not it still tells only of an innate potential, of an athletic sense. Years later, that instinct remains.

It remains as part of a comprehensive golfing system and a thoroughly schooled and still searching golfing mind. Refinements to Woods's technique, forged under the close watch of his coach Butch Harmon, have not blunted his creativity. One thinks of the many shots Woods has succeeded in making at just the right times. A biography of Woods's shots is a tale of excellence when excellence was required.

It is this possibility – of excellence at the defining moments – that Woods brings to Glen Abbey. Jones was as smooth a swinger as one could hope to find, and made golf look easy, though he was so nervous during a championship that he lost weight. Hogan was a clinician, a scientist of the swing who turned golf into a chess game while checkmating courses during championships. Nicklaus overwhelmed courses with his power, putted better than anybody when he had to, and knew he was a supreme player; his will would not allow him to believe anything else. These golfers snarled at the challenges golf presented. They looked forward to them.

So it is with Woods. Of all the fine golfers at the Canadian Open, only Woods conveys the possibility to his fans of creating that moment, when he plays an unforgettable shot. It is enjoyable to watch golf, a slow game, because of the tension that waiting for an explosive moment generates.

Woods more than any golfer makes waiting fraught with suspense, anticipation, and expectation. It is a devastating combination that makes one feel – crazy as it might sound – more alive as a spectator, keener of eye and emotion. Yes, Woods could fail. "I've messed up a couple of times," he said earlier this year. But one does not expect failure when he stands over a shot.

There was a choice moment, for instance, when Woods stood over a 256-yard shot in the sixteenth fairway of the NEC Invitational last month at the Firestone course in Akron, Ohio. This hole is 625 yards, and is meant to play driver, lay-up, and short iron. As Woods stood over his ball, an analyst on the telecast mentioned that Woods was laying up. He had an iron in his hands, after all.

But then, unexpectedly, Woods took a ferocious swing at the ball, nearly coming off his feet at the end. As he did so it was clear he was going for the green. His two-iron shot soared over the water in front of the green, over the flag, and just into the rough behind. Woods got up and down for birdie and went on to win the NEC by eleven shots. That two-iron shot brought him plenty of satisfaction.

Woods has made a habit of making shots when he needed them. In April of 1997 he shot four-over-par 40 the front nine in the first round of the Masters. The skeptics who felt the young man would not fulfill the promise as a pro that he had shown as an amateur smirked. But then Woods shot 30 on the back nine, making the shots to get back into the frame. He won that Masters by twelve shots.

Yet Woods felt his swing needed improvement if he were to contend regularly in majors and to win them. Woods decided to change his swing under Harmon, seeking complete trust in himself on the course. Why not? Who would not want that belief in oneself, whether it is attainable in golf over a long period or not? Perhaps Woods is the test case.

Some years ago George Knudson said he wanted security on the course. He didn't mean men watching out for hooligans. He meant the feeling of security in his swing. He wanted to know if he made such and such a move with his swing then he would get such and such a result. He wondered how golfers who played for their liveli-hoods could put up with less.

Woods, by the end of 1997, had lived with less, and craved more. He tightened his long, relatively loose swing and improved his swing plane. Into the golfer's lexicon came a phrase he likes when discussing the swing he built – "wide, tight, and rip it." He didn't win for fifteen months while making changes, and has since won regularly.

Yet he wants more – more control, that is, more improvement wherever he feels it's warranted. Woods said so after his fifteen-shot win in the U.S. Open in June, his eight-shot win in the British Open in July, and his playoff win over Bob May in the PGA Championship in August.

Here, then, we have a golfer who is brutally honest with himself. He once hit a 276-yard iron to a par-five green and finished left of the hole, thirty feet away, then made the putt for an eagle. This was at a tournament in Arizona that he won. But Woods had aimed thirty feet to the right of the hole. He had missed his target by sixty feet.

Later, Woods said he didn't like the shot he had hit, and that he had gotten away with a mistake. There was trouble left of the green, and he nearly found it. He wanted a swing that would not produce a mistake such as the one he had made, short-siding himself. What if he were on the final hole of a major and needed to hit a long iron to a green where there was trouble to one side? Security. That's what he wanted.

Jones, Hogan, Nicklaus – they all built swings they could count on when the pressure was so high less reliable swings would burst. Byron Nelson, Sam Snead, Lee Trevino, Tom Watson, Nick Faldo, and Nick Price also built nearly error-free swings, for longer or shorter periods. They came to tournaments during their best years feeling those swings belonged to them, as their signatures belong to them.

Woods comes to the Canadian Open bearing such a swing, and a registry of perfect shots – perfect because they happened at the right times: the eight-foot par putt he holed on the seventy-first green of the 1999 PGA Championship to maintain his one-shot lead over Sergio Garcia – he went on to win; the ninety-seven-yard wedge shot he holed on the fifteenth hole the final day on his way to winning the AT&T National Pro-Am in Pebble Beach last winter, after which his caddy Steve Williams said, "The game is on"; the six-foot putt that he holed on the seventy-second green last month to get into the playoff at the PGA Championship with May. The list expands.

In 1994, Price, to cite one golfer who for a couple of years was the best player in the world, holed a fifty-foot putt on the seventy-first green of the British Open at Turnberry in Scotland for eagle. He parred the last hole and won that Open. Later, somebody said to Price, "You could stand there on that green and not make that putt once in a hundred tries."

Price answered, "True enough, but I made it the one time I needed it."

Ben Crenshaw, a two-time Masters winner, said Price at that time was a golfer "in full flight." Woods is in full flight now. He's soaring. And should anybody point out that he couldn't make a particular shot again, he might say, "Sure, but I made it the one time I needed it."

Woods comes to Glen Abbey in full flight, all right. He comes bearing the weight of many successful shots hit at just the right moment. But it must be a bearable weight, a light weight, a weight that gives confidence.

His successful shots are merely foundation stones, and Woods continues to add more, tournament after tournament. The pleasure in watching Woods is in watching him construct a monumental edifice, shot by memorable shot.

There is more building to do, and the work continues this week. At Glen Abbey, the course that Jack Nicklaus built, Tiger Woods has come to learn more; to learn more about the range of his abilities, by discovering what shots he can hit. Jones, Hogan, Nicklaus, and now Woods: masters all, in pursuit of an excellence beyond excellence.

• • •

Tiger held a one-shot lead over Grant Waite as they played the par-five, 508-yard eighteenth hole in the last round. Waite had hit his drive into the fairway while Woods was in a bunker to the right, 218 yards from the hole across the pond. Waite hit a five-iron from 224 yards, leaving himself 30 feet away from the hole with an eagle putt. Woods had 218 yards to the hole, and selected a six-iron. He picked the ball clean, and pushed it just slightly. But it covered the flag and finished in the short fringe behind the green, 15 feet from the hole. Waite missed his eagle putt, and then Woods made his birdie to win by a shot. He had again demonstrated excellence at the defining moment. He had again played an unforgettable shot. Golfers at Glen Abbey since have examined the shot he faced from the bunker, and many have placed a ball to play from there.

"It's such a great feeling to be in that position and see what you've got inside you," Woods said after his win. "You focus on what you need to do at that moment, and you give it absolutely everything you have."

The Globe and Mail | April 15, 2002

AUGUSTA, GEORGIA
Call the doctors – psychoanalysts, psychiatrists, psychologists, that is. Make appointments for golf's best players, who stand tier two behind Tiger Woods.

These players must be totally frustrated after Woods took the Masters with ease yesterday, notwithstanding a round of only one-under-par 71 at the unforgiving, sodden Augusta National Golf Club.

His fellow professionals beat themselves. Sure, they had to take chances, once Woods zipped away to a commanding lead with birdies at the second and third holes. The ever-precocious one went on to win by three shots over Retief Goosen with a twelve-under-par 276.

Was there any doubt who would win?

Woods started out tied for the lead with Goosen at eleven under par. Goosen didn't have his usual impeccable timing, and fell to eight-under after the front nine. Woods was thirteen-under by then. Goosen was no longer a factor, although he made a couple of birdies coming in to claim second place. The 2001 U.S. Open champion beat himself with wayward shots.

Ditto for Vijay Singh, the winner of the 1998 PGA Championship and the 2000 Masters. He started two behind Woods and Goosen, and was within striking distance of the lead for much of the afternoon. But he missed a six- or seven-foot par putt at the eleventh, hit a conventional (under most circumstances) 216-yard iron shot into the creek at the par-five thirteenth, and whacked his drive into the trees on the fourteenth. Singh was sunk.

Did Woods intimidate these players? You'd have to think so. He doesn't beat himself, or at least hasn't in majors, and precious few other tournaments. Woods is a golfing Buddha when a major is on the line. He's at ease while others appear ill at ease. They fall out of their comfort zones into uncomfortable zones.

Neither Phil Mickelson nor Ernie Els, who started four shots behind Woods, seemed comfortable. Mickelson birdied the first two holes, but, mixing birdies and splendid play with bogeys and poor shots, fell six behind by the end of the front nine.

As for Els, who won the 1994 and 1997 U.S. Opens, he was one battered, shattered man after finding the creek twice on the thirteenth hole. Upset, he held his face in his hands after triple-bogeying the hole. His Masters was over.

The collective collapse of so many top golfers was hard to watch, even weird. Singh found the water in front of the green twice on the fifteenth, and went for a quadruple-bogey nine. The air had gone out of him on the thirteenth and fourteenth.

Yesterday's events demonstrated how much better Woods is than anybody else, especially in a major. He's won six of his past ten majors.

Woods plays intelligent golf that is a pleasure to watch. He goes and wins majors while, so often, his opponents make shots that guarantee they will lose.

Woods now holds seven majors, at twenty-six years old. He's got a leg up on an authentic Grand Slam – wins in all four majors in a calendar year. That could happen, and nobody would be surprised.

Woods wins his majors, in part, because other players crumble as he plays his crafty game. He crept up the leaderboard all week, playing a waiting game. Scores of 70, 69, 66 – tied for the lead after fifty-four holes. He's relentless in majors, as Jack Nicklaus was for some twenty-five years while winning eighteen professional majors. They included six Masters, the first in 1963 and the last in 1986.

Woods has so many shots. He wasn't going to miss his approach shot right off the pin on the seventh hole, because a ridge would take the ball spinning away. So he played left and past the hole. He wasn't going to hit his approach below the hole at the ninth, as Els did, only to find his ball recoil and spin off the green and down a hill a few yards. Woods flew his approach past the hole. Brilliant stuff.

He didn't even need his best stuff down the final holes yesterday. He did mis-hit some shots – a little – but you had the feeling he would have nailed them if he'd had to. He missed the fifteenth fairway from the tee, laid up short of the pond in front of the green, then nearly holed his third and got his birdie.

Nicklaus said after playing a practice round with Woods when he was an amateur that Woods would win more Masters than he and

Arnold Palmer together. That would mean at least eleven green jackets for Woods. He has three already.

Woods carves up a course like a chess grandmaster, moving pieces around the board, waiting for the kill. In doing so, he carves up other golfers.

Checkmate, guys, checkmate. Call in the shrinks.

The Globe and Mail | July 21, 2005

If it's a treat to watch Tiger Woods play golf – and "play" is what he does – it's also enjoyable to hear him talk about his game. The 2005 Masters and British Open champion has always had his own vocabulary.

"I'm using the true loft of the club," Woods said the day before the 1998 Tour Championship. "When you're not coming into the ball as steep, I'm not getting the shooters like I used to get."

Woods was then altering the swing with which he had won the 1997 Masters by twelve shots. He started doing that not long after the Masters, under the guidance of Butch Harmon, then his swing coach. Woods won only one tournament in 1998, and so most observers thought he was nuts to change. He persevered.

Who wants shooters?

By the spring of 1999 Woods was finding the swing he craved. He was on the range a week before the Byron Nelson Classic that spring when everything clicked in one swing. He called Harmon to tell him about his eureka experience.

"It was just a perfect shot, a perfect trap," Woods told Harmon of his swing of beauty. "It was very flat, a very thin, very shallow divot. That's just right where I wanted to be."

Woods also spoke that spring of getting "sweet rolls," and he wasn't referring to visits to a bakery. Even with his altered and more efficient swing he knew that any golfer needs good breaks. He'd received one when his ball bounced through a bunker and ran up near the hole. A "sweet roll." Sweet-talking Tiger.

Not every shot worked out as he wanted. Woods, contrary to popular belief, isn't Superman. So it was that he referred to a tee shot during the 1999 Memorial Tournament in Dublin, Ohio, as a "high flamer out to the right in the trees." Woods won the tournament.

That same event Woods went into quite a riff about a shot that he wanted to carry 163 yards over a bunker. He spoke about catching the ball "flush" and about a "knuckling effect" and his concern about hitting a "hot one."

Woods has discussed "swirly" grass. He's mentioned his interest in "letting the blade release," about wanting to "hit a low ball and dig it," about going for a "picker," where he shallows out the clubface to make sure the ball doesn't "juice" on him. When he won the 2000 U.S. Open by a mere fifteen shots at Pebble Beach Golf Links he often spoke again about shots he hit "flush," and putts he "buried."

That year he won his first British Open at the Old Course in St. Andrews. Asked, after his eight-shot victory, whether there was any shot he was leery of hitting, Woods answered quickly and fully.

"One of the shots I've been struggling with for most of the year has been sweeping the ball and arcing the plane off properly to sweep the ball from right to left," Woods said. He added that he'd been able to pull off the shot that week, much to his delight.

Golf Digest's Dave Kindred noticed that Woods talks a weird and wonderful game. In a March 2003 piece, he recalled words by Woods. Shots, he wrote, are "blistered, bombed, chunked, fatted, half-fatted, shaved, squirted, ripped, skipped, yipped." Woods said he "raked" a shot, and on another occasion he hit a "bleeder."

The master linguist of the game demonstrated more vivid lingo last week when he won the Open by five shots. He'd incorporated swing changes that he's worked on for the past sixteen months with Hank Haney, his swing coach post-Harmon. He and Harmon parted company three years ago.

Woods described trying "to hit a low, skipping spinner where it hit on top and released on down." He spoke of using "one of the spinniest balls out here on tour." He "three-ripped a green," three putts in more usual language. Woods is worth listening to as well as watching. Call him Tiger Wordsworth, the golf poet and ten-time major champion.

To tell the truth, however, words fail when trying to describe what he's doing in the game. All that remains is to see whether Woods will drive the ball where he wants to during next month's PGA Championship at tree-lined Baltusrol Golf Club in Springfield, New Jersey.

Should that happen, Woods will surely find the words to describe what everybody will have to agree is a complete game. Or maybe he'll fall silent, because his game will have spoken for itself. Eloquently.

Earl Woods: A Father's Influence

The Globe and Mail | May 5, 2006

Tiger Woods was four holes down to Trip Kuehne after the morning round of their scheduled thirty-six-hole final match in the 1994 U.S. Amateur when his father, Earl, told him, "Let the legend grow." He had won three consecutive U.S. Juniors and fought back to win his first of three consecutive U.S. Amateurs.

He was letting the legend grow.

His father, who died Wednesday, has long been a legend himself, and he both pushed his son and left him alone to let him grow. Of course, most every father is a legend to his own children, and in some fundamental way it's probably not right to lionize Earl. But at the same time, there's no denying that he was a fascinating and complex individual who, with his wife Kultida, raised golf's best player. Tiger could yet break all the important golf records and, perhaps, transcend his sport in significant ways.

Earl saw an artist in his son when Tiger was only an infant. Tiger was six months old when his father plunked him in a high chair, took it out to the garage at the family home in Cypress, California, set up a net there, and started hitting balls. He figured his son might learn by osmosis.

The infant was mesmerized. His father would say years later when Tiger was a champion that he had an attention span of two hours. Who knows if that was a proud father exaggerating, but the fact is that Tiger watched and watched as his father whacked balls into the net. It wasn't long before he was hitting balls, first left-handed. But he was a natural right-hander, so that soon changed.

Earl was forty-three when his wife gave birth to Tiger, on December 30, 1975. She called him Eldrick, but Earl had another name in mind: Tiger. It was meant as a nickname to honour Nguyen Phong, a fellow soldier of Earl's in Vietnam whose nickname was Tiger. When Saigon fell and the war ended, Earl vowed he would so nickname his son should he have one. He had three children from a first marriage.

Earl was a tough-minded man who wasn't afraid of a battle, and who faced more than a few during two tours of duty in Vietnam. His first was in 1967–68 and his second 1972–73. He was a personnel officer during his first tour and advised Phong, a commander of South Vietnamese military forces, during his second tour.

Tiger Phong and Earl eventually lost touch, and Earl never did see him again. But he came to see the steely soldier in his son, although it's far-fetched to compare the battlefield of a golf course to that of a killing field. Still, Earl brought what he had learned in those fields to bear in the training of his son. He didn't call one of his books *Training a Tiger* without thinking about it. He trained him, but good.

By the time he was five, Tiger could discern a reverse weight transfer in a golfer. At six, he was listening to subliminal tapes. Tim Rosaforte wrote in his fine book *Tiger Woods: The Making of a Champion* that the prodigy taped messages to his desk. The messages can sound trite and silly, but they went into the training of a champion, according to Earl.

One message, Rosaforte wrote, was, "My decisions are strong! I do it all with my heart!" Another was, "I focus and give it my all!"

Lieutenant-Colonel Earl Woods was a talented athlete himself. He attended Kansas State University and was the first black scholarship baseball player in the old Big Eight conference. He liked what he was seeing in his child.

The making of a champion meant the making of the mind, not only the swing.

The swing was important, but for a long time the least of it. Sure, Earl directed his son to proper coaching, especially when Tiger, then seventeen, got together with Butch Harmon. But he wouldn't have had the resolve to change his swing then, and again after he had won multiple majors, had he not developed the discipline to stick with the program.

His father drilled discipline into him, but didn't push him over the edge. That's the edge where kids learn to hate what they're doing because their parents are insistent and because they're afraid of being punished or losing their love.

Earl incorporated techniques he'd learned in the military, and called the regimen "psychological warfare." He rolled golf balls into Tiger's line while he was trying to make three-foot putts. According to Rosaforte, he would suddenly say, "Better not hook it" on holes where the out-of-bounds was to the left.

"There's a dark side to me," Earl told Rosaforte. "I pulled every nasty, dirty, ungodly trick on him. He'll tell you today it was one of the toughest periods of his life."

But he also pulled back. He didn't berate Tiger for missing shots when he was trying his best. He did once scold him hard when he felt he'd given up in the last round of a junior tournament. But that was different. Tiger wasn't trying his best.

The contrast between the ways different parents handle their kids in high-level amateur golf becomes apparent all too often. One example: A former U.S. Amateur champion who was touted as a tremendous prospect in pro golf had shot 71 in the first round of a recent Masters. His father was seen berating him in the parking lot after the round for missing a few short putts.

Earl, by all accounts, and by the natural affection one always saw between him and his son, never acted in such a manner. He knew when to pull back, and wrote in *Training a Tiger* that his plan with his son wasn't to raise a golfer, but to raise a good person.

That in itself sounds a bit strange, since Earl was certainly raising a golfer. But he meant that he wanted to raise his son so that he would act properly on the world stage for which his father felt he was destined. Earl wasn't shy about declaring his son a "chosen one," and predicted he would have a major impact on the world, and not by winning major championships.

For one thing, he predicted in *Golf Digest*'s November 2001 issue that Tiger "would have an impact upon the world, in a humanitarian aspect, very similar to that of Gandhi. Tiger will be interested in kids like that. He will be like an ambassador at large, without portfolio. It would not be political. He's not a very political person, at this stage."

It's four and a half years since Earl said that, and his son remains first and foremost a golfer. Tiger has won ten major championships; his father predicted after his third U.S. Amateur that he would win fourteen, and he could be low there. He's shown no inclination toward politics, yet with his father's guidance and $3 million (US) of his own money, he started the Tiger Woods Learning Center in Anaheim, California. The 35,000-square-foot educational facility opened February 10.

It remains to be seen whether Tiger will transcend his sport and contribute beyond golf. For now, he is a grieving son who has lost a father to whom he was very close. The lasting image to anybody who has been around Tiger at tournaments is of his eyes searching for his father, and the two of them locking in an embrace when they find one another.

They'll embrace no more, and it will become apparent in the years to come whether Tiger embraces his father's vision for him. "Pop gave me many great lessons, not only about golf, but about life," Tiger wrote in his book *How I Play Golf.* "His greatest advice to me was to always be myself."

That's a pretty good lesson for a father to pass on to his child, prodigy or otherwise.

The Globe and Mail | July 26, 2006

Mastermind of the game that he is, it was no surprise to see Tiger Woods develop a nuanced strategy during last week's British Open that effectively took Royal Liverpool Golf Club's ninety-four bunkers out of play. The surprise is that so few players, professional and amateur, really get it when it comes to playing links golf.

Woods hit but one driver, out of fifty-six opportunities. His two-iron, for the most part, played the role of his driver. Jack Nicklaus did something similar when he won the 1966 British Open at the Muirfield Golf Club in Gullane, Scotland, except that he used his driver seventeen times out of fifty-six opportunities. The ball didn't fly as far then, even for Nicklaus, so the strategies are comparable.

Nicklaus, then twenty-six and golf's powerhouse, as Woods is today, used his driver on most holes during his first practice round. He used the driver fewer and fewer times in subsequent practice sessions, until, as he wrote in *The Greatest Game of All*, his early autobiography, he came to a conclusion.

"By the eve of the championship there was only one hole, the long fifth, where I planned to drive with my driver in any wind, and there were only a handful of other holes, all lengthy par-fours, where I planned to take my driver in certain kinds of wind," Nicklaus said. "Everything considered, this amounted to the best preparation I had ever given a tournament in terms of learning a specific course."

Nicklaus used his one-iron frequently, and controlled it beautifully in winds that ranged from mild to blustery over Muirfield's difficult holes. He won by a shot over Dave Thomas and Doug Sanders. It was his first of three Open wins, the other two coming at the Old Course in St. Andrews in 1970 and 1978.

Forty years before Woods wept after holing his winning putt, owing to the emotions that he had so impressively restrained down the stretch, Nicklaus was also overcome. Woods was in tears because he felt the presence of his late father, Earl. Nicklaus's reason was more prosaic.

"I got so choked up [during the trophy presentation] that tears came into my eyes and I couldn't talk," Nicklaus wrote. He added, "I hadn't been at all sure that I would ever be up there standing beside that trophy – a high-ball player like me who couldn't handle hard linksland fairways and who had always found a way to lose the British Open and probably would continue to."

But Nicklaus, and now Woods, grasp links golf. And, perhaps more than any modern architect, Donald Steel has brought its features into his work. Steel was hired to do some work on Royal Liverpool for the Open, but he was never going to mess with its essential character. The work that Steel, along with his former young associates Martin Ebert and Tom Mackenzie, who now have their own company, did, won high praise from the players.

"The easiest thing to do is to make a golf course impossible, but golf course architecture is the art of the possible," Steel wrote during a series of e-mail exchanges during the Open. "All Winged Foot had was a spooky finish."

Steel was referring to Phil Mickelson's debacle on the final hole of last month's U.S. Open at the Winged Foot Golf Club. Mickelson had very few options from left of the fairway, and chose a couple of nearly impossible ones. He double-bogeyed the hole, and Geoff Ogilvy won.

"This is the way it all started and how I think that it should be played," Woods said of possible rather than impossible golf after his win on Sunday. "You should have options to run the ball on the ground. But we play all around the world, and that's not normally the case."

Golf needs a new normal. Steel, the president of the English Golf Union, and adamantly not retired from architecture – "far from it," he wrote – will continue to work in that direction. He designed the Fiddlers' Ridge course now under construction in Goodwood, Ontario. Ebert has taken over, and, like Steel, knows that the landscape will yield links-like, hugging-the-ground conditions. Ebert is on site this week.

"From an old dog in which there is still some life," is how Steel signed an e-mail Sunday, before watching Woods shoot 67 to claim his third Open.

Woods's shrewd strategy, and the way Royal Liverpool opened up the game, demonstrates that there's life in another old dog. That's the traditional ground game, which represents the art of the possible. No other style comes close to being as interesting and entertaining.

Golfobserver.com | April 1, 2007

The Royal and Ancient Golf Club of St. Andrews is considering a date change for this year's Open Championship at the Carnoustie Golf Club, which is currently scheduled for July 19–22. The organization might take this unprecedented step because Tiger Woods has said he will miss the championship he has won three times should his wife Elin give birth around that time. Her due date is sometime in July.

"If she's going to have it during the week of the Open, I just don't go," Woods said earlier this year. "That's the most important thing, not a golf tournament."

R&A secretary Peter Dawson and championship secretary David Hill are taking seriously the possibility that Woods will not play. Dawson tipped the R&A's hand on March 6 in Glasgow, during an Open-related meeting.

"Tiger is a big draw," Dawson said. "He's going for his third consecutive championship, and you don't get that happening very often. If he doesn't come, then it would be bound to affect things."

More golfers around the world follow the Open Championship than any of the other three majors. Attendance at the event is also huge. Dawson said he expects attendance at Carnoustie this year to increase by 10 to 15 per cent over the 160,000 who were on site in 1999, when Paul Lawrie won in a playoff over Jean Van de Velde and Justin Leonard.

However, Dawson is well aware that attendance figures, not to mention worldwide interest on television, would suffer dramatically should Woods not play. Media coverage would also diminish sharply. Companies that have committed substantial investments in the Open for entertainment on site already fear the worst.

Dawson knows that in today's golf scene, there's Woods, and then there's everybody else. Still, he respects the decision that Woods said he will make should he find himself a father for the first time come Open Championship week.

"I know he'll be there if he possibly can," Dawson said. "Family, though, comes first and we quite understand that."

Since March 7 in Glasgow, Dawson has thought further on the matter. He and Hill have met with PGA Tour commissioner Tim Finchem and European Tour chief executive George O'Grady. They are considering moving the Open to August 16–19. The PGA Tour's Wyndham Championship in Greensboro, North Carolina, would still be played that week. Dawson and Hill will meet again with Finchem and O'Grady, and other key officials in the golf world, during the Masters.

"We appreciate the spot that the R&A finds itself in, and of course we understand how important Tiger Woods is to the championship, and how much he would like to be there," James Lanik, the Wyndham Championship's general chairman, said.

The Wyndham Championship will remain the last tournament on the FedEx Cup schedule. The playoff series of four tournaments that will culminate in the Tour Championship begins the following week.

It's highly unlikely that the Wyndham Championship would have been on Woods's schedule this year. It follows the PGA Championship, for one thing. Should the Open move to the same week, it would make for an awkward end to the majors, with two in a row.

"That's hardly the ideal situation," Dawson said, "but it's the best alternative we've been able to find."

Television, of course, is playing a titanic role in the R&A's thinking. The BBC has agreed to move its coverage to August 16–19. The BBC will work around its August 18 coverage of the ECB Trophy final cricket match at Lord's in London, and the EuroHockey Men's and Women's Nations Championship, which begins August 18.

The week also makes sense for U.S. networks that a decision will affect. CBS is telecasting the Wyndham, so there's no issue with the network. ABC, which telecasts the Open in the United States, does not have any major sporting events on during the July 19–22 period, and has agreed to switch its coverage.

Meanwhile, Woods has agreed to play the Wyndham event two of the next five years, in return for its magnanimous gesture. He has also agreed to play the Scandinavian Masters, which will be held August 16–19 at the Arlandastad Golf Club in Stockholm, Sweden, at least once in the next five years.

Some of his fellow players feel the PGA Tour has already done enough for Woods, what with the new tournament in Washington that he will host next year, which will include a limited field of 120 players. The tournament will replace the International, a full-field event.

"Look, Tiger's done amazing things for the PGA Tour and for golf around the world," Phil Mickelson said. "But to change the date of the Open? That's going way too far. Really, it's off the charts."

Still, the R&A simply wants to do whatever it can so that the world's number-one golfer will play.

"We are continuing to study the ramifications of moving the Open," Dawson said. "This is the last thing we wanted to do. But we know that the Open's millions of followers around the world, and those who have already purchased tickets for the Open and made their plans for Carnoustie, expect Tiger to play."

Discussions on the possible date change are ongoing. Dawson and Hill will meet again with Finchem and O'Grady, and other key officials in golf, during the Masters. Dawson said a decision will follow soon after the Masters.

Finally, Dawson made a statement that reveals without ambiguity how seriously the R&A is taking the issue of Woods's possible absence.

"Only a fool would think we should not examine every possible means of ensuring that Tiger will play," Dawson said.

• • •

Many people didn't get this April Fool's joke. That didn't surprise me, given Tiger Woods's influence. The piece could only have worked for a golfer as prominent as Woods; it was almost possible to believe the R&A would make such a move. It helped that Woods and Dawson made the actual comments I used at the top of the piece. Great fun. I continued to hear about this piece for some time.

The Globe and Mail | July 12, 2008

Twenty-six days have passed since Tiger Woods won the U.S. Open Championship in a playoff over Rocco Mediate while in obvious pain, and nineteen days since he had surgery to repair a torn anterior cruciate ligament in his left knee.

Larry Holt, a retired professor of Kinesiology in the School of Health and Human Performance at Dalhousie University in Halifax, has been paying close attention to Woods's career. Holt's research and observations have led him to a conclusion that he knows is hardly mainstream.

"His type of injuries were self-inflicted," Holt said in a recent interview, "and are not related to practising or playing golf, but through his non-specific training that has virtually no positive influence on how he plays the game."

Holt is the lead author of *Scientific Stretching for Sport (3S)* and a new book called *Flexibility: A Concise Guide to Conditioning, Performance Enhancement, Injury Prevention, and Rehabilitation*. He has not worked with Woods, nor does he have any more knowledge of his injuries than what Woods has revealed publicly. Woods said shortly after winning the U.S. Open that he had suffered a double stress fracture in his left leg before the championship and that he had torn an ACL, the major stabilizing ligament in the knee, while running the week after the 2007 British Open.

Woods told CBS last weekend that he doesn't know when he will return to competition, let alone begin his rehabilitation. "I've been laid up pretty much every day, all day," he said, "moving from the bedroom to the couch and back to the bedroom and maybe a few bathroom stops along the way, but that's pretty much how my day goes."

In Holt's view, Woods put too much stress on his lower body over the years by lifting weights, adding muscle and therefore weight to his upper body. Holt said that Woods "placed his ectomorphic body [long and slender, like that of a marathon runner] through intense resistance training, bringing out the mesomorphic [muscular, "ripped" look by nature] component, adding muscle tissue, body weight that increased the forces on landing every time he ran. The stress fractures had nothing to do with golf, and neither did the knee problems."

Holt added: "Look how many golfers get stress fractures. Not many. It makes no sense. It's the running with the added weight on his upper body [that led to Woods's stress fractures]. He's a basically lean guy who has put on upper-body mass. It's like putting a twenty-pound sack of sand on your upper body. When he runs, it stresses his lower body. His body and legs are designed for a guy twenty, twenty-five pounds lighter.

"But Tiger feels he has to do these things to be a complete athlete. I think he's losing sight of his real goal, which is to be the greatest golfer. He thinks he has to be the greatest athlete."

Holt has consulted with the Calgary Flames and the defunct Minnesota North Stars and Quebec Nordiques, along with the Canadian Swimming Association. He is a past president of the International Society of Biomechanics in Sports. He wrote a book called *An Experimenter's Guide to the Full Golf Swing*. Holt is no fan of what he calls the "optimization" myth in sports, which suggests that athletes can improve by becoming stronger.

"You have to ask the question, 'What are the demands of a sport?' I'm not against non-specific training [such as heavy lifting], just against doing things that cause injuries or predispose a person to them, without any evidence that the exercise program actually improves performance."

He added: "Doing intense muscle-bulking exercise has not been shown to improve anyone's golf game, and may contribute to injuries if the program is one of progressive resistance training, where more mass and more strength are expected to continuously develop."

Holt pointed out that, according to an article in the August 2007 issue of *Men's Fitness* magazine, Woods weighed only 158 pounds when he won the 1997 Masters by twelve strokes. His weight fluctuates now between 182 and 185 pounds.

He questions whether Woods's bigger muscles have "added anything substantial to his game." Holt pointed out that Woods frequently misses fairways with the driver when he tries for extra distance. Holt doesn't pretend to be a swing coach, but he believes the speed with which Woods snaps his lower body to the left is an issue, because, according to him, Woods's natural ectomorphic frame can't support the movement.

"Golfers and other athletes often don't get the connection between their working out and their injuries," Holt said. "They sometimes set themselves up for injury on the course by working in the weight room."

Holt is aware that his ideas are controversial. The fundamental question is: Are his ideas valid? Can intense strength training harm even a golfer as strong as Woods? Might it have contributed to Woods's injuries?

Holt referred to golf as a "sedate" game, except for the desire many players have to maximize clubhead speed, and said, "The idea that you have to be in great shape to play great golf is ridiculous. Tiger just duelled it out with an overweight, mid-forties guy [Mediate] who couldn't pass a fitness test. People just won't see what is plainly in front of their eyes."

It's clear that Woods's trainer, Keith Kleven, believes his client's program is not the culprit in his injuries. Kleven could not be reached yesterday at his institute in Las Vegas. However, he told *Men's Fitness* that Woods's training program aims for "balance, control, endurance, and speed," and that it includes extensive stretching, manipulation, and mobilization of his muscles and joints, involving "everything from his cervical spine to his toes."

Marvin Tile, the past chief of orthopedic surgery at Sunnybrook Hospital in Toronto and professor emeritus of Surgery at the University of Toronto, responded to Holt's views this week. He said what happened to Woods is "a difficult read" because, for one thing, "You're dealing with the most famous athlete in the world and you're only going to know what he tells you." He, like other orthopedic specialists, is baffled by Woods's stress fractures and also by the manner in which he tore his ACL.

"I'm not sure how he tore his ACL running," Tile said. "That's unusual for an athlete in good shape. The main way an ACL tears is by hyperextension, as in skiing. But the knee is mostly flexed in running. There are a lot of unknowns with what's going on here."

With those caveats, Tile addressed Holt's views.

"I don't agree with what he says about the cause of Tiger's injuries," Tile said. "I think it's a stretch to say his upper-body weight caused the stress on his knee. But I do agree with him that knee injuries aren't common in golf, and that you don't have to be in great shape for golf. But I don't think it's a straight line from there to Tiger."

Chris Broadhurst, the head athletic therapist at the Toronto Athletic Club and most recently the head athletic therapist for the Phoenix Coyotes, also doesn't think Woods's upper-body workouts have caused his injuries.

"I don't think it would be fair to Tiger to say that any imbalance was created through his training," Broadhurst said. "Golfers do have to be leery of muscle imbalances, though. Are you tightening in a way that would put stress on your joints? Are you putting too much stress on your hips? Tiger's profile has been pretty good up to this knee incident."

Jeff Handler, who holds a degree in Exercise Science and has been Mike Weir's trainer since 2005, also weighed in.

"I don't agree with any of this," Handler said of Holt's views. "There isn't one athlete in pro sports, in hockey, basketball, baseball, or golf, who isn't trying to get stronger. Are Tiger's injuries a result of golf? No. Are they a result of his conditioning? No. A change in his physique? No."

Handler also doesn't agree with Holt's central premise that Woods's increased upper-body weight led to his knee and leg injuries. "Keith [Kleven] understands as well as anybody that if you add weight through increased muscle mass to the upper body that you have to balance it with lower-body work," Handler said. "Tiger's glutes and quads and hamstrings are much stronger than they were. Keith is one of the best in the business. There's no way he would allow Tiger to put on twenty pounds of upper-body mass without lower-body improvement. We all do foundation-based exercises that aren't golf-specific."

Holt, however, argued: "That is exactly the problem. Just about every trainer sets up a program that maximizes all parts of the body and all systems. In their view, a balance is maintained because intense exercises for all the gross musculature have been prescribed and followed. There's no consideration of the interactive effects of these programs. Increasing one dimension might negatively impact another, which might end up decreasing performance in the specific sport."

In this contentious arena, it's impossible yet to come up with a reasonable conclusion. There aren't any randomized, double-blind studies about the effect of intense training on performance.

"You can't take half of the Boston Red Sox and put them on a training program and leave the other half out," Tile said. "But my feeling is that if you did, there would be no difference in the groups. In golf, pot-bellied guys also shoot subpar."

Woods will surely continue to work out hard once he's ready to resume training, although he may well modify his program. That's his nature. He decided long ago to treat golf as a sport. "I let other people treat it like a hobby," he told *Men's Fitness*. "It would be asinine for someone not to work out and go play football. It doesn't make sense for golf, either."

Holt remains unconvinced. For him, intense resistance training for golf not only doesn't make sense. For him, it's nonsense.

• • •

Tiger continued to work on recovering from his knee surgery for the rest of 2008, while keeping busy with his various business activities. He visited the Al Ruwaya course in Dubai, which he designed. He met Michael Phelps, the winner of eight gold medals during the Summer Olympics in Beijing. He watched his friend Roger Federer win the U.S. Open tennis championship, and kept his eyes on the telecast of the Ryder Cup in September as the U.S. team defeated the European side. Tiger texted U.S. captain Paul Azinger throughout the event, offering encouragement and also ribbing him good-naturedly. He looked forward to returning to competition during the 2009 season, and so did everybody else who has followed his career. Young stars such as Anthony Kim and Camilo Villegas had emerged in his absence, but he remained the star of stars. He topped BusinessWeek magazine's second annual "Power 100" list of the most influential people in sports. Was there ever any doubt?